HOLLYWOOD
PICKS *the* CLASSICS

HOLLYWOOD
PICKS *the* CLASSICS

A GUIDE
FOR THE BEGINNER & THE AFICIONADO

AFTON FRASER

PREFACE BY
ESTHER WILLIAMS

MANOAH BOWMAN
PHOTO EDITOR

Bulfinch Press
New York • Boston

Bulfinch Press

Time Warner Book Group
1271 Avenue of the Americas, New York, NY 10020
Visit our Web site at www.bulfinchpress.com

First Edition

All images, unless otherwise noted, courtesy Independent Visions.

Library of Congress Cataloging-in-Publication Data

Fraser, Afton.
    Hollywood picks the classics : a guide for the uninitiated and the aficionado /
Afton Fraser ; preface by Esther Williams.-- 1st ed.
        p. cm.
    Includes bibliographical references and index.
    ISBN 0-8212-6190-8
  1.   Motion pictures--United States--Catalogs. I. Title.

    PN1998.F75 2004
    791.43'75'0973--dc22

                                                                2004009012

DESIGN
BY MIRIAM SMITH

PRINTED IN CHINA

To Brendan,
my leading man

CONTENTS

Movie stars— real movie stars— always had their names above the title. Their names told the audience what to expect. In the days when M-G-M, Warner Bros., 20th Century Fox, and Paramount ran the film business, the studios created well-honed images for their movie stars, who defined the content and the look of a movie. Personalities were synonymous with themes, indicative of a style. A Bette Davis movie was clearly different from a Betty Grable movie. You wouldn't find Ingrid Bergman swimming in a sequined costume any more than you would expect to see me in a nun's habit. These movie stars were more than just "talent." They were the story, the look, the production, all tied up in a name. If you were going to see a Cary Grant movie and you forgot the title, it didn't matter. Once you knew it was Cary Grant, you'd swoon with pleasure and anticipation of knowing exactly what to expect—a classy affair with an actor who exuded charm, good humor, and, well, class.

THOSE WERE THE DAYS

The name above the title could create fashions and attitudes that would sweep the country. If shoulder pads looked good on Joan Crawford, every woman in America would be wearing them. When Clark Gable undressed and showed his bare chest, undershirt factories closed across the nation. Such was the power of the movie star!

Stars were box office—big box office! Sometimes in combination they were double dynamite: Tracy and Hepburn, Astaire and Rogers, Gable and Lombard, Gable and Turner, Gable and Garbo. Gable and . . . anybody! These entertainers were the magical, mysterious draw that would bring audiences into theaters.

And I was lucky enough to be in that fraternity, that sorority. When a director worked with me, he knew what he had to do. Take Esther Williams out of the pool? That was dangerous! Positively unthinkable! Knowing what the public expected is what kept the studios humming to the tune of more than 400 pictures a year! They said, "She swam her way through twenty-six sparkling aquamusicals. Keep Esther in a one-piece, gold-lame swimsuit, a Pepsodent smile, and flowers in her hair and she'll never disappoint."

They spared no expense. For my favorite movie, **Million Dollar Mermaid**, they went all out. To create the red and yellow smoke streams for the movie's most spectacular water ballet, dance director Busby Berkeley employed 400 electrically controlled smoke pots. For the number's closing effect, he used 500 lighted sparklers that emerged from the water and formed a background for me. My chain-mail bathing suit was made of 50,000 gold flakes. Berkeley produced the geyser-like effect in the fountain number by having me in a huge water tank beneath a canopy of 400 jet streams of water that shot up thirty feet. Now *that* was attention to detail!

It worked. All my movies, even though the locations, co-stars and scripts changed, gave the audiences the same thing. They knew what they'd get: Esther underwater—impeccable, unsinkable, balletic, filmed in beautiful Technicolor. I didn't disappoint my fans. And they were faithful.

I was blessed to be part of that star system and the marvelous, memorable, mythical movies they made in the halcyon days of Hollywood, the days when "there were more stars at the studios than in the heavens."

—*Esther Williams*

HOLLYWOOD PICKS

June Allyson
Actress (b. 1917)

The Glen Miller Story
Good News
Little Women (1949)
Strategic Air Command

David Arquette
Courteney Cox
Actors (b. 1964, 1971)

All About Eve
Ben-Hur (1959)
Casablanca
Citizen Kane
Gone with the Wind
It's a Wonderful Life
Now, Voyager
Sunset Boulevard
The Wizard of Oz

Sean Astin
Actor (b. 1971)

All the King's Men
Citizen Kane
The Front Page
The Treasure of the
Sierra Madre
The Wizard of Oz

Elizabeth
Banks
Actress (b. 1975)

Abbott & Costello
Meet Frankenstein
Double Indemnity
Giant
The Gold Rush
Mogambo
The Philadelphia
Story
Roman Holiday
Shane
Snow White and
the Seven Dwarfs
The Women

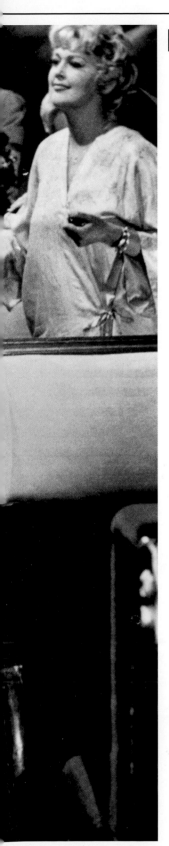

"I LOVE old movies!" exclaimed my eighteen-

year-old stepsister, Emily.

"Really? Which is your favorite?" I asked.

"**Sixteen Candles**," she replied.

I needed a few seconds to compose myself.

"**Sixteen Candles**? **Sixteen Candles** isn't an old movie. It was made in 1984!"

It was clear that she needed my help.

Not too long after, my brother-in-law Matt, a cinephile when it comes to the multiplex era but an old-movie-neophyte, decided he was ready to study the classics to round out his film repertoire.

"What should I watch?" he asked. "I need a list. I want to see all the important old movies. I'm just not sure where to start."

And so this book was born.

The films of the 1930s, '40s and '50s were the foundation upon which all great future directors built their movies. Without these classics, the renaissance brought forth by next-generation masters such as Spielberg, Scorsese, Coppola, and Lucas would not have been possible. There are constant allusions and winks to the past in all their work. Spielberg put a modern-day spin on **The Wizard of Oz** theme that there's no place like home when he gave us **E.T.** And how different are Shane or Robin Hood from Han Solo? Lucas used the horse operas and swashbucklers of Hollywood's golden age as the inspiration for his **Star Wars** trilogy, replacing six-shooters and swords with lasers, while recapturing the same zest for action for the modern generation.

Studying the classics enriches our viewing today. We wouldn't have brilliant films such as **Goodfellas** or **The Godfather** were it not for the gangster films of the '30s. The crude but clever special effects of the sci-fi and horror films that shocked audiences may seem rudimentary to us, but without them we might not have **The Lord of the Rings**.

Those years also gave us a gold mine of material to remake: **Sabrina, Born Yesterday, The Postman Always Rings Twice, Frankenstein, Wuthering Heights, King Kong,** and **Stella Dallas**, to name a few. **A Star is Born** and **Love Affair** were each remade twice. Often these reincarnations made us appreciate the originals even more.

I was introduced to classic films at age eleven, growing up in New York. Local television stations offered a treasure trove of classics back then. Whenever I heard "Tara's Theme," the signature tune on channel 9's Million Dollar Movie, I knew it was magic time. I would see a film five times as they repeated it every night of the week.

That same year, I remember watching **That's Entertainment** with my grandmother. This dazzling, colorful collection of highlights from the golden age of M-G-M musicals was glorious in scope yet frustrating in that I yearned for more after the movie ended. Back then those grand musicals weren't easily available. There were no DVD or video rentals, and cable had yet to give birth to Turner Classic Movies (or, as I call it, Movie Heaven). I scoured the television listings to find showings of the old films, and stayed up past my bedtime to catch them whenever I could. While my friends had posters of David Cassidy in their rooms, I had posters of James Dean, my teen idol.

When I moved to Hollywood, I started having old movie nights at my home. We'd have a theme. On Katharine Hepburn night, I showed **The Philadelphia Story** and served a high society meal to match. There were calla lilies and candles on the table. I made a toast telling about her life and her career. Over vichyssoise, my guests talked about their favorite classic films.

It was fascinating to hear their top ten lists. I thought it would be a delightful addition to my book to share actors' lists of favorites, which are sprinkled throughout. I asked them for favorites pre-1960, to fit in our time frame.

How I love that era! The distinctive actors, the lush productions, the glamorous costumes, artful direction, creative cinematography, and original screenplays of these classics never fail to captivate. Knowing these films helps us to see the evolution of the cinema we know today.

So Matt, if you want to know where to start your classic movie viewing, you cannot do better than these films. I hope you're going to love them as much as I do. Or to steal a line from **Casablanca**, "I think this is going to be the beginning of a beautiful friendship."

OPENING LINES

MUST SEE

Halle Berry
Actress (b. 1966)

Bringing Up Baby
Cat on a Hot Tin Roof
**Of Human
Bondage (1934)**
Porgy and Bess

Thora Birch
Actress (b. 1982)

For Heaven's Sake
The Hanging Tree
Holiday
Lust for Life
Mister Roberts
Phone Call
From a Stranger
A Place in the Sun
The Rainmaker
This Gun for Hire
Warlock

Jeff Bridges
Actor (b. 1949)

**Abbott & Costello
Meet Frankenstein**
Carousel
Citizen Kane
High Noon
Mister Roberts
On the Waterfront
Out of the Past
Sunset Boulevard
Twelve Angry Men
Vertigo

Carol Burnett
Actress (b. 1933)

All About Eve
The Bridge
on the River Kwai
It's a Wonderful Life
A Letter to Three Wives
The Philadelphia Story
Rear Window
**Seven Brides
for Seven Brothers**
Singin' in the Rain
A Star Is Born (1954)
Strangers on a Train

Will I watch it any time it comes on TV?

This is my first criterion for a must-see movie. From the gripping opening scene in **Sunset Boulevard** to the snappy surprise ending of **Some Like It Hot**, these ten have top-shelf screenplays, direction, cinematography, and acting. They have fully developed, rich characters who are endlessly watchable.

All About Eve was one of the first classic movies I ever saw and loved. Today I can see that the theme of the inevitability of being replaced by a more ambitious, younger talent is universal. We are all afraid of the Eves in our lives. I can also see the brilliance of the casting and the writing. But why did I love it when I was twelve years old? Because the emotions, the fear, and ambition are so raw, the inside look at the world of theater rings so true, how could I not be seduced? And, of course, there was Margo Channing in that satin dress at the bottom of the stairs, right before she says, "Fasten your seat belts—it's going to be a bumpy night!"

Casablanca and **Citizen Kane** are obvious choices. They are regarded as the greatest films of all time by critics and movie buffs —and rightly so. "Rosebud . . ." "Play it, Sam." "Here's looking at you, kid." "I think this is the beginning of a beautiful friendship." These have become embedded in our collective consciousness. These movies are important to know. In **Casablanca**, principles prevail over love; in **Citizen Kane**, the reverse is true.

Double Indemnity is my favorite film noir. Murder! Betrayal! Lust! All this and the most crackling dialogue of any movie ever. And it's got a message: Crime doesn't pay.

Gone with the Wind—nearly four hours long and I still want more. I care so much about these characters and long to know what happens to them after the final credits. A spoiled Southern belle gains my sympathy by her spunk, style, and dogged optimism. And she designed that dress out of the green velvet curtains. Rhett is my macho hero. He is every woman's fantasy, or mine, anyway. He is amused by Scarlett's petulance and loves her unconditionally— up to a point . . . until he doesn't give a damn.

Marlon Brando tore at my heartstrings in **On the Waterfront**. I felt his pain. "I coulda been a contender," he laments to his weakling brother. "Instead of a bum, which is what I am." What a thrill for me to watch him act.

The Philadelphia Story—this is the one that critics might question. No quotable quotes, no fancy cinematography, no sweeping spectacle. Well, what can I say. I've seen it a zillion times and it never fails to satisfy. This is Katharine the Great at her most Hepburnesque—sparkling, sophisticated, witty.

Some Like It Hot is perhaps the most clever, funny movie of all time. In the thick of the comedy, Marilyn in her slinky see-through dress with strategically placed beads sings "I'm Through With Love." She's riveting, luscious, vulnerable. Tony Curtis, Jack Lemmon, and Joe E. Brown are utterly hilarious. It is one of Billy Wilder's masterpieces.

Sunset Boulevard is a legendary piece about a legend in her own mind. "I'm ready for my closeup." It's almost embarrassing, but you can't look away.

When the young Judy Garland sings "Over the Rainbow" in **The Wizard of Oz**, it is beyond moving. No performer has matched this brilliance and it never gets corny. The actors, the music, the sets—it is perfect. I grew up with this movie and only today do I realize that it has great messages in it without being preachy: You have your strength within you. Follow your dream. There's no place like home.

To me, these ten films represent the human spirit—our frailties and flaws, life's highs and lows, the desire to make something of yourself and fit in, the longing to be loved and to give love. Watch them. "Close your eyes and tap your heels together three times. . ."

WHY THESE TEN?

ALL ABOUT EVE

20th CENTURY-FOX 1950

AGING stage diva Margo Channing (Davis) is part of a successful team: her director and younger lover Bill Sampson (Merrill), her playwright and friend Lloyd Richards (Marlowe), and his wife, Karen (Holm). A cunning younger actress Eve Harrington (Baxter), who is Margo's biggest fan, ingratiates herself into their world, securing a job as Margo's assistant and a room in her home. Eve

soon makes it apparent that she wants everything Margo has, including Bill and the lead in Lloyd's next play. Eve is abetted by two people in her plans: Karen, who wants to give Margo a little harmless comeuppance, and manipulative theater critic Addison DeWitt, who is interested in more than just Eve's career.

The Cast

Bette Davis
Margo Channing

Anne Baxter
Eve Harrington

George Sanders
Addison DeWitt

Celeste Holm
Karen Richards

Gary Merrill
Bill Sampson

Hugh Marlowe
Lloyd Richards

Gregory Ratoff
Max Fabian

Barbara Bates
Phoebe

Marilyn Monroe
Claudia Caswell

Thelma Ritter
Birdie Coonan

Director
Joseph L. Mankiewicz

Producer
Darryl F. Zanuck

Academy Awards

14 NOMINATIONS 6 OSCARS ✱

✱ Best Picture
✱ Director (Mankiewicz)
Actress (Davis and Baxter)
✱ Supporting Actor (Sanders)
Supporting Actress (Holm and Ritter)
✱ Writing, Screenplay (Mankiewicz)
Cinematography, Black and White
(Milton Krasner)
Art Direction-Set Decoration, Black and White
(Lyle Wheeler and George Davis;
Thomas Little and Walter M. Scott)
✱ Sound Recording
(20th Century-Fox Sound Department)
Scoring of a Dramatic or Comedy Picture
(Alfred Newman)
Film Editing (Barbara McLean)
✱ Costume Design, Black and White
(Edith Head and Charles LeMaire)

THE BUZZ

All About Eve's 14 nominations remained an Oscar record until 1998 when **Titanic** tied it.

The best actress nominations for Davis and Baxter marked the first time two women from the same film ever competed against each other in that category. Not long before she died in 1985, Baxter admitted she should have campaigned for a supporting actress nomination so Davis might have won a third Oscar. Upon hearing this, the outspoken Davis replied, "Yes, she should have."

"**M**iss Caswell is an actress, a graduate of the Copacabana School of Dramatic Arts.—Addison"

Screen Team

Davis and Merrill co-starred in the 1952 dramas **Another Man's Poison** and **Phone Call From a Stranger**.

The Stars

Bette Davis
Margo

DAVIS' reign as the queen of Warner Bros. ended in 1949 when she left the studio after a series of box-office flops. She was forever grateful to Mankiewicz for offering her the role of Margo. "Mankiewicz resurrected me from the dead," she said.

"**F**asten your seat belts—it's going to be a bumpy night."
—Margo

Anne Baxter
Eve

SHE was a reliable Fox contract player whose other great screen role was her Oscar-winning turn as the tragic Sophie in **The Razor's Edge** (1946). Her other claim to fame is that she was the granddaughter of architect Frank Lloyd Wright.

George Sanders
Addison

ADDISON DeWitt was the most memorable in a long line of screen cads played by Sanders in such classics as **Rebecca** (1940), **The Picture of Dorian Gray** (1945), and **The Ghost and Mrs. Muir** (1947). Appropriately, his autobiography was called *Memoirs of a Professional Cad.*

Gossip

Claudette Colbert was all set to play Margo Channing but injured her back filming **Three Came Home,** and had to turn down the role.

Fox's favorite girl next door Jeanne Crain was Zanuck's choice to play Eve Harrington, but Mankiewicz didn't think she had the "bitch virtuosity" the role required.

George Sanders' wife at the time, thirty-ish Zsa Zsa Gabor, asked her husband to suggest to Zanuck that she play the teenage Phoebe who worms her way into Eve's graces.

Bette Davis and Gary Merrill fell in love while making **Eve.** They were wed in 1951, a stormy union that ended in divorce ten years later.

'Of all the gin joints in all the towns in all the world, she walks into mine.--*Rick*'

CASABLANCA

WARNER BROS. 1942

RICK BLAINE (Bogart), a cynical, moody, American expatriate in Casablanca, Morocco, during World War II, owns a popular club. The charming but sleazy police captain Renault (Rains) ingratiates himself with Nazi Major Strasser (Veidt) and detains Czech underground resistance leader Victor Laszlo (Henreid). The upright, unexciting Laszlo has arrived in Casablanca to meet with other rebels at Rick's bar. He is married to virtuous beauty Ilsa (Bergman), Rick's old flame from Paris. Sam (Wilson), Rick's piano player, plays Rick and Ilsa's love song. Rick wants to reunite and run off with Ilsa, using his two valuable letters of transit. Another possibility would be to give the letters of transit to Ilsa and her husband. Rick and Ilsa must choose between their honorable principles and their love.

Screen Team

Bogart, Lorre, and Greenstreet also worked together in **The Maltese Falcon** (1941) and **Passage to Marseilles** (1944). Bogart appeared with Lorre in **All Through the Night** (1941) and **Beat the Devil** (1954), and only with Greenstreet in **Across the Pacific** (1942) and **Conflict** (1945). Lorre and Greenstreet's other teamings were **The Mask of Dimitrios** (1944), **Hollywood Canteen** (1944), **Three Strangers** (1946), and **The Verdict** (1946).

Bergman and Rains co-starred in **Notorious** (1946).

Academy Awards

8 NOMINATIONS 3 OSCARS

✱ Best Picture
✱ Director (Curtiz)
Actor (Bogart)
Supporting Actor (Rains)
✱ Writing, Screenplay (Julius J. Epstein, Philip G. Epstein, and Howard Koch)
Cinematography, Black and White (Arthur Edeson)
Music, Scoring of a Dramatic or Comedy Picture (Max Steiner)
Film Editing (Owen Marks)

THE BUZZ

The film's producer, Hal B. Wallis, was upset that Jack Warner accepted the Oscar that Wallis should have gotten. Industry insiders claimed that the incident was a factor in Wallis' decision to move to Paramount in 1945.

The Stars

Paul Henreid
Victor

Having scored as a leading man in the 1942 dramas **Joan of Paris** and **Now, Voyager**, Henreid feared playing the second male lead in **Casablanca** would hurt his career. His fears were groundless, and throughout the '40s he starred opposite several of Warners' top actresses including Ida Lupino in **In Our Time** (1944) and Bette Davis in **Deception** (1946).

Ingrid Bergman
Ilsa

Bergman had been a sensation in films in her native Sweden when David O. Selznick brought her to Hollywood in 1939 for the remake of her 1936 Swedish drama **Intermezzo**. Her natural beauty and endearing presence made her an immediate favorite with American audiences.

Humphrey Bogart
Rick

Having apprenticed in B movies for five years at Warners, Bogart became a bona fide star with the double-punch of **High Sierra** and **The Maltese Falcon** in 1941. The success of **Casablanca** and his best actor Oscar nomination for the film earned him a place in the studio's upper echelon of stars with Bette Davis and Errol Flynn.

Gossip

Conrad Veidt received the highest salary of the cast, $225,000. He died soon after the film opened.

Warners announced early on that Ronald Reagan, Dennis Morgan, and Ann Sheridan would star in the movie. It was a ploy to generate publicity for her 1942 films, **Juke Girl** with Reagan and **Wings for the Eagle** with Morgan.

The song "As Time Goes By" was not supposed to be in the film. Composer Max Steiner was working on another film at the time **Casablanca** was in production, and said he'd write an original song when the film was completed. Once **Casablanca** wrapped, Bergman had her hair cut short for **For Whom the Bells Tolls**. Since her **Casablanca** scenes couldn't be reshot, "As Time Goes By" remained.

Wallis considered making the character Sam a woman, and singer-pianist Hazel Scott was favored for the role.

"Louie, I think this is the beginning of a beautiful friendship. —*Rick*"

RKO RADIO
1941

ORSON WELLES
CITIZEN KANE
Jo Terrific!

The Cast

Orson Welles
Charles Foster Kane

Joseph Cotten
Jedediah Leland

Dorothy Comingore
Susan Alexander

Everett Sloane
Mr. Bernstein

Ray Collins
J.W. Gettys

George Coulouris
Walter Parks
Thatcher

Agnes Moorehead
Kane's mother

Paul Stewart
Raymond

Ruth Warrick
Emily Norton Kane

Director and Producer
Orson Welles

CITIZEN KANE

CHARLES FOSTER KANE (Welles), a newspaper tycoon, dies in his opulent mansion Xanadu, murmuring his last word "Rosebud." His life is explored, as his biographers search for the meaning of his dying word. Young Kane's friend Jedediah Leland (Cotten) helps him build a newspaper empire specializing in sensational tabloid-style news. Kane marries upstanding Emily Norton (Warrick), but his affair with Susan Alexander (Comingore) destroys his marriage and his promising future in politics. He marries Susan and tries to make her an opera star and control her life. Her terrible singing gets good reviews only from his newspapers. She is a joke. Kane's ruthless climb to riches and power is overshadowed by his yearning for love and the innocence of his early years.

'*Mr. Kane was a man who got everything he wanted, and then lost it.* —Thompson'

> ❝Love. That's all he really wanted out of life . . . That's Charlie's story. You see, he didn't have any to give. —*Leland*❞

Comingore and Welles.

Academy Awards

9 NOMINATIONS 1 OSCAR ✳

Best Picture
Director (Welles)
Actor (Welles)
✳ Writing, Original Screenplay
(Herman J. Mankiewicz and Welles)
Cinematography, Black and White (Gregg Toland)
Interior Decoration, Black and White
(Perry Ferguson and Van Nest Polglase;
Al Fields and Darrell Silvera)
Sound Recording (John Aalberg)
Music, Scoring of a Dramatic Picture
(Bernard Herrmann)
Film Editing (Robert Wise)

THE BUZZ

When Welles and Mankiewicz were announced as the winners of the screenplay award, the people at Louella Parsons' table began booing.

Neither Mankiewicz nor Welles attended the ceremony. The former was afraid he'd lose and might do something drastic in anger.

Gossip

Despite Welles' denial, gossip columnist Louella Parsons insisted **Kane** was an unflattering and thinly veiled portrait of her boss, newspaper titan William Randolph Hearst. In retaliation, Hearst did his best to suppress the film by refusing to run ads for it or any other RKO films in his papers. He also threatened to ban ads for theater chains that ran the film, which made it difficult for **Kane** to get bookings.

Welles, Cotten, Moorehead, Stewart, and Warrick all made their film debuts in **Kane**.

John Citizen, U.S.A. was a working title for **Citizen Kane**.

Alan Ladd has a brief cameo as a reporter.

The Stars

Orson Welles
Kane

Joseph Cotten
Leland

Though he had his share of ardent admirers and envious detractors, no one in Hollywood could dismiss Welles' innovative gifts as an actor, director, and storyteller. Though **Kane** was his masterpiece, directorial follow-ups **The Magnificent Ambersons** (1942), **The Stranger** (1946), **The Lady From Shanghai** (1948), and **Touch of Evil** (1958) each have their brilliant moments. At the same time, he continued to impress as an actor, most notably as the sinister Mr. Rochester in **Jane Eyre** (1944).

Like many of the **Kane** cast, Cotten's ticket to Hollywood was as a member of Welles' Mercury Players from radio. With his lean, good looks, Cotten became the breakout star of the group, finding steady film work as the love interest of Jennifer Jones, Deanna Durbin, Ginger Rogers, and other top leading ladies throughout the 1940s. His finest hour came in an uncharacteristic role as the mysterious Uncle Charlie in Alfred Hitchcock's **Shadow of a Doubt** (1943).

Screen Team

Cotten, Moorehead, Sloane, Warrick, and Welles all appeared together in **Journey Into Fear** (1942). Welles also worked with Cotten in **The Third Man** (1950) and with Sloane in **The Lady From Shanghai** (1948).

> ❝Rosebud!❞ —*Kane*

DOUBLE INDEMNITY

COLD-BLOODED femme fatale Phyllis Dietrichson (Stanwyck) hates her oilman husband (Powers). Walter Neff (MacMurray), an insurance agent, comes to renew her husband's automobile policy. When Phyllis learns of her husband's life insurance policy with a double indemnity clause for an accident on a train, she starts to see a way out of her marriage. She seduces Neff and convinces him to help her kill her husband. They have a steamy

PARAMOUNT 1944

affair and hatch the perfect plan. But things turn sour. After they commit the murder, Mr. Dietrichson's dishy daughter, Lola (Heather), falls for Neff, while Walter's friend and co-worker Barton Keyes (Robinson) smells a rat. These two obstacles affect Walter's relationship with Phyllis, leading to mutual suspicion and betrayal.

Gossip

Wilder wrote the role of Phyllis with Stanwyck in mind, and though she loved the script, she was reluctant to play a hard-boiled killer. When Wilder asked "Are you a mouse or an actress?" her mind was made up.

Breezy comedy had been MacMurray's forte, so he at first said no to playing Walter. "I can't do that," he said, "it requires acting."

Wilder's usual script collaborator, Charles Brackett, thought the story too grim and didn't want to work on the screenplay. The director then hired Raymond Chandler, which Wilder called an unhappy experience. "If I did not work with a writer twice," Wilder said, "that's a clue."

The movie originally ended with MacMurray dying in the gas chamber. After the scene was filmed, Wilder decided it was unnecessary because the previous scene between MacMurray and Robinson was so effective.

The Cast

Barbara Stanwyck
Phyllis Dietrichson

Fred MacMurray
Walter Neff

Edward G. Robinson
Barton Keyes

Jean Heather
Lola Dietrichson

Tom Powers
Mr. Dietrichson

Porter Hall
Mr. Jackson

Byron Barr
Nino Zachetti

Richard Gaines
Edward S. Norton

Director
Billy Wilder

Producer
Joseph Sistrom

"This has got to be perfect—straight down the line." —*Walter*

The Stars

Barbara Stanwyck
Phyllis

STANWYCK admitted that she never took an acting class. "Life was my teacher," she said. And she obviously studied it well based on her gift for comedy in films such as **The Lady Eve** (1941), villainy in **The Strange Love of Martha Ivers** (1946), and her ability to wring tear ducts dry in **So Big** (1932) and **Stella Dallas** (1937).

Fred MacMurray
Walter

THE insurance agent with murder on his mind was light-years away from his most famous role, as the lovable, pipe-smoking dad of TV's **My Three Sons**. Still, MacMurray was never better than when he veered into dark waters in films like **The Caine Mutiny** (1954) and **The Apartment** (1960).

Edward G. Robinson
Keyes

THOUGH best known as a movie tough guy, Robinson was one of the screen's most versatile actors whose parts ranged from the ruthless killer **Little Caesar** (1930) and a gang lord in **The Hatchet Man** (1932) to the discoverer of the syphilis vaccine in **Dr. Ehrlich's Magic Bullet** (1940) and a vengeful Italian banker in **House of Strangers** (1949).

Academy Awards

Best Picture
Director (Wilder)
Actress (Stanwyck)
Writing, Screenplay
(Wilder and Raymond Chandler)
Cinematography, Black and White (John Seitz)
Sound Recording (Loren Ryder)
Scoring of a Dramatic or Comedy Picture
(Miklos Rozsa)

7 NOMINATIONS

THE BUZZ

Stanwyck lost the best actress award to Ingrid Bergman for **Gaslight**, but Stanwyck could not have been more gracious when asked how she felt about the outcome: "I don't feel bad about the award because my favorite actress won it and has earned it by all her performances."

> They've committed a murder and it's not like taking a trolley ride together where they can get off at different stops. —*Keyes*

Screen Team

Stanwyck and MacMurray also co-starred in **Remember the Night** (1940), **The Moonlighter** (1953), and **There's Always Tomorrow** (1956).

Stanwyck and Robinson were reunited for **The Violent Men** (1954).

GONE WITH THE WIND

SELZNICK-M-G-M
1939
-COLOR-

The Cast

Clark Gable
Rhett Butler

Vivien Leigh
Scarlett O'Hara

Olivia de Havilland
Melanie Hamilton

Leslie Howard
Ashley Wilkes

Hattie McDaniel
Mammy

Thomas Mitchell
Gerald O'Hara

Barbara O'Neil
Ellen O'Hara

Butterfly McQueen
Prissy

Evelyn Keyes
Suellen O'Hara

Ann Rutherford
Careen O'Hara

Laura Hope Crews
Aunt Pittypat
Hamilton

Jane Darwell
Mrs. Merriwether

Rand Brooks
Charles Hamilton

George Reeves
Stuart Tarleton

Cammie King
Bonnie Blue Butler

Director
Victor Fleming

Producer
David O. Selznick

SCARLETT O'Hara (Leigh), a beautiful, willful Southern belle, lives on the plantation Tara. She loves Ashley Wilkes (Howard), who favors honey-sweet, frail Melanie Hamilton (de Havilland). Rhett Butler (Gable), a handsome, gambling adventurer, admires Scarlett. The Civil War breaks out. Scarlett marries twice: once, to make Ashley jealous, and next to save Tara from the destruction inflicted during the war. Eventually, she marries Rhett and they have a daughter. Scarlett behaves badly, flouting convention and still yearning for Ashley. Rhett grows indifferent to her, but devoted to their daughter. After tragedy strikes, Scarlett realizes her true love. Alas, it is too late. Her survivor instincts, however, never flag.

In new screen splendor...
The most magnificent picture ever!

"GONE WITH THE WIND"

CLARK GABLE
VIVIEN LEIGH
LESLIE HOWARD OLIVIA de HAVILLAND

> "I can't go all my life waiting to catch you between husbands. —*Rhett*"

Academy Awards

✻ Best Picture
✻ Director (Fleming)
Actor (Gable)
✻ Actress (Leigh)
Supporting Actress (de Havilland)
✻ Supporting Actress (McDaniel)
✻ Writing, Screenplay (Sidney Howard)
✻ Cinematography, Color
(Ernest Haller and Ray Rennahan)
✻ Interior Direction (Lyle Wheeler)
Sound Recording (Thomas T. Moulton)
Original Score (Max Steiner)
✻ Film Editing (Hal C. Kern and James E. Newcom)
Special Effects—Photographic and Sound
(John R. Cosgrove; Fred Albin and Arthur Johns)

13 NOMINATIONS 8 OSCARS ✻

THE BUZZ
Hattie McDaniel was the first black performer to win an Oscar and also the first of her race to attend an Academy Awards banquet.

Gossip

George Cukor began as director of the film, but was fired during filming at Clark Gable's insistence. Leigh and de Havilland pleaded with Selznick to keep Cukor, but to no avail. Both actresses would visit Cukor at his home during their off-hours for his advice on scenes.

Among the ninety actresses who tested for Scarlett were Jean Arthur, Lucille Ball, Joan Bennett, Frances Dee, Susan Hayward, and Lana Turner. The front-runner for the role was Paulette Goddard, but fear of negative publicity surrounding her living arrangements with Charlie Chaplin hurt her chances.

The Stars

Clark Gable
Rhett

As the box-office king of the 1930s, Gable's raw masculinity appealed to both men and women. He was also the public's overwhelming choice to play Rhett when news got out that Selznick had purchased the film rights to Margaret Mitchell's best-seller.

Leslie Howard
Ashley

An accomplished actor of stage and screen, Howard preferred more flamboyant roles, such as Henry Higgins in **Pygmalion** (1938) and the title hero in **The Scarlet Pimpernel** (1935), to the wan Ashley.

Vivien Leigh
Scarlett

Leigh had made a handful of films in England before being "discovered" by Myron Selznick, who introduced her to his brother, David, as Scarlett the night that the burning of Atlanta was being shot. Leigh went on to win a second Oscar for playing a different type of Southern belle in **A Streetcar Named Desire** (1951).

Olivia de Havilland
Melanie

De Havilland was possibly the only actress in Hollywood who coveted the role of Melanie rathe than Scarlett. "I knew I was going to have to earn my own living and be self-reliant and independent and self-supporting," she once said. "And when I made **Gone with the Wind,** that's exactly what I was. So was Scarlett. Since I was myself leading that life, the role didn't interest me at all."

Screen Team

Howard and de Havilland also co-starred in **It's Love I'm After** (1937).

De Havilland and McDaniel worked together again in the 1942 films **The Male Animal** and **In This Our Life.**

'Scarlett: Rhett, if you go, where shall I go? What shall I do?
Rhett: Frankly, my dear, I don't give a damn. '

ON THE WATERFRONT

COLUMBIA
1954

TERRY MALLOY (Brando), a washed-up ex-boxer, is a gofer for racketeer union boss Johnny Friendly (Cobb), whose lawyer Charley Malloy (Steiger) is Terry's brother. The scene is Hoboken's waterfront, where dock workers have to grovel to get work from the corrupt unions. Terry witnesses the boss' men murdering a potential informant, whose sister Edie (Saint) makes friends with Terry. The courageous local priest, Father Barry (Malden), tries to get the men to fight the crooked union. Edie urges Terry to help find her brother's killers. His conscience and his love for Edie on the one hand and his loyalty to his brother and fear of the mob on the other make for a tense decision for Terry.

The Cast

Marlon Brando
Terry Malloy

Eva Marie Saint
Edie Doyle

Karl Malden
Father Barry

Lee J. Cobb
Johnny Friendly

Rod Steiger
Charley Malloy

Pat Henning
"Kayo" Dugan

Leif Erickson
Clover

James Westerfield
Big Mac

John Heldabrand
Mutt

Rudy Bond
Moose

Director
Elia Kazan

Producer
Sam Spiegel

"I coulda had class. I coulda been a contender."
—Terry

Gossip

Kazan claimed the script was based on actual events, and was not modeled after his own involvement with the Communist Party and eventual testimony before the House Un-American Activities Committee.

Frank Sinatra was considered for the role of Terry, but Kazan decided Brando looked more like a fighter and also had what the director called "absolute vulnerability."

Grace Kelly turned down the role of Edie so that she could star in **Rear Window** for Alfred Hitchcock.

Kazan first presented the **Waterfront** screenplay to an unenthusiastic Darryl F. Zanuck. "Who gives a damn about labor unions?" the Fox chief said after reading it. The script was then turned down by every other major studio until Spiegel agreed to produce it.

On the Waterfront was shot on location in Hoboken, N.J., the film's setting. Many actual longshoremen were used as extras.

Screen Team

Brando and Malden co-starred in **A Streetcar Named Desire** (1951) and **One-Eyed Jacks** (1961).

Malden and Cobb both appeared in **Boomerang** (1947).

The Stars

Marlon Brando
Terry

BRANDO'S brooding, explosive brand of Method acting caught Hollywood's eye after his performance on Broadway in **A Streetcar Named Desire.** He repeated the role in the 1951 film and by the time he made **On the Waterfront** established himself as the rebellious icon of his generation.

Karl Malden
Father Barry

THE pug-nosed Malden was a Kazan favorite who worked with the director on three other films: **Boomerang** (1947), **A Streetcar Named Desire** (1951), and **Baby Doll** (1956).

Eva Marie Saint
Edie

LIKE Brando, she hailed from New York's Actors Studio and was a student of the Method school. After **Waterfront,** she excelled in equally demanding roles in **A Hatful of Rain** (1957) and **Exodus** (1960), and showed her glamorous side in Hitchcock's **North by Northwest** (1959).

Academy Awards

✳ Best Picture
✳ Director (Kazan)
✳ Actor (Brando)
Supporting Actor (Cobb, Malden, and Steiger)
✳ Supporting Actress (Saint)
✳ Writing, Story and Screenplay
(Budd Schulberg)
✳ Cinematography, Black and White
(Boris Kaufman)
✳ Art Direction-Set Decoration, Black and White
(Richard Day)
Scoring of a Dramatic or Comedy Picture
(Leonard Bernstein)
✳ Film Editing (Gene Milford)

12 NOMINATIONS 8 OSCARS ✳

THE BUZZ

With such heavyweights as Judy Garland **(A Star Is Born)** and Grace Kelly **(The Country Girl)** being touted for best actress, Spiegel listed his leading lady Saint in the supporting actress category, where he believed her odds of winning would be more favorable.

On the Waterfront was the first film to ever have three nominees up for supporting actor.

Brando's Oscar was misplaced. He was later contacted by a London auction house that uncovered the award and wanted to sell it.

❝ **Y**ou want to know what's wrong with our waterfront? It's the love of a lousy buck. — *Father Barry* ❞

THE PHILADELPHIA STORY

M-G-M
1940

SPOILED, sassy, wealthy socialite Tracy Lord (Hepburn) is preparing to marry boring George Kittredge (Howard) at her family's estate. Tabloid *Spy Magazine* threatens to expose her father's infidelity if she doesn't let them cover the wedding. Cynical reporter Mike Connor (Stewart), who disdains the rich, shows up with down-to-earth, pretty photographer Elizabeth Imbrie (Hussey) and handsome, suave, rich playboy C. K. Dexter Haven (Grant), Tracy's first husband, who wants to win her back. Mike falls in love with Tracy, while Liz pines for him. Tracy discovers the heart beneath her haughty exterior.

> "Well, you may not believe this, but there are people in this world that must earn their living. —*Mike*"

Screen Team

The main leads, Hepburn and Grant, worked together in three previous films: Cukor's **Sylvia Scarlett** (1935) and **Holiday** (1938) and Howard Hawks' **Bringing Up Baby** (1938).

Academy Awards

6 NOMINATIONS 2 OSCARS
✳

Best Picture
Director (Cukor)
✳ Actor (Stewart)
Actress (Hepburn)
Supporting Actress (Hussey)
✳ Writing, Screenplay (David Ogden Stewart)

THE BUZZ

This was James Stewart's only performance to earn an Oscar, but he always said that his friend Henry Fonda should have won instead for **The Grapes of Wrath.** Stewart mailed his Oscar to his father, who displayed the award in his hardware store in Indiana, PA., in a glass case that had been used to house kitchen knives.

The Stars

James Stewart
Macaulay "Mike"

1940 was a busy year for Stewart. He also starred with Margaret Sullavan in **The Mortal Storm** and **The Shop Around the Corner,** and in **No Time for Comedy** with Rosalind Russell.

Cary Grant
C.K. Dexter

GRANT showed his versatility in three other 1940 films: as a rugged colonist in **The Howards of Virginia,** a scheming editor in **His Girl Friday,** and a man with two wives in **My Favorite Wife.**

Katharine Hepburn
Tracy

HEPBURN had a string of film flops before heading to Broadway in 1938. **The Philadelphia Story** marked her screen comeback.

Gossip

Hepburn starred in the stage version of **The Philadelphia Story** and bought the rights to the play from author Philip Barry.

Warner Bros. offered $225,000 for the rights to **The Philadelphia Story,** but didn't want Hepburn, who was still considered box-office poison. She sold the play to M-G-M for $250,000 — $175,000 for the film rights and $75,000 for playing the lead.

In order to sign Cary Grant, M-G-M agreed to give him top billing and to donate his $137,500 salary to the British War Relief Fund.

Clark Gable and Spencer Tracy were Hepburn's first choices to play the Grant and Stewart roles, but neither was available.

George Cukor shot the film in only eight weeks with virtually no retakes.

> "You'll never be a first-class human being or a first-class woman, until you've learned to have some regard for human frailty. —*Dexter*"

SOME LIKE IT HOT

UNITED ARTISTS 1959

JOE (Curtis) and Jerry (Lemmon), out-of-work musicians in 1920s Chicago, witness a gangland shootup by Spats Colombo (Raft) and need to flee town. Disguised in women's garb, they head to Miami by joining Sweet Sue's all-girl orchestra, where they're known as Josephine and Daphne. Both men are attracted to Sugar Kane (Monroe), the lead singer, but it's Joe who tries to woo her by disguising himself as a rich oil man. Meanwhile, goofy millionaire Osgood Fielding III (Brown) falls in love with Jerry/Daphne. Joe uses Osgood's yacht for a date with Sugar while Jerry/Daphne distracts Osgood by dancing the night away. By the end of the night, Osgood proposes marriage to Jerry/Daphne. Meanwhile, the gangsters arrive. Revelations are made all around, leading to the madcap escape where all is resolved—sort of.

The Cast

Marilyn Monroe
Sugar Kane Kowalczyk

Tony Curtis
Joe/Josephine

Jack Lemmon
Jerry/Daphne

Joe E. Brown
Osgood Fielding III

George Raft
Spats Colombo

Pat O'Brien
Mulligan

Joan Shawlee
Sweet Sue

Nehemiah Persoff
Little Bonaparte

Billy Gray
Sig Poliakoff

George E. Stone
Toothpick Charlie

Dave Barry
Beinstock

**Mike Mazurki
Harry Wilson**
Spats' henchmen

Director and Producer
Billy Wilder

"It's the story of my life. I always get the fuzzy end of the lollipop." —Sugar

Mitzi Gaynor was Wilder's first choice to play Sugar until he learned Monroe was interested. "We just had to have her," Wilder said.

The original title of the movie was **Not Tonight, Josephine.**

It took more than fifty takes before Wilder was satisfied with Monroe's reading of the line, "Where's that bourbon?"

Wilder originally considered Frank Sinatra for one of the two male leads.

Cary Grant called Wilder after seeing **Some Like It Hot.** The actor said how much he loved Curtis' imitation of him in the movie.

> *Jerry:* You don't understand, Osgood! I'm a man!
> *Osgood:* Well, nobody's perfect.

Marilyn Monroe
Sugar

IN **Some Like It Hot,** Monroe sings "I Wanna Be Loved by You," a title which sums up her relationship with her legions of fans. How could we not fall in love with her, whether she's vamping it up in **Gentlemen Prefer Blondes** (1953), tickling our funny bone in **How to Marry a Millionaire** (1953), or touching our heart in **Bus Stop** (1956).

Jack Lemmon
Jerry/Daphne

HE was one of the screen's most beloved performers, who played comedy and drama with equal ease. Lemmon was also one of Wilder's favorite actors and the two collaborated on six more films: **The Apartment** (1960), **Irma La Douce** (1963), **The Fortune Cookie** (1966), **Avanti** (1972), **The Front Page** (1974), and **Buddy Buddy** (1981).

Tony Curtis
Joe/Josephine

BORN Bernie Schwartz in a tough section of the Bronx, Curtis' street-tough manner served him well with a chilling performance in the searing **Sweet Smell of Success** (1957). But it was his farcical side that was more frequently his fortune in comic fare such as **Operation Petticoat** (1959) and **Sex and the Single Girl** (1964).

Director (Wilder)
Actor (Lemmon)
Writing, Screenplay—Based on Material From Another Medium (Wilder and I.A.L. Diamond)
Cinematography, Black and White (Charles Lang Jr.)
Art Direction-Set Decoration, Black and White (Ted Haworth; Edward G. Boyle)
＊**Costume Design, Black and White** (Orry-Kelly)

6 NOMINATIONS 1 OSCAR ＊

THE BUZZ

In his acceptance speech, designer Orry-Kelly paid special thanks to Curtis and Lemmon, "who, as Louella [Parsons] would say, never looked lovelier."

Jack Lemmon and Tony Curtis co-starred again in **The Great Race** (1965).

❝I am big. It's the pictures that got small.❞ *—Norma*

SUNSET BOULEVARD

PARAMOUNT 1950

DOWN-AND-OUT screenwriter Joe Gillis (Holden), running from some repo men, pulls his car into the Sunset Boulevard mansion belonging to Norma Desmond (Swanson). The older, imperious, former silent film star lives in a delusional state with her sycophantic, stoic butler Max (von Stroheim), who is also her former husband and director. She is dreaming of her next role and her return to the big screen. Joe moves in to edit the awful

screenplay she has written and becomes her gigolo. Meanwhile, he has a crush on Betty, his friend's fiancee. Betty seems perfect for Joe, but grows disgusted with his situation. Joe tries to leave his rich life with Norma, who flies into a murderous rage and descends into complete insanity.

The Stars

Gloria Swanson
Norma

William Holden
Joe

Erich von Stroheim
Max

HE WAS billed as "The Man You Love to Hate" because of his stern demeanor. Though he occasionally acted in films, von Stroheim is more renowned as the iron-fisted director of such classics as **Greed** (1924), **Foolish Wives** (1925), and **The Wedding March** (1928).

LIKE Norma Desmond, Swanson was a major star of the silent screen. Unlike her screen alter ego, Swanson continued to enjoy a full, rich life after her peak years in Hollywood. Though **Sunset** was her high-water mark, she made occasional returns to the stage and screen and penned a best-selling autobiography.

FOLLOWING a successful film debut in **Golden Boy** (1939), Holden spent most of the '40s playing the all-American boy, or what he called "Smilin' Jack" roles. As the somewhat unscrupulous screenwriter in **Sunset Boulevard,** he showed a darker, more intense side to his personality and became one of the top male stars of the '50s.

"There's nothing tragic about being fifty. Not unless you're trying to be twenty-five. *—Joe*"

Screen Team

On the heels of **Sunset Boulevard,** Holden and Olson were reteamed in **Union Station** (1950) and **A Force of Arms** (1951).

Academy Awards

11 NOMINATIONS 3 OSCARS ✻

Best Picture
Director (Wilder)
Actor (Holden)
Actress (Swanson)
Supporting Actor (von Stroheim)
Supporting Actress (Olson)
✻ Writing, Story and Screenplay
(Wilder, Brackett and D.M. Marshman Jr.)
Cinematography, Black and White (John F. Seitz)
✻ Art Direction-Set Decoration, Black and White
(Hans Dreier and John Meehan;
Sam Comer and Ray Moyer)
✻ Scoring of a Dramatic or Comedy Picture
(Franz Waxman)
Film Editing
(Arthur Schmidt and Doane Harrison)

THE BUZZ

When von Stroheim learned he received a supporting rather than a best actor nomination, he threatened to sue Paramount.

"All right, Mr. DeMille. I'm ready for my close-up. *—Norma*"

Gossip

Montgomery Clift was Wilder's first choice to play Joe, but Clift said no because the role of a kept man mirrored his own relationship with New York socialite Libby Holman. Wilder then approached Fred MacMurray, who also said no.

Mae West, Mary Pickford, and Pola Negri all turned down the role of Norma.

The original opening scene took place at a morgue where Gillis' corpse converses in voice-over with the other dead bodies. After preview audiences laughed at the scene, it was rewritten.

It was von Stroheim's idea to make Max the author of the fan letters to Norma.

The silent film sequence Norma screens for Joe is from Swanson's 1928 movie **Queen Kelly,** which was directed by von Stroheim.

After seeing **Sunset Boulevard,** M-G-M boss Louis B. Mayer told Wilder he should be run out of Hollywood.

THE WIZARD OF OZ

A TORNADO sweeps Dorothy (Garland) and her dog Toto from their farm in Kansas to a fantastical place, beautiful and full of exotic creatures, but she's homesick. The Wizard of Oz (Morgan) can help her, but the only way to get to him is by following the Yellow Brick Road. Dorothy is joined on the journey by a scarecrow (Bolger) who wants a

brain, a tin man (Haley) who wants a heart, and a cowardly lion (Lahr) who wants courage. They encounter Glinda the Good Witch of the North (Burke), who gives Dorothy magic ruby slippers, and the Wicked Witch of the West (Hamilton) and her monkey guards. The witch is killed and Dorothy and her friends are off to see the wizard, who grants each of them a wish. Dorothy clicks her ruby slippers together and is returned home.

M-G-M 1939 B&W/COLOR

> " Toto, I've a feeling we're not in Kansas anymore.
> —*Dorothy* "

The Stars

Judy Garland
Dorothy

SHE LANDED the coveted role of Dorothy after Fox refused to loan Shirley Temple to M-G-M.

Screen Team

Garland and Haley co-starred in **Pigskin Parade** (1936). Garland and Bolger appeared together in **The Harvey Girls** (1946).

Bert Lahr
Zeke, The Cowardly Lion

A VETERAN comic of burlesque, vaudeville, and the legitimate stage, he made only a few films. Of his role in **Oz**, he said, 'It hurt my picture career. After that, I was type-cast as a lion, and there just weren't many *parts* for lions.'

Jack Haley
Hickory, The Tin Woodsman

HALEY, a popular song-and-dance man under contract to Fox, was ordered by that studio to replace Buddy Ebsen as the Tin Woodsman after Ebsen was poisoned by the aluminum dust in his makeup.

Ray Bolger
Hunk, the Scarecrow

HE was originally assigned to play the Tin Woodsman, but at his urging, switched roles with Buddy Ebsen, who was first cast as the Scarecrow.

> ' I'll get you my pretty, and your little dog, too! '
> —*The Wicked Witch*

CHAPTER 2

DRAMA

HOLLYWOOD PICKS

Michael Caine
Actor (b. 1933)

All About Eve
Casablanca
Gone with the Wind
The Great Dictator
The Maltese Falcon
On the Waterfront
The Third Man
To Have and Have Not
The Treasure of the
Sierra Madre

Erika Christensen
Actress (b. 1982)

Adam's Rib
The African Queen
Casablanca
Guys and Dolls
It's a Wonderful Life
North by Northwest
The Philadelphia Story
Singin' in the Rain
Some Like It Hot

John Cleese
*Actor, Comedian
(b. 1939)*

The Great Dictator
Kind Hearts and
Coronets
The Ladykillers (1955)
The Third Man

Jackie Collins
Writer (b. 1939)

The African Queen
Citizen Kane
The Killers
The Postman Always
Rings Twice
Rebel Without a Cause
Shane
Singin' in the Rain
A Streetcar Named
Desire
Sunset Boulevard
The Wild One

The producers, directors, and screenwriters of the 1930s, '40s and '50s were smart, political, and firmly grounded in the history that they lived through. The Depression, World War II, and McCarthyism influenced the films that were made during those decades. These ten dramas deal with powerful subject matter and emotions: poverty, alcholism, adultery, political corruption, greed, dysfunctional families, the media, social class, returning veterans, and anti-Semitism.

In **The Grapes of Wrath**, the Depression has ravaged Oklahoma, home of the Joad family, who decide to move West hoping they'll find work. The most poignant scene: Worn-down Ma Joad goes through her things. She must choose what to pack, as space on the truck is scarce. She picks a pair of earrings and holds them to her ears, looking wistfully at herself in the mirror. Her pain and loss radiate. Jane Darwell deserved her Oscar.

Harold Russell also deserved his Oscar for his portrayal of Homer, a returning veteran who has lost both his hands, in **The Best Years of Our Lives**. The most touching, intimate scene: Homer's fiancée Wilma sees him without his prosthetics but she doesn't flinch. Instead, she gently helps him button up his pajamas. I cry every time.

Angry, rebellious soldiers rage, drink, fight, and make love in **From Here to Eternity**. The most smoldering scene: Burt Lancaster and Deborah Kerr at the beach, rolling around on the sand, as the waves crash into them.

Prejudice was rampant in the '40s. Many Jewish actors such as John Garfield (nee Julius Garfinkle) changed their names just to get work. **Gentleman's Agreement** addresses the issue of anti-Semitism head on. The most insightful scene: Gregory Peck, who is pretending to be Jewish to write a magazine story, learns that his secretary has also changed her name to pass as gentile. She then rails against the "kikey" Jews, disdaining her heritage in order to succeed.

Montgomery Clift also wants to make it. He is anxious to move up from his factory job in

A Place in the Sun. The most riveting scene: Pregnant Shelley Winters confronts him in a boat near his rich girlfriend's estate. His disgust for Shelley—and his desire for Elizabeth Taylor and her upper-class life—is palpable.

Social strata are explored in the all-star classic **Grand Hotel**. The strangers, all flawed but dignified, touch each other's lives. The most human scene: Depressed diva Greta Garbo contemplates suicide and discovers John Barrymore stealing her jewelry. Her outrage turns to love as the two strangers get to know each other.

James Dean as Cal desires his father's love in the Cain and Abel tale **East of Eden**. The most heartbreaking scene: The father, in financial straits, still rejects Cal's birthday gift of money, since the money was made from the war. Cal retaliates by lashing out. His brother's girlfriend Abra, whom Cal also loves, defends him. The devastated look on Cal's face makes me want to take him in my arms.

Alcoholism makes Ray Milland crazy in **The Lost Weekend**. He rants and regrets as he bounces from barstools to Bellevue. The most gritty and unflinching scene: Milland hallucinating about rats and bats.

Power corrupts. Fame corrupts. Television gives Lonesome Rhodes both in **A Face in the Crowd**. The most satisfying comeuppance: Steely Patricia Neal quietly exposes Lonesome for the monster that he is by leaving off a mute button on his microphone while he reveals his true contemptuous feelings for his audience.

Incorruptible Jimmy Stewart fights the powerful politicians in **Mr. Smith Goes to Washington**. The most inspiring moment: Stewart's voice getting hoarse just before he collapses from his patriotic, idealistic filibuster to the Senate. "Great principles don't get lost once they come to light. They're right here. You just have to see them again!"

Mr. Jefferson Smith's speech is a tribute to democratic values. It moves us to be better. These films go deep, emotionally, visually, and ideologically. They tell us how to live and how to see. Their messages are still relevant today.

BUT SERIOUSLY, FOLKS

THE BEST YEARS OF OUR LIVES

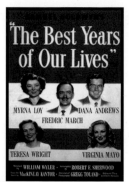

**GOLDWYN-
RKO RADIO
1946**

AFTER three years overseas fighting in World War II, three veterans return home to their small city. Sophisticated, wealthy banker Al Stephenson (March) has a beautiful, loyal wife (Loy) and two attentive children who have grown and changed. His job at the bank is frustrating, because he wants to do good. Dashing Fred Derry (Andrews) has a low-paying job and is married to a floozy (Mayo). He falls in love with Al's daughter Peggy (Wright). Homer Parrish (Russell) lost his hands in the war, and worries that his fiancee Wilma (O'Donnell) will be repulsed. His parents are oversolicitous and unaccepting of his disability. They all have to learn to adjust and renew their lives.

The Cast

Fredric March
Al Stephenson

Myrna Loy
Milly Stephenson

Dana Andrews
Fred Derry

Teresa Wright
Peggy Stephenson

Virginia Mayo
Marie Derry

Harold Russell
Homer Parrish

Cathy O'Donnell
Wilma Cameron

Hoagy Carmichael
Uncle Butch

Gladys George
Hortense Derry

Roman Bohnen
Pat Derry

Ray Collins
Mr. Milton

Director
William Wyler

Producer
Samuel Goldwyn

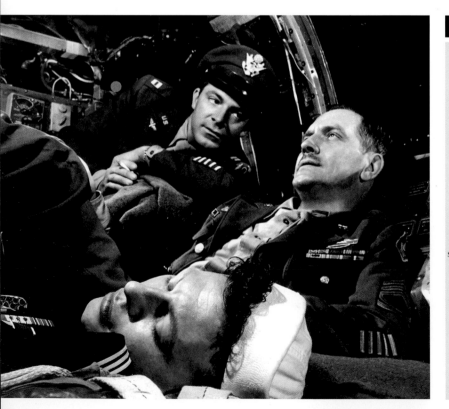

Academy Awards

✱ Best Picture
✱ Director (Wyler)
✱ Actor (March)
✱ Supporting Actor (Russell)
✱ Writing, Screenplay (Robert E. Sherwood)
Sound Recording (Gordon Sawyer)
✱ Music, Scoring of a Dramatic or Comedy Picture (Hugo Friedhofer)
✱ Film Editing (Daniel Mandell)

**8
NOMINATIONS
7 OSCARS
✱**

THE BUZZ

Goldwyn picked up two Oscars— the Irving G. Thalberg Memorial Award and another for best picture. In his acceptance speech for the latter, Wyler thanked everyone in the cast, including Hoagy Carmichael, whom he called Hugo Carmichael.

Russell received a special Oscar for "bringing hope and courage to his fellow veterans."

In 1992, Russell was forced to sell his supporting actor Oscar to pay for his wife's medical expenses.

The Stars

Myrna Loy
Milly

LOY wasn't concerned about the size of a role. Even though she was allotted less screen time than the other female lead, Teresa Wright, Loy was sold on **Best Years** as soon as she read the script. The actress was forty-one, and after playing Asian vamps, Nora Charles, a bevy of screwball cutups, and socialites, Loy was ready to play the mother of two grown children.

Fredric March
Al

WITH an assortment of characters from Dr. Jekyll and Mr. Hyde, Mark Twain, Christopher Columbus, and even Death personified, March never ran into the danger of being typecast. He also had screen triumphs in **A Star Is Born** (1937) and **Death of a Salesman** (1951), but his greatest screen success, in terms of critical and commercial success, was in **Best Years.**

Dana Andrews
Fred

ANDREWS had been a fixture in Goldwyn films since **The Westerner** (1940). Though he never reached the heights of James Stewart or Henry Fonda, he had a similar everyman quality that served him nicely in films like **The Purple Heart** (1944) and **A Walk in the Sun** (1945).

Teresa Wright
Peggy

TERESA Wright wasn't a flamboyant actress in the Davis or Stanwyck manner. Starting with her debut in **The Little Foxes** (1941), Wright liked to let her emotions simmer and then bubble over in the film's climax. At no time did she do it better than with her performance in Alfred Hitchcock's gripping **Shadow of a Doubt** (1943).

Goldwyn's inspiration for the film came from a 1944 article he read in *Time* magazine that detailed the difficulties encountered by servicemen returning home.

Russell, a veteran who lost his hands during an explosion in 1944, was discovered when Goldwyn saw him in an army film about the rehabilitation of veterans.

Screenwriter Robert E. Sherwood had conceived a scene involving GIs rioting over the housing shortage, but Goldwyn told him to delete it because he wanted a simple, believable story.

Loy was only twelve years older than her screen daughter, Teresa Wright.

> *All I want is for people to treat me like anybody else instead of pitying me.*
> —*Homer*

> " I guess there's just a certain amount of good and bad you get from your parents and I just got the bad. —*Cal* "

EAST OF EDEN

The Cast

James Dean
Cal Trask

Julie Harris
Abra

Raymond Massey
Adam Trask

Burl Ives
Sam

Richard Davalos
Aron Trask

Jo Van Fleet
Kate

Albert Dekker
Will Hamilton

Lois Smith
Anne

Harold Gordon
Gustav Albrecht

Nick Dennis
Rantani

Director and Producer
Elia Kazan

**WARNER BROS.
1955
-COLOR-**

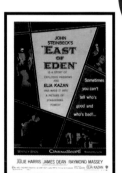

ℝELIGIOUS Adam Trask (Massey) lives on a modest lettuce farm in California with his two sons: his favorite, the sensitive Aron (Davalos), and the tortured bad boy Cal (Dean), who must compete with Aron for their father's approval and love. Cal finds his estranged mother, savvy, rebellious Kate (Van Fleet), running a brothel, and asks her for a stake to invest, turning it into a fortune with a war-related venture. Although successful, Cal still cannot win his father's affection. His frustration hits its apex when his father, ruined by a money-making scheme, rejects Cal once again by not taking his offer of money.

The Stars

James Dean
Cal

IF EVER an actor spoke to a generation, it was Dean. Even though **East of Eden** took place during World War I, Dean's troubled Cal instantly connected with the disillusioned youth of the Eisenhower era. His popularity mushroomed following his volatile performances in **Rebel Without a Cause** (1955) and **Giant** (1956); ironically he assumed cultish proportions after his fatal car crash on Sept. 30, 1955.

Julie Harris
Abra

LIKE Dean, the gifted Harris was trained in the Method style of acting. She came to Hollywood in 1952 for the screen version of her stage hit **The Member of the Wedding**, and nabbed an Oscar nomination. Though mostly known for her work on Broadway, her sporadic film appearances have been worth the wait, especially her turn as one of the spooked houseguests in **The Haunting** (1963).

Gossip

During the making of **East of Eden**, Dean was depressed over his breakup from actress Pier Angeli. To keep an eye on him, Kazan moved into a dressing room on the Warners lot and had Dean live in the adjoining one.

Kazan only used the last third of John Steinbeck's huge novel as the basis for the movie.

To get the proper outburst from Massey in the scene where Dean is reading the Bible, Kazan had Dean spout a stream of profanity. In another scene, Massey was genuinely surprised when Dean improvised giving him an embrace.

Dean's salary for **East of Eden** was $18,000.

East of Eden was Kazan's first film in color and CinemaScope.

> "If you want to give me a present, give me a good life. That's something I could value. —*Adam*

> "It's awful not to be loved . . . makes you mean and violent and cruel." —*Abra*

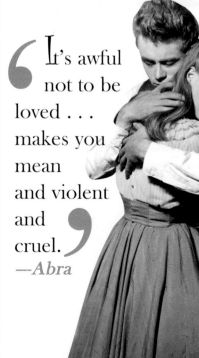

Academy Awards

Director (Kazan)
Actor (Dean)
✱ **Supporting Actress** (Van Fleet)
Writing, Screenplay (Paul Osborn)

4 NOMINATIONS 1 OSCAR ✱

THE BUZZ

Dean was the first performer since Jeanne Eagels in 1929 to earn a posthumous Oscar nomination. The following year, he was nominated again for **Giant**.

Columnist Hedda Hopper was pushing for the Academy to give Dean an honorary award, but the Academy president pointed out that current nominees were ineligible from receiving such tributes.

A FACE IN THE CROWD

REPORTER Marcia Jeffries (Neal) discovers charming, folksy drifter Lonesome Rhodes (Griffith) while working on her local Arkansas radio show, "A Face in the Crowd." Marcia helps him get his own show and he becomes an overnight sensation and moves on to national television. But his down-home entertainment masks a corrupt, cynical, right-wing megalomaniac and as the power and celebrity goes to his head he becomes unbearable. Marcia loves Rhodes, but is shattered when he shows up with a sexy young bride, baton-twirling champion Betty Lou Fleckum (Remick). Both his head writer Mel Miller (Matthau) and Marcia start to see through Rhodes and they both fear that he is dangerous. Marcia must stop the sinister autocrat she helped create.

WARNER BROS.
1957

POWER! He loved it! He took it raw in big gulpfuls... he liked the taste, the way it mixed with the bourbon and the sin in his blood!

AN ELIA KAZAN PRODUCTION
BUDD SCHULBERG'S
a Face in the Crowd
ANDY GRIFFITH · PATRICIA NEAL

The Cast

Andy Griffith
Lonesome Rhodes

Patricia Neal
Marcia Jeffries

Walter Matthau
Mel Miller

Anthony Franciosa
Joey Kiely

Lee Remick
Betty Lou Fleckum

Percy Waram
Gen. Haynesworth

Paul McGrath
Macey

Rod Brasfield
Beanie

Marshall Neilan
Sen. Worthington
Fuller

Alexander Kirkland
Jim Collier

Charles Irving
Mr. Luffler

Howard Smith
J.B. Jeffries

Director and Producer
Elia Kazan

'This whole country's just like my flock of sheep! Hillbillies, hausfraus — everybody that's got to jump when someone else blows a whistle! They're mine! — *Lonesome*

Gossip

Screenwriter Budd Schulberg did extensive research to create the atmosphere of "grass-roots fascism" that Kazan called the theme of **A Face in the Crowd.** They attended Young & Rubicam product meetings, talked to ad execs, visited the Grand Ole Opry, and met stand-up comics, several of whom appear in the movie.

Stand-up comic Griffith attracted Kazan and Schulberg's attention when they heard one of his recordings, and Kazan spotted Remick dancing the samba on a television show.

For the final scene in which Lonesome goes insane, Kazan wanted Griffith to be completely out of control. Since the easy-going Griffith was a relatively inexperienced actor, Kazan decided the only way he'd get the desired wild behavior was to get Griffith drunk.

Many television and news personalities appear in cameos as themselves, including Mike Wallace, Bennett Cerf, Faye Emerson, Walter Winchell, and John Cameron Swayze.

> **"I**llegal? Honey, nothing's illegal if they don't catch you!**"**
> *—Joey*

The Stars

Andy Griffith
Lonesome

MOST people know Griffith as television's honest, dependable Andy Taylor, which makes Griffith's portrait of power-hungry Lonesome Rhodes all the more astonishing. It was Griffith's follow-up, **No Time for Sergeants** (1958), in which he recreated his stage success as a dimwitted private, that paved the way for his sitcom success as a lovable, down-home sheriff.

Patricia Neal
Marcia

STAGE-trained actress Neal meshed nicely with Kazan, who also had his roots in the theater. Though she came to Hollywood eight years earlier, she got her best notices for playing the hapless Marcia. **A Face in the Crowd** was not a commercial success, but it did jump-start Neal's film career, and led to her Oscar-winning performance in **Hud** (1963).

Walter Matthau
Mel

BROADWAY actor Matthau had appeared in three undistinguished films before Kazan gave him his first screen role of note as the intellectual Mel. Matthau held his own dramatically, but comedy was really his forte, especially when paired with Jack Lemmon in **The Fortune Cookie** (1966) (for which he copped a supporting actor Oscar) and **The Odd Couple** (1968).

Screen Team

Griffith and Matthau starred in the comedy **Onionhead** (1958).

Franciosa and Remick played husband and wife in **The Long Hot Summer** (1958).

COLUMBIA

1953 FROM HERE TO ETERNITY

IN 1941, JUST before World War II, bugler and former middleweight boxer, Pvt. Robert E. Lee Prewitt (Clift) transfers to an army base in Pearl Harbor. He stubbornly refuses to get in the ring, even though his superior, cruel boxing coach Capt. Dana Holmes (Ober) goes to great lengths to get him on the team.

Prew's friend, Pvt. Angelo Maggio (Sinatra) has his own problems with the sadistic Sgt. James R. "Fatso" Judson, and on the home front, Holmes' straying wife (Kerr) embarks on an affair with charismatic Sgt. Milton Warden (Lancaster). Prew meanwhile falls for pretty hostess Alma (Reed). The Japanese attack of December 7, 1941 changes everything.

The Cast

Burt Lancaster
Sgt. Milton Warden

Montgomery Clift
Pvt. Robert E. Lee
Prewitt

Deborah Kerr
Karen Holmes

Frank Sinatra
Pvt. Angelo Maggio

Donna Reed
Alma Burke
aka Lorene

Ernest Borgnine
Sgt. James R.
"Fatso" Judson

Jack Warden
Cpl. Buckley

Director
Fred Zinnemann

Producer
Buddy Adler

Gossip

The Production Code Office suggested that before Kerr and Lancaster embrace on the beach, one of them should don a robe. When Zinnemann refused, he was told to cut four seconds showing the water coming up on the two actors rather suggestively.

Ava Gardner, then married to Sinatra, spoke to Columbia boss Harry Cohn's wife, and the two women convinced the reluctant Cohn to test Sinatra. Sinatra agreed to make **Eternity** for the bargain-basement price of $8,000.

Joan Crawford turned down the part of Karen because she objected to the costumes.

While shooting in Honolulu, Sinatra, Clift, and author James Jones would go out drinking most nights. Lancaster usually had to carry the two actors to their rooms each night and put them in bed.

Screen Team

Lancaster worked with Kerr again in **The Gypsy Moths** (1969) and with Clift in **Judgment at Nuremberg**.

Academy Awards

⭕ **13 NOMINATIONS 8 OSCARS** ✱

✱ Best Picture
✱ Director (Zinnemann)
Actor (Clift and Lancaster)
Actress (Kerr)
✱ Supporting Actor (Sinatra)
✱ Supporting Actress (Reed)
✱ Writing, Screenplay (Daniel Taradash)
✱ Cinematography, Black and White
(Burnett Guffey)
✱ Sound Recording (Columbia Sound
Department; John P. Livadary)
Music, Scoring of a Dramatic or Comedy Picture
(Morris Stoloff and George Duning)
✱ Film Editing (William Lyon)
Costume Design, Black and White
(Jean Louis)

THE BUZZ

Sinatra returned home from the ceremony with his kids, then took a walk around Beverly Hills with Oscar in tow. During the stroll, police stopped him, thinking he had swiped the award.

The Stars

Deborah Kerr
Karen

THE ladylike Kerr seemed odd casting to play a nymphomaniac, especially after her virtuous roles in **The Hucksters** (1947) and **King Solomon's Mines** (1950). But her regal demeanor belied her inner passion, and she surprised the naysayers, including Harry Cohn, who agreed to cast her only at Zinnemann's urging.

Montgomery Clift
Prewitt

LANCASTER said the only time he was ever nervous was filming his first scene with Clift, who he feared would blow him off the screen. Clift gave one of his complex performances in **Eternity**. After a bad car crash during the filming of **Raintree County** (1957) that marred his boyish good looks and left him addicted to painkillers, he never had another role or film of as much substance, with the exception of **Judgment at Nuremberg** (1961) for which he was nominated for an Oscar.

Burt Lancaster
Warden

HUNKY Lancaster was forty when he made **From Here to Eternity**. He kept in shape for the beach scene by jogging and working out with weights. The result was one of the most scorching scenes ever put on film. Lancaster got his start in film noir, and in ten years played everything from a drunk (**Come Back Little Sheba**) to a legendary athlete (**Jim Thorpe—All American**), but will always be known for his heavyweight performances in **Eternity** as well as **Sweet Smell of Success** (1957) and **Elmer Gantry** (1960).

‘I'm a private no-class dogface. The way most civilians look at that, that's two steps up from nothin.'– *Prewitt*

GENTLEMAN'S AGREEMENT

WIDOWED magazine writer Phil Green (Peck), a Christian, has an assignment to write an exposé on anti-Semitism. He pretends to be Jewish, takes the name Greenberg, and sees the prejudice first-hand—from his delicate fiancee Kathy (McGuire), who shows her prejudice in subtle ways, to his son Tommy (Stockwell) being called a "kike" in school. Phil's old friend, insightful, charming Dave (Garfield), shares the frustrating prejudice he has endured without bitterness. Brassy, witty fashion writer Anne (Holm) is also in love with Phil; he must choose between Kathy and Anne while writing his heart-felt, righteous story.

20th CENTURY-FOX 1947

The Cast

Gregory Peck
Phil Green

Dorothy McGuire
Kathy Lacey

John Garfield
Dave Goldmann

Celeste Holm
Anne Dettrey

Anne Revere
Mrs. Green

Dean Stockwell
Tom Green

Albert Dekker
Mr. Minify

June Havoc
Elaine Wales

Jane Wyatt
Jane

Nicholas Joy
Dr. Craigie

Sam Jaffe
Professor Lieberman

Harold Vermilyea
Mr. Jordan

Director
Elia Kazan

Producer
Darryl F. Zanuck

' *Phil:* **I**'m just going to let everybody know that I'm Jewish. **'**
Kathy: Jewish? Phil, you're not. Are you?

Screen Team

Revere worked with Garfield in another 1947 hit **Body and Soul**, and with Stockwell in **Deep Waters** (1948).

Academy Awards

8 NOMINATIONS 3 OSCARS ✳

✳ Best Picture
✳ Director (Kazan)
Actor (Peck)
Actress (McGuire)
✳ Supporting Actress (Holm)
Supporting Actress (Revere)
Writing, Screenplay (Moss Hart)
Film Editing (Harmon Jones)

THE BUZZ

Kazan also won a best director Oscar for **On the Waterfront** (1954). Far more controversial was his honorary Oscar in 1999, which sparked dissension among the Academy, as many members had not forgiven him for cooperating with the House Un-American Activities Committee in the '50s.

Holm's husband was so excited over her win that he locked the Oscar in their car for safekeeping and then lost the key.

Gossip

Zanuck paid $75,000 for the rights to Laura Z. Hobson's bestseller. The other studio moguls tried to persuade him not to make the movie because they didn't want to draw attention to anti-Semitism and the fact that many of them were Jewish.

Garfield was the only Jewish leading man in Hollywood who wanted to play Dave, even though it was a supporting role.

Gentleman's Agreement was Fox's top moneymaker in 1948, and paved the way for other social dramas that tackled such previously taboo topics as mental illness (1948's **The Snake Pit**) and racism (Kazan's 1949 film **Pinky**).

After completing this film, Peck and McGuire established the La Jolla Playhouse in California with Mel Ferrer.

The Stars

Dorothy McGuire
Kathy

Though McGuire had a string of hits since her 1943 film debut, she took a three-year sabbatical after **Gentleman's Agreement** to do some stage work and take care of her children. Her maternal instincts served her well, and from the '50s on played a host of memorable screen moms in **Friendly Persuasion** (1956), **Old Yeller** (1957), **Swiss Family Robinson** (1960), and **Summer Magic** (1963).

Gregory Peck
Phil

With rare exception, most notably **Duel in the Sun** (1946), Peck usually played the valiant knight, explaining that he liked the challenge of playing good guys because "it's harder to make them interesting." He was also one of Hollywood's most outspoken liberals and sought out projects that melded with his beliefs such as **Gentleman's Agreement** and his greatest film, **To Kill a Mockingbird** (1962).

John Garfield
Dave

Amiable Dave Goldmann was a welcome departure for Garfield, who had become a poster boy for brooding outcasts in Warner movies such as **They Made Me a Criminal** (1939). Still, it wouldn't be a Garfield film without some of his fireworks, and he ignites the film's most powerful scene involving an anti-Semitic drunk.

The Cast

GRAND HOTEL

The Cast

Greta Garbo
Grusinskaya

John Barrymore
Baron Felix von Gaigern

Joan Crawford
Flaemmchen

Wallace Beery
Preysing

Lionel Barrymore
Otto Kringelein

Director
Edmund Goulding

Producer
Irving Thalberg

"I want to be alone."
—*Grusinskaya*

1932

M-G-M

ERLIN'S opulent, exclusive, teeming Grand Hotel is home to charming, down-and-out Baron Felix von Gaigern (John Barrymore), who wants to steal from self-centered, suicidal ballet diva Grusinskaya (Garbo), but falls in love with her. The baron is kind to terminally ill, working-class bookkeeper Otto Kringelein (Lionel Barrymore), who is spending all his hard-earned money to have a final taste of the good life.

Kringelein's boss, upright and uptight business-man Preysing (Beery), bullies him. Preysing's mistress, stenographer and aspiring starlet Flaemmchen (Crawford), falls for the baron. These lives intertwine for a brief time.

The Stars

Greta Garbo
Grusinskaya

John Barrymore
The Baron

AT the time she made **Grand Hotel,** Garbo was at the crest of her most rewarding period with **Queen Christina** (1933), **Anna Karenina** (1935), **Camille** (1937), and **Ninotchka** (1939) on the horizon. The enigmatic Swedish siren retired in 1941, nearly vanishing from the public eye. Still, the occasional Garbo spotting in New York City never failed to create headlines.

NO ONE ever did more with half a face than Barrymore, except maybe Claudette Colbert. "The Great Profile" proved the perfect romantic partner for the usually reserved Garbo, who was so smitten that she once shocked cast and crew by giving him an impromptu kiss at the end of shooting a scene.

Joan Crawford
Flaemmchen

THOUGH Crawford made her box-office mark playing a flapper in **Our Dancing Daughters** (1928), and a poor working girl turned kept woman in **Possessed** (1931), **Grand Hotel** elevated her to the big leagues as she proved she could hold her own opposite the upper crust of the M-G-M star roster.

Wallace Beery
Preysing

BEERY'S rigid Preysing was a 180-degree turn from the actor's previous role, as a down-and-out boxer with two loves—booze and his son—in the sentimental **The Champ** (1931). In a bid to outshine the other actors who checked into **Grand Hotel,** Beery was the only one who adopted a German accent.

Lionel Barrymore
Kringelein

"**I**'VE got a lot of ham in me" was Barrymore's critique of himself, and to a certain extent that could be said of his performance in **Grand Hotel,** which was mostly moving, and at times whining. Still, it's hard not to enjoy the moment when he finally overcomes his timidity and blasts Beery.

Academy Awards

1 NOMINATION 1 OSCAR

✳ Best Picture

THE BUZZ
Grand Hotel is the only film to be named best picture and not receive a nomination in any other category.

Screen Team

The two Barrymores appeared together again in two more 1932 releases, **Arsene Lupin** and **Rasputin and the Empress.**

Lionel Barrymore worked with Crawford in **The Gorgeous Hussy** (1936) and Beery in **Dinner at Eight** (1933).

Gossip

Garbo had the crew rearrange the furniture in Grusinskaya's suite so that Barrymore's famed left profile would be favored.

Buster Keaton was M-G-M's original choice to play Kringelein.

To avoid any chance of either Garbo or Crawford trying to upstage one another, Goulding made sure they never played a scene together.

'**G**rand Hotel. . . always the same. . . Nothing ever happens.'
— Dr. Otternschlag

THE GRAPES OF WRATH

20th CENTURY-FOX

1940

THE DESTITUTE Joads, having lost their farm in the Dust Bowl of Oklahoma, must pack up and leave. Tom Joad (Fonda), just home from jail, leads the family to California in search of promised work, but the Depression has forced thousands of other poor,

desperate families to seek jobs in the orange groves as well. The family endures terrible hardships, but somehow finds the strength to go on.

The Cast

Henry Fonda
Tom Joad

Jane Darwell
Ma Joad

John Carradine
Casy

Charley Grapewin
Grandpa

Dorris Bowdon
Rosasharn

Russell Simpson
Pa Joad

O.Z. Whitehead
Al

Eddie Quillan
Connie

Zeffie Tilbury
Grandma

Frank Sully
Noah

Frank Darien
Uncle John

Darrell Hickman
Winfield

Director
John Ford

Producer
Darryl F. Zanuck

'Wherever you can look, wherever there's a fight so hungry people can eat, I'll be there.
—*Tom*'

Screen Team

Fonda and Carradine shared screen time on many occasions, including **Jesse James** and **Drums Along the Mohawk** (1939), and **The Return of Frank James** and **Chad Hanna** (1940).

Academy Awards

7 NOMINATIONS 2 OSCARS ✱

Best Picture
✱ Director (Ford)
Actor (Fonda)
✱ Supporting Actress (Darwell)
Writing, Screenplay (Nunnally Johnson)
Sound Recording (E.H. Hansen)
Film Editing (Robert E. Simpson)

THE BUZZ

Fonda had to wait another forty-one years to be Oscar-nominated. Sadly, he died four months after receiving his Oscar for **On Golden Pond** (1981).

Instead of saying how happy she was to win an Oscar, Darwell, who claimed she hadn't worked in seven months, told reporters, "Awards are nice, but I'd much rather have a job."

The Stars

Henry Fonda
Tom

"I AIN'T really Henry Fonda! Nobody could be. Nobody could have that much integrity," the gangly, soft-spoken actor once said about himself. But try getting anyone to believe it after seeing how much conviction he brought to parts such as **Young Mr. Lincoln** (1939) and the lone-wolf juror in **12 Angry Men** (1957).

Jane Darwell
Ma

MA JOAD was Darwell's favorite role and the pinnacle of a career that spanned more than 175 films from **The Capture of Aguinaldo** (1913) to **Mary Poppins** (1964) with her touching performance as the Bird Woman.

Gossip

Beulah Bondi and Walter Brennan were originally considered for Ma and Pa Joad.

Zanuck paid $75,000 for the rights to **The Grapes of Wrath**, the highest price for any novel up to that point.

Screenwriter Nunnally Johnson had to clean up much of the book's raw language to meet censor approval.

PARAMOUNT
1945

The Cast

Ray Milland
Don Birnam

Jane Wyman
Helen St. James

Phillip Terry
Wick Birnam

Howard Da Silva
Nat

Doris Dowling
Gloria

Frank Faylen
"Bim" Nolan

Mary Young
Mrs. Deveridge

Anita Sharp-Bolster
Mrs. Foley

Director
Billy Wilder

Producer
Charles Brackett

THE LOST WEEKEND

ALCOHOLIC, insecure writer Don Birnam (Milland) is trying to stay sober. His girlfriend, successful writer Helen St. James (Wyman), and his solicitous brother, Wick (Terry), try to help him. As Don's craving for liquor becomes overpowering, he pushes them away and goes on a four-day bender. His descent into alcoholic hell is swift. He remembers opportunities in his life ruined by his drinking, enabled by Wick with money and excuses. This spree will be his last. Either he will kill himself or recover and write his book.

> "One's too many and a hundred's not enough.
> —Nat"

Screen Team

Milland and Wyman co-starred once more in the appropriately titled **Let's Do It Again** (1953), a musical remake of **The Awful Truth** (1937).

Academy Awards

7 NOMINATIONS 4 OSCARS

* Best Picture
* Director (Wilder)
* Actor (Milland)
* Writing, Screenplay
(Wilder and Charles Brackett)
Cinematography, Black and White (John F. Seitz)
Music, Scoring of a Dramatic or Comedy Picture
(Miklos Rosza)
Film Editing (Doane Harrison)

THE BUZZ

The occupants of the Writers' Building on the Paramount lot really knew how to say congratulations. When Wilder and Brackett showed up the morning after the Oscar ceremony, dozens of liquor bottles were hanging from every window.

> "What I'm trying to say is, I'm not a drinker . . . I'm a drunk. —*Don*"

The Stars

Jane Wyman
Helen

Ray Milland
Don

CASTING the amiable Welsh actor, whose career had been built on racy comedies such as **The Major and the Minor** (1942), as a struggling alcoholic seemed like a gamble, especially to Wilder who had wanted Broadway actor Jose Ferrer. But Paramount insisted on Milland; for once, someone knew better than the brilliant director.

WYMAN'S stock in trade had been playing the wisecracking best friend to the likes of Priscilla Lane in **Brother Rat** (1938) and Olivia de Havilland in **My Love Came Back** (1940). In **The Lost Weekend**, she played it straight, and directors finally began tapping her dramatic range, casting her as farmer Gregory Peck's stern wife in **The Yearling** (1946) and as a deaf mute in **Johnny Belinda** (1948), for which she won an Oscar.

Gossip

Wilder asked for Wyman based on her performance as a devoted war wife in **Princess O'Rourke** (1943).

Wilder's decision to film in Manhattan around Bellevue Hospital and along the grungy streets of Third Avenue, with its seedy bars and derelicts, gave **The Lost Weekend** a bleak and realistic atmosphere.

The director met his future wife, Audrey Young, on the set. She had a bit as a hatcheck girl at a nightclub from which Milland is ejected.

The liquor industry offered Paramount $5 million to "bury" the movie. In his typical sardonic manner, Wilder said "If they'd offered me the $5 million, I would have."

The optimistic ending of the film is different from the somber novel. Another key change: In the novel, Don's bisexuality is a direct cause of his drinking rather than writer's block.

COLUMBIA
1939

MR. SMITH GOES TO WASHINGTON

GOV. HOPPER (Kibbee) appoints naive, earnest, Boy Ranger leader Jefferson Smith (Stewart) to replace a late senator, assuming that Smith will be his pawn. In Washington, wide-eyed Smith unites with his hero, the state's patrician senior senator Joseph Paine (Rains) and manipulative media boss Jim Taylor (Arnold), who tries to corrupt Smith. When the powerful men in the capital cannot co-opt him, they try to drive him out with a scandal. But Mr. Smith fights back.

The Cast

James Stewart
Jefferson Smith

Jean Arthur
Clarissa Saunders

Claude Rains
Sen. Joseph Paine

Edward Arnold
Jim Taylor

Guy Kibbee
Gov. Hopper

Thomas Mitchell
Diz Moore

Eugene Pallette
Chick McGann

Beulah Bondi
Ma Smith

H.B. Warner
Senate Majority Leader

Harry Carey
Senate President

Astrid Allwyn
Susan Paine

Ruth Donnelly
Mrs. Hopper

Grant Mitchell
Sen. MacPherson

Porter Hall
Sen. Monroe

Director and Producer
Frank Capra

"You think I'm licked. Well, I'm not licked. I'm going to stay right here and fight for this lost cause. — *Smith*"

Screen Team

Stewart and Arthur teamed with Capra on the previous year's Best Picture **You Can't Take It With You**.

Arthur worked with Arnold in **Diamond Jim** (1935), **Easy Living** (1937), and **You Can't Take It With You**, and with Mitchell in **Adventure in Manhattan** (1936) and **Only Angels Have Wings** (1939).

Academy Awards

10 NOMINATIONS 1 OSCAR ✱

Best Picture
Director (Capra)
Actor (Stewart)
Supporting Actor (Carey)
Supporting Actor (Rains)
✱ **Writing, Original Story** (Lewis R. Foster)
Writing, Screenplay (Sidney Buchman)
Interior Decoration (Lionel Banks)
Sound Recording (John Livadary)
Film Editing (Gene Havlick and Al Clark)

THE BUZZ

At the time of the 1939 ceremony, Capra was winding up his stint as Academy president. The position didn't give him or **Mr. Smith** an edge in the voting. As he said in his autobiography, "Don't make the best picture you ever made in the year that someone makes **Gone with the Wind**."

The Stars

James Stewart
Mr. Smith

WITH his all-American looks, "golly-gee" demeanor, and country-boy drawl, Stewart was a perfect fit for the wide-eyed idealist who takes on Washington. His bravura perform-ance, especially his famous filibuster sequence, secured his position as a first-class star and an American original for the next six decades.

Jean Arthur
Saunders

DAFFY, squeaky-voiced Arthur was Capra's favorite actress, and he also worked with her on **Mr. Deeds Goes to Town** (1936) and **You Can't Take It With You** (1938). Though she was often jittery before going in front of the camera, her performances always seemed effortless, whether it was drama (**History is Made at Night** in 1937) or comedy (1943's **The More the Merrier**, her sole Oscar nod).

> ❝ Either I'm dead right or I'm crazy. ❞
> — *Smith*

Gossip

The U.S. Senate was horrified about the way its members were portrayed and denounced **Mr. Smith** as "belittling the American system of government."

Capra originally intended the movie to be a sequel to **Mr. Deeds Goes to Town**, with Gary Cooper repeating his title role. But when Cooper had other film commitments, he cast Stewart and adapted the script.

To make Stewart sound hoarse during the filibuster sequence, the actor's throat was swabbed twice a day with a vile mercury solution that swelled and irritated his vocal cords.

U.S. ambassador to England Joseph P. Kennedy urged Columbia chief Harry Cohn to withdraw the film overseas because it was generating negative foreign public opinion about the American mode of life.

> ❝ I've loved you since the first moment I saw you. I guess maybe I've even loved you before I saw you. —*George* ❞

A PLACE IN THE SUN

DAILY EXPRESS

I WOULDN'T STOP AT MURDER!

FROM THE FILM: 'A PLACE IN THE SUN'

THROUGH his successful relative, working-class George Eastman (Clift) gets a factory job, with the promise of promotion.

He meets vivacious, upper-class Angela Vickers (Taylor) and her elite wealthy crowd; he and Angela fall madly in love, but George is entangled with plain, poor, unsophisticated Alice Tripp (Winters), who is pregnant after a liaison with George. Alice pursues him to Angela's family estate, threatening to expose their secret if he doesn't marry her. But George wants the rich life with beautiful Angela, and is caught in a dilemma. An accident on the lake propels him into a tragic place.

PARAMOUNT 1951

The Cast

Montgomery Clift
George Eastman

Elizabeth Taylor
Angela Vickers

Shelley Winters
Alice Tripp

Anne Revere
Hannah Eastman

Keefe Brasselle
Earl Eastman

Fred Clark
Bellows

Raymond Burr
Frank Marlowe

Herbert Heyes
Charles Eastman

Director and Producer
George Stevens

The Stars

Elizabeth Taylor
Angela

TAYLOR was that rare child star who achieved greater stardom as an adult, thanks in no small part to her off-screen exploits— in particular, keeping everyone wondering whom she would marry next. But her innate gift for acting cannot be discounted, given her intelligent performances in **A Place in the Sun, Giant** (1956), **Cat on a Hot Tin Roof** (1958), and **Who's Afraid of Virginia Woolf?** (1966).

Montgomery Clift
George

IN A MERE three years, Clift earned Oscar nominations for his moving film debut as a soldier trying to reunite a war orphan with his mother in **The Search** (1948), a fortune hunter in **The Heiress** (1949), and the social-climbing George Eastman. His intense acting style influenced Taylor, who said she never cared about acting until she worked with him.

Shelley Winters
Alice

WINTERS never thought of herself as a love goddess, yet that was the build-up she was given in forgettable potboilers like **South Sea Sinner** (1949). Finally with **He Ran All the Way** (1951) and her follow-up, **A Place in the Sun,** she was taken seriously as an actress; she would go on to win supporting actress Oscars for **The Diary of Anne Frank** (1959) and **A Patch of Blue** (1965).

Gossip

Taylor's white debutante gown caused a sensation, and thousands of teenage girls wore copies of it to their senior proms.

To convince Stevens she could look dowdy, Winters dyed her blonde hair mousy brown and pinned it back, donned a frumpy dress, and carried a sack lunch to her meeting with him at the Hollywood Athletic Club. Stevens was there almost an hour before he finally spotted Winters.

Winters' drowning scene was shot during a chilly November at Lake Tahoe. She and Clift agreed beforehand to have stunt people do the scene. To get them to change their minds, Stevens plunged into the lake. When he emerged from the water, soaked and teeth a-chattering, Stevens said, "Never mind."

❝If you're an Eastman, you're not in the same boat with anyone. *—Alice* **❞**

Screen Team

Clift and Taylor teamed up again in **Raintree County** (1957) and **Suddenly, Last Summer** (1959).

Academy Awards

9 NOMINATIONS 6 OSCARS ✳

Best Picture
✳ **Director** (Stevens)
Actor (Clift)
Actress (Winters)
✳ **Writing, Screenplay**
(Michael Wilson and Harry Brown)
✳ **Cinematography, Black and White**
(William C. Mellor)
✳ **Music, Scoring of a Dramatic or Comedy Picture** (Franz Waxman)
✳ **Film Editing** (William Hornbeck)
✳ **Costume Design, Black and White**
(Edith Head)

THE BUZZ

Head's Oscar was one of eight in her career. In all, she received thirty-four costume design nominations.

SUSPENSE

SUSPENSE

Nail-biting, edge-of-your-seat, heart-pounding suspense. Knots in your stomach.

Nobody does it better than the master, Alfred Hitchcock. He draws you right in. Will the spies discover that Ingrid Bergman is an agent in **Notorious**? Are they trying to kill her? Will dashing Cary Grant save her? There's no break in the uneasy tension. As soon as we see her escape from the missing-key incident, we need to worry about Claude Rains catching them in the wine cellar. "Watch it! Get OUT of there," we want to yell at the screen.

In **Rear Window,** when evil neighbor Raymond Burr is about to surprise snooping Grace Kelly in his apartment, we want to scream "Hurry! Just LEAVE!" Hitchcock plans every frame, every close-up to draw you in and keep you in his grip.

Gaslight fills us with foreboding. Will insecure heiress Ingrid Bergman intuit that she's not insane? Can the suspicious detective expose Boyer? "Wise up! HE'S the loony!" we scream at her. Will she prevail?

Who was trying to kill **Laura**? Slithery Clifton Webb? Spineless Vincent Price? Two-faced Judith Anderson? Otto Preminger keeps us guessing to the tune of **Laura**'s haunting theme song.

Why is Marlene Dietrich so evil in **Witness for the Prosecution**? You just have to wait for its ending that never fails to surprise and dazzle.

Plots twist as we try to piece together the puzzle, unravel the cliffhanger, solve the mystery. Angst, willies, panic, butterflies, heebie-jeebies, sweaty palms. Bring it on.

WHO DONE IT?

NOTORIOUS

PARTY GIRL Alicia Huberman (Bergman) is devastated when her German father is convicted of crimes against the United States. At a drunken party after the trial, charming undercover agent Devlin (Grant) talks her into spying on her father's Nazi friends in Rio and marrying the boss, Alex Sebastian (Rains), to gain access to the spy ring, even though she is falling in love with Devlin. The team makes an important discovery about the spies. Alicia's life is in danger as Alex and his mother (Konstantin) try to slowly poison Alicia. Although Devlin at first disapproves of her loose ways, he becomes smitten and tries to rescue her and get the spies.

**RKO RADIO
1946**

The Cast

Cary Grant
T.R. Devlin

Ingrid Bergman
Alicia Huberman

Claude Rains
Alexander "Alex" Sebastian

Louis Calhern
Capt. Paul Prescott

Leopoldine Konstantin
Madame Anna Sebastian

Director and Producer
Alfred Hitchcock

Gossip

Hitchcock gave Rains the choice of whether or not to adopt a German accent. Rains decided against it.

Bergman and Grant's telephone kissing scene defied Production Code censors, who only allowed three seconds for a screen kiss. Hitchcock extended the scene by interrupting their kiss with talking, nibbling, and other diversions.

The Stars

Cary Grant
T.R. Devlin

NO woman could resist Grant in his Hitchcock films: in **Suspicion** (1941), Joan Fontaine succumbs to his charms; in **To Catch a Thief** (1955) it's Grace Kelly. And in **North by Northwest** (1959), Eva Marie Saint lets him share her train compartment.

Ingrid Bergman
Alicia

LIKE Grace Kelly, Bergman is one of the most fondly remembered Hitchcock heroines. Another distinction Bergman shared with Kelly: she worked with Hitchcock three times and remained a lifelong friend.

Academy Awards

2 NOMINATIONS

Supporting Actor (Rains)
Writing, Original Screenplay (Ben Hecht)

Alicia: This is a strange love affair.
Devlin: What's strange about it?
Alicia: The fact that you don't love me!

GASLIGHT

NEWLYWED and impressionable heiress Paula Anton (Bergman) moves with her cunning, manipulative, evil husband Gregory (Boyer) to her Gothic childhood home in London, which was once the site of her aunt's brutal murder. Paula believes the house is haunted but Gregory dismisses her, insisting that she is mad. He is uninterested in Paula, except to torment her

M-G-M
1944

psychologically, and gets the servants, especially sassy Nancy Oliver (Lansbury), to unwittingly help him. Paula, terrified and isolated, starts to think that she is going crazy. Detective Brian Cameron (Cotten) begins to wonder whether there is a connection between Gregory and the earlier murder and comes to Paula's aid.

The Cast

Charles Boyer
Gregory Anton

Ingrid Bergman
Paula Alquist Anton

Joseph Cotten
Brian Cameron

Angela Lansbury
Nancy Oliver

Dame May Whitty
Miss Thwaites

Barbara Everest
Elizabeth

Emil Rameau
Maestro Mario Guardi

Edmund Breon
Gen. Huddleston

Halliwell Hobbes
Mr. Muffin

Tom Stevenson
Williams

Heather Thatcher
Lady Dalroy

Lawrence Grossmith
Lord Dalroy

Director
George Cukor

Producer
Arthur Hornblow Jr.

‘ If I could only get inside that brain of yours and understand what makes you do these crazy, twisted things. — *Gregory* ’

Joseph Cotten
Brian

Angela Lansbury
Nancy

LIKE Bergman, Cotten also belonged to David O. Selznick's stable of stars, and he headlined many of the producer's biggest hits, both romantic (**Since You Went Away** and **I'll Be Seeing You** from 1944) and epic (the 1946 western **Duel in the Sun**).

LANSBURY was only eighteen when she made her film debut in **Gaslight,** but she quickly became one of M-G-M's most reliable actresses, enlivening several important productions including **The Picture of Dorian Gray** (1945) and **The Harvey Girls** (1946). She had even greater success on the stage in shows such as **Mame** (1966) and **Sweeney Todd** (1979), and a twelve-year run on TV's **Murder, She Wrote.**

Charles Boyer
Gregory

BERGMAN once called Boyer "the most intelligent actor I ever worked with, and one of the very nicest," a sentiment echoed by several of his leading ladies, including Joan Fontaine and Alexis Smith. His suave manners and continental looks made him an irresistible screen lover, whether playing Napoleon in **Conquest** (1937) or the notorious Pepe Le Moko in **Algiers** (1938).

Ingrid Bergman
Paula

DURING her peak Hollywood years from 1939 to 1946, Bergman's diverse screen incarnations ranged from a Cockney trollop in **Dr. Jekyll and Mr. Hyde** (1941) and a freedom fighter in **For Whom the Bell Tolls** (1943) to a nun in **The Bells of St. Mary's** (1945) and a party girl working undercover for the F.B.I. in **Notorious** (1946).

Academy Awards

7 NOMINATIONS 2 OSCARS ✻

Best Picture
Actor (Boyer)
✻ Actress (Bergman)
Supporting Actress (Lansbury)
Writing, Screenplay (John L. Balderston, Walter Reisch and John Van Druten)
Cinematography, Black and White (Joseph Ruttenberg)
✻ Interior Decoration, Black and White (Cedric Gibbons and William Ferrari; Edwin B. Willis and Paul Huldschinsky)

THE BUZZ

Bergman's Oscar for **Gaslight** was her first of three. She earned a second best actress Oscar for **Anastasia** (1956) and had a supporting actress win for **Murder on the Orient Express** (1974).

Screen Team

Boyer and Bergman were reunited for **Arch of Triumph** (1948).

Gene TIERNEY
Dana ANDREWS

Laura

CLIFTON VINCENT JUDITH
WEBB · PRICE · ANDERSON
20th
CENTURY-FOX
OTTO PREMINGER

The Cast

Dana Andrews
Mark McPherson

Gene Tierney
Laura Hunt

Clifton Webb
Waldo Lydecker

Vincent Price
Shelby Carpenter

Judith Anderson
Ann Treadwell

Dorothy Adams
Bessie

Kathleen Howard
Louise

Director and Producer
Otto Preminger

> " I must say, for a charming, intelligent girl, you certainly surrounded yourself with a remarkable collection of dopes. "
> *– Mark*

LAURA

HARD-BOILED detective Mark McPherson (Andrews) investigates the murder of beautiful Laura Hunt (Tierney). McPherson interviews suspects Waldo Lydecker (Webb), her prissy, witty, manipulative mentor; Shelby Carpenter (Price), her wimpy playboy fiance; and her aunt, Ann Treadwell (Anderson). McPherson develops an obsessive crush on Laura with the help of a painted portrait of her. Halfway through, in a suspenseful twist, McPherson finds that all is not as it seems, which makes him rethink the compelling mystery of **Laura**.

20th CENTURY-FOX 1944

The Stars

Dana Andrews
Mark

THE hard-boiled police lieutenant with a necrophiliac bent was a departure for Andrews, who'd played all-American types in films such as **Swamp Water** (1941) and **The Ox-Bow Incident** (1943). His dark side came through again in Preminger's **Fallen Angel** (1945) and **Where the Sidewalk Ends** (1950).

Gene Tierney
Laura

THOUGH **Laura** established Tierney as a top leading lady at Fox, she didn't think much of her role as Laura Hunt, since the character is absent for nearly half the film.

Clifton Webb
Waldo

LAURA marked Webb's return to the screen after a nineteen-year absence. In the next eighteen years at Fox, he played several variations of the effete Waldo, most memorably the pompous baby-sitter Lynn Belvedere in **Sitting Pretty** (1948).

Academy Awards

5 NOMINATIONS 1 OSCAR *

Director (Preminger)
Supporting Actor (Webb)
Writing, Screenplay (Jay Dratler, Samuel Hoffenstein, and Betty Reinhardt)
✱ **Cinematography (Black and white)** (Joseph LaShelle)
Interior Decoration (Black and white) (Lyle Wheeler, Leland Fuller, and Thomas Little)

THE BUZZ

Laura failed to get a Best Picture nomination because Zanuck was plugging his pet project, **Wilson**, which did get nominated.

> "I write with a goose quill, dipped in venom."
> —*Waldo*

> "I can afford a blemish on my character, but not on my clothes."
> -- *Shelby*

Gossip

THE film was begun by director Rouben Mamoulian, but Fox chief Darryl Zanuck was unhappy with the rushes and turned the production over to producer Otto Preminger.

Both Jennifer Jones and Hedy Lamarr were offered the title role and turned it down.

Zanuck was against casting Webb as Waldo because the actor was homosexual, but Preminger insisted on his old friend Webb.

The painting of Laura was actually a photograph done over with oil paint.

Screen Team

The main leads, Dana Andrews and Gene Tierney, worked together in four other films: **Tobacco Road** (1941), **Belle Starr** (1941), **The Iron Curtain** (1948), and **Where the Sidewalk Ends** (1950).

REAR WINDOW

PARAMOUNT

1954

-COLOR-

The Cast

James Stewart
L.B. "Jeff" Jeffries

Grace Kelly
Lisa Carol
Fremont

Thelma Ritter
Stella

Wendell Corey
Lt. Thomas
J. Doyle

Raymond Burr
Lars Thorwald

Judith Evelyn
Miss Lonelyhearts

Ross Bagdasarian
Songwriter

Georgine Darcy
Miss Torso

Sara Berner
Woman
on fire escape

Frank Cady
Man on fire escape

Jessalyn Fax
Miss Hearing Aid

Rand Harper
Newlywed husband

Havis Davenport
Newlywed wife

Director and Producer
Alfred Hitchcock

PHOTOGRAPHER L. B. "Jeff" Jeffries (Stewart) is wheelchair-bound in his apartment with a broken leg. With nothing to do, he watches his neighbors, a dramatic cast of characters, across the courtyard. His nurse, Stella (Ritter) disapproves of his spying as does his doting but frustrated girl-friend, fashionista Lisa Fremont (Kelly). Jeff becomes obsessed with salesman Lars Thorwald (Burr) whom Jeff believes has murdered his bedridden wife. Jeff's detective friend (Corey), Stella and Lisa are unconvinced. Eventually, Lisa and Stella tentatively enter Thorwald's apartment to get a closer look. Jeff watches the intense drama unfold on both sides of the courtyard.

> *Jeff, you know if someone came in here, they wouldn't believe what they'd see. You and me with long faces plunged into despair because we find out a man didn't kill his wife. —Lisa*

Gossip

The director made a cameo winding a clock in the songwriter's apartment.

Hitchcock wanted Thorwald to be a chain smoker and to sport glasses, short curly hair and white button-down shirts to evoke David O. Selznick, the producer to whom Hitchcock had been unhappily under contract.

Hitchcock suggested that Kelly wear falsies under her peignoir. Instead designer Edith Head altered the garment to achieve the same effect. When they returned to the set, Hitchcock said, "See what a difference they make?"

Academy Awards

Director (Hitchcock)
Writing, Screenplay (John Michael Hayes)
Cinematography, Color (Robert Burks)
Sound Recording (Loren Ryder)

4 NOMINATIONS

THE BUZZ

Hitchcock earned one of his five best director nominations for **Rear Window**, but somehow a win always eluded him. He was finally recognized by the Academy with the Irving G. Thalberg Memorial Award in 1968 for his body of work.

The Stars

Grace Kelly
Lisa

LONG before she became Princess of Monaco, Grace Kelly reigned as the ultimateHitchcock blonde.The elegance and eloquence she acquired growing up in Philadelphia's Main Line served her well in **Dial M for Murder** (1954), **Rear Window**, and **To Catch a Thief** (1955), where she played ice princesses whose inner flames were stirred up by the likes of Stewart and Cary Grant.

"We've become a race of Peeping Toms.

—*Stella*

James Stewart
Jeff

STEWART'S everyman persona was a perfect fit for the trademark Hitchcock hero: the innocent man who gets drawn into unseemly situations. Murder was the game for Stewart in **Rope** (1948) and **Rear Window** (1954), and in **The Man Who Knew Too Much** (1956) he dealt with a kidnapping and a political assassination. His most complex role was in Hitchcock's **Vertigo** (1958), where Stewart had to cope with a fear of heights and a perverse obsession for Kim Novak.

Thelma Ritter
Stella

RITTER was a Bronx housewife for so long before hitting Hollywood in the late '40s, it was only natural that she would end up playing an assortment of maids, mothers-in-law, and matchmakers. In **All About Eve** (1950), **The Mating Season** (1951), and **Pillow Talk** (1959), she had a knack for meddling as well as stealing every scene she was in.

Screen Team

Stewart and Corey also worked together in **Carbine Williams** (1952).

WITNESS FOR THE PROSECUTION

E STEEMED, aging, sickly barrister Sir Wilfrid Robarts (Laughton) is recuperating from a heart attack. His cheerfully hovering, nagging nurse Miss Plimsoll (Lanchester) tries to keep the cigars and brandy at bay and hold his tension level down, a task made more difficult when he takes on a sensational murder case. Charming, unemployed Leonard Vole (Power) is accused of murdering a rich widow, Emily French (Varden), who left him all her money. His only alibi is his bitchy, haughty wife, Christine (Dietrich), who announces she will not testify for him, but for the prosecution. The trial at the Old Bailey is filled with tension and surprises.

UNITED ARTISTS

1957

The Cast

Tyrone Power
Leonard Vole

Marlene Dietrich
Christine Vole

Charles Laughton
Sir Wilfrid Robarts

Elsa Lanchester
Miss Plimsoll

John Williams
Mr. Brogan-Moore

Henry Daniell
Mr. Mayhew

Ian Wolfe
Mr. Carter

Torin Thatcher
Mr. Myers

Norma Varden
Emily French

Una O'Connor
Janet McKenzie

Director
Billy Wilder

Producer
Arthur Hornblow Jr.

> *Leonard:* But this is England, where I thought you never arrest, let alone convict, people for crimes they have not committed.
> *Sir Wilfrid:* We try not to make a habit of it.

Gossip

Wilder was reluctant to make a movie that he felt was essentially just a filmed play. At the urging of Dietrich and with the producers' assurance that he could adapt Agatha Christie's tale to his own style, he took the helm.

Ava Gardner and Rita Hayworth were considered for Christine.

William Holden was the first choice to play Leonard, but he was unavailable. Power originally turned down the part, but changed his mind when he was offered the leads in both **Witness** and **Solomon and Sheba,** also to be executive-produced by Edward Small, and paid $300,000 for each. **Witness** wound up being Power's last film—he suffered a fatal heart attack in 1958 while working on **Solomon and Sheba** in Spain.

When **Witness** was screened at a special command performance for the Royal Family in London, Hornblow asked all of the royals to sign a pledge stating that they would not divulge the surprise ending.

The Stars

Marlene Dietrich
Christine

EVEN though she was fifty-six when she made **Witness,** Dietrich was still as alluring and magnetic as she had been working with her mentor, Josef von Sternberg, at Paramount in the '30s. By the 1950s, she had matured as an actress after working with masters such as Wilder on **A Foreign Affair** (1948) and Alfred Hitchcock on **Stage Fright** (1950).

Charles Laughton
Sir Wilfrid

FROM Quasimodo to Henry VIII to the *veh-ry* proper valet Ruggles of Red Gap, Laughton could transform himself into any character. In addition to his cornucopia of character roles, Laughton's sole directing effort, the haunting and horrifying **Night of the Hunter** (1955), showed that he was equally adept behind the camera.

Tyrone Power
Leonard

DASHING Tyrone Power was Fox's top male star from 1936 to 1947 as well as the studio's answer to Errol Flynn. Power wielded a sword with gusto in **The Mark of Zorro** (1940), dallied with bulls and Rita Hayworth in **Blood and Sand** (1941), and buckled his swash in **The Black Swan** (1942). But his favorite role was anything but heroic — a carnival con artist that he performed to chilling effect in the gripping **Nightmare Alley** (1947).

Screen Team

The husband-and-wife team of Laughton and Lanchester made numerous films together including **The Private Life of Henry VIII** (1933), **Rembrandt** (1936), **The Beachcomber** (1938), **Tales of Manhattan** (1942), and **The Big Clock** (1948).

Academy Awards

6 NOMINATIONS

Best Picture
Director (Wilder)
Actor (Laughton)
Supporting Actress (Lanchester)
Sound (Gordon Sawyer, Samuel Goldwyn Studio Sound Department)
Film Editing (Daniel Mandell)

THE BUZZ

Dietrich seemed certain she'd get a best actress nomination and had the recording of her 1958 Las Vegas show open with the announcer presenting "Academy Award nominee for **Witness for the Prosecution,** Miss Marlene Dietrich!" Once the nominations came out, the introduction was rerecorded

'LIAR!' —*Sir Wilfrid*

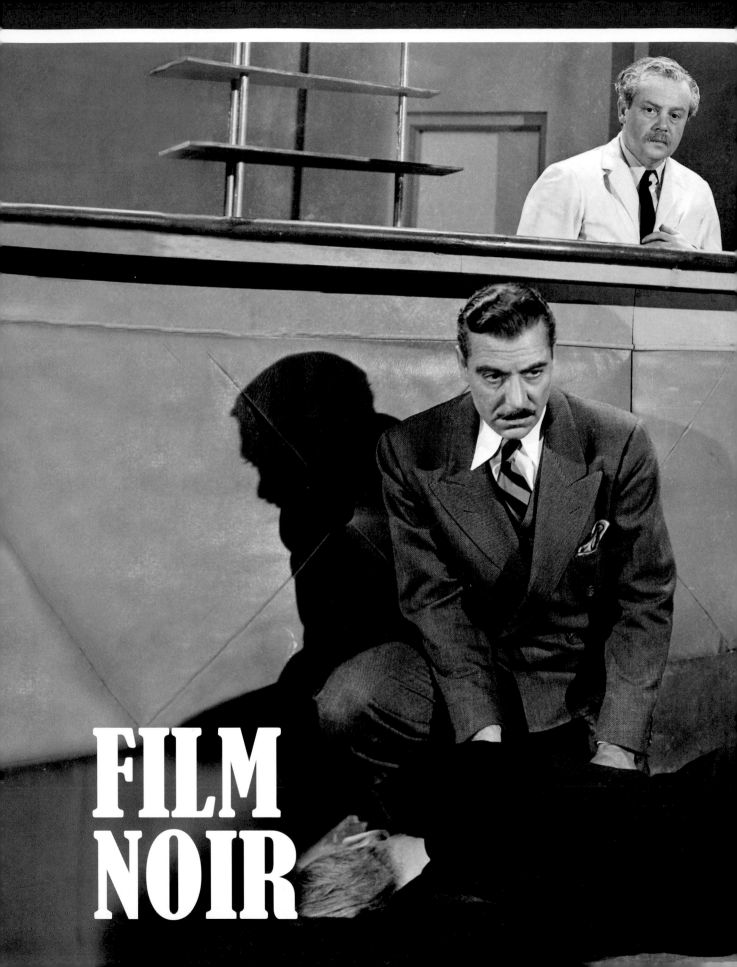

FILM
NOIR

FILM NOIR

French film critics first used the term Film Noir, which means "black cinema," to describe the Hollywood films of the '40s, which were dark, visually and thematically.

The cinematography was dramatic. Lighting came from a single source, such as a light bulb, which cast ominous shadows, or streamed through Venetian blinds. Expenses were cut by the spare techniques, which helped with wartime budgets. In the process, a visual style was created. Cigarette smoke and odd camera angles added to the moody effect. Exteriors were often shot at night, with wet streets and neon signs, in black and white.

Plots were suspensefully theatrical. The leading men were morally conflicted, hard-boiled loners: gangster, detective, criminal or just a Joe Schmo who got mixed up with the wrong dame. The women were sultry femme fatales, sometimes deadly double-crossers like Cora in **The Postman Always Rings Twice**, Kitty in **The Killers**, and **Gilda**, played by steamy Rita Hayworth. When she sings "Put the Blame on Mame," one of the sexiest songs on film, we know Glenn Ford is in for trouble.

The ultimate film noir is **Out of the Past**, with the quintessential film noir hero, Robert Mitchum. The story is told in flashback, another typical device of the genre.

The Third Man won an Oscar for its breathtaking, powerful cinematography. The impressive underground sewer scene should not be missed.

Film noir's strong images are embedded in our visual psyche. Notice the composition of each frame, the affecting angles, the play of light and shadow. It's art.

BUT IS IT ART?

GILDA

COLUMBIA
1946

"I was true to one man once... and look what happened!"

COLUMBIA PICTURES presents

Rita HAYWORTH
Gilda
Glenn FORD
GEORGE MACREADY · JOSEPH CALLEIA
VIRGINIA VAN UPP · CHARLES VIDOR

ENTICING redhead Gilda (Hayworth) is married to wealthy, powerful Ballin Mundson (MacCready), but her heart belongs to drifter Johnny Farrell (Ford), her old beau who now works for the ruthless Ballin in his South American casino.

Gilda and Johnny have a love-hate relationship. She has many flirtations. Ballin mysteriously disappears and his wife gets together with Johnny, only to find out a terrible secret, which resolves the steamy love triangle and the political intrigue.

The Cast

Rita Hayworth
Gilda

Glenn Ford
Johnny Farrell

George Macready
Ballin Mundson

Joseph Calleia
Det. Maurice Obregon

Steven Geray
Uncle Pio

Joe Sawyer
Casey

Gerald Mohr
Capt. Delgado

Robert Scott
Gabe Evans

Director
Charles Vidor

Producer
Virginia Van Upp

Gossip

When shooting began on **Gilda** in September 1945, no one had yet been cast as Johnny.

The movie was shot without a completed script. Usually only a couple of pages were delivered to the set each day, just before those scenes were to be filmed.

Anita Ellis dubbed Hayworth's singing.

The Stars

Rita Hayworth
Gilda

COLUMBIA'S premiere love goddess was never more seductive than as the lusty Gilda, which was a stark contrast to her shy, reserved demeanor off the set. The luscious Hayworth was also an accomplished dancer, a talent that was used to great effect in musicals like **Cover Girl** (1944) with Gene Kelly.

Glenn Ford
Johnny

FORD spent most of his early career languishing in B movies before his star-making turn as the smoldering Johnny Farrell. His no-nonsense performance in **Gilda** led to more tough guy roles in noirs such as **Framed** (1947) and **The Big Heat** (1953).

❝**I**f I'd been a ranch, they would have named me the Bar Nothing.❞
—Gilda

THE KILLERS

WASHED-UP boxer Ole "the Swede" Andersen (Lancaster) is murdered by two killers. Tenacious insurance investigator Jim Reardon (O'Brien) tries to find out why Ole's been killed. A series of flashbacks show scenes from his life: a robbery with three other men led by Big Jim Colfax (Dekker), and a stint in prison taking the rap for a heist and

protecting femme fatale Kitty Collins (Gardner), who has an erotic hold over the Swede. As Reardon pieces together the mystery, we come to understand why Ole submitted to his gangland execution without a struggle.

UNIVERSAL 1946

" I'm poison, Swede, to myself and everybody around me. --*Kitty*

The Cast

Burt Lancaster
Ole "The Swede" Andersen

Ava Gardner
Kitty Collins

Edmond O'Brien
Jim Reardon

Albert Dekker
Big Jim Colfax

Sam Levene
Lt. Sam Lubinsky

Virginia Christine
Lily Harmon Lubinsky

Vince Barnett
Charleston

Charles D. Brown
Packy Robinson

Jack Lambert
Dum-Dum Clarke

Donald MacBride
R.S. Kenyon

Phil Brown
Nick Adams

Charles McGraw
Al (one of the killers)

William Conrad
Max (one of the killers)

Director
Robert Siodmak

Producer
Mark Hellinger

Academy Awards

4 NOMINATIONS

Director (Siodmak)
Writing, Screenplay (Anthony Veiller)
Music, Scoring of a Dramatic or Comedy Picture
(Miklos Rosza)
Film Editing (Arthur Hilton)

THE BUZZ

The Killers lost to The Best Years of Our Lives
in all four categories
for which it was nominated.

Screen Team

Lancaster, Gardner, and O'Brien all worked
together again in **Seven Days in May** (1964).
O'Brien also reteamed with Gardner for
The Barefoot Contessa (1954) and with
Lancaster for **Birdman of Alcatraz** (1962).

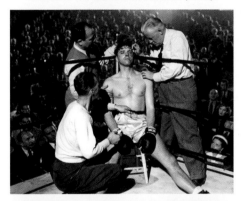

Gossip

Hemingway's short story upon which the
film was based was only a few pages.
Except for the killers and the
Swede, all of the characters were
written for the film.

John Huston helped work on the screenplay,
but he didn't receive screen credit.

Siodmak had Gardner play her climactic
final scene so many times that she said
she really did become hysterical,
and she credited him with eliciting
a stronger performance from her.

While filming **The Killers,** Gardner also
took extension courses from UCLA
in English literature and economics,
and made a big show of her
B-plus report card to cast and crew.

The Stars

Ava Gardner
Kitty

"Until I
played Kitty Collins,
I'd never worked
very hard in
pictures, never
taken my career
very seriously,"
Gardner wrote in
her autobiography.
And no wonder.
For five years she
had been doing bits
at M-G-M in the
likes of **Maisie Goes
to Reno.** Then she
landed the lead in
Whistle Stop (1946),
playing a loose
woman, and critics
finally took notice.
But **The Killers**
was her real
breakthrough:
As she huskily
warbled "The More
I Know of Love,
the Less I Know"
in a slinky black
gown, a fiery sex
symbol was born.

Edmond O'Brien
Reardon

O'Brien started
out playing boyish
heartthrobs
opposite such
lovelies as
Maureen O'Hara,
Lucille Ball, and
Deanna Durbin,
but his foray into
noir territory in
The Killers proved
he was better suited
to tough guy roles.

Burt Lancaster
The Swede

Lancaster's
training in acrobatics
and a stint with a
circus troupe helped
him develop a
Herculean physique
that made him the
ideal choice for the
prizefighter in
The Killers, his film
debut. For the next
four decades he
remained an
audience favorite,
along the way
winning a best
actor Oscar for
Elmer Gantry (1960)
and producing hits
such as **Marty** (1955).

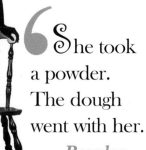

"She took
a powder.
The dough
went with her."
—Reardon

RKO RADIO

1947 OUT OF THE PAST

FORMER private eye Jeff Bailey (Mitchum) runs a gas station under an alias. He wants to forget his unsavory past working for sleazy thug Whit Sterling (Douglas), who hired Jeff to find his paramour, femme fatale Kathie Moffat (Greer). Jeff fell in love with her and they ran away together. Whit sent his henchmen after them to try to catch them and bring them back. Now Jeff has a new girl, small-town Ann Miller (Huston). Whit wants Jeff to steal from tax attorney Leonard Eels (Niles). Eels' scheming secretary (Fleming) has betrayed her boss and set up Jeff, who is wary of the plan. In the end, Jeff learns Kathie robbed and double-crossed both Whit and him. Their manipulations end in betrayal and murder.

> "My feelings? About ten years ago, I hid them somewhere and haven't been able to find them."
> —*Whit*

Screen Team

Mitchum worked once more with Greer in **The Big Steal** (1949) and with Douglas in **The Way West** (1967).

Douglas and Fleming co-starred again in **Gunfight at the O.K. Corral** (1957).

The Stars

Kirk Douglas
Whit

THOUGH Douglas is often remembered as the virile hero of dozens of westerns and war flicks, he was at his best playing a heel in **Out of the Past** and in the gritty boxing yarn **Champion** (1949); Billy Wilder's attack on sleazy journalists, **The Big Carnival** (1951); and Vincente Minnelli's **The Bad and the Beautiful** (1952), in which Douglas played an unscrupulous producer.

Jane Greer
Kathie

AS THE luscious viper of **Out of the Past,** Greer carved a place for herself in cinema history as one of the screen's great femme fatales. She came to Hollywood in 1943 after catching the eye of billionaire Howard Hughes, who signed her to a personal contract. When Greer, who was happily married, later spurned Hughes' advances, she declared her independence and established herself as a formidable actress in such dramas as **Man of a Thousand Faces** (1957).

Robert Mitchum
Jeff

WITH HIS sleepy eyes, square jaw and who-gives-a-damn attitude, Mitchum never conformed to Hollywood's image of a leading man. His tough guy image in noirs like **Out of the Past** and **Crossfire** (1947) was actually enhanced by scandals that might have ruined other stars. His 1948 arrest for smoking marijuana and reports of his sexual conquests only served to make him more appealing and defined him as Hollywood's ultimate bad boy.

Gossip

Though Mitchum had a reputation as a womanizer, Greer said he acted more like a big brother to her. Since this was her first lead role, Mitchum worked with her on scenes and made sure makeup and hair stylists were always nearby to keep Greer looking her best.

Greer had a small role in the 1984 remake **Against All Odds,** with Jeff Bridges and Rachel Ward.

Dick Powell and John Garfield both turned down the role of Jeff.

Out of the Past was shot on location in Reno, Lake Tahoe, San Francisco, Los Angeles, Mexico City, and Acapulco.

> "You're like a leaf that the wind blows from one gutter to another."
> —*Jeff*

THE POSTMAN ALWAYS RINGS TWICE

DRIFTER Frank Chambers (Garfield) stops at a California roadside gas station/diner and gets a job as handyman/mechanic from the owner, good-hearted, bumbling

M-G-M
1946

Nick Smith (Kellaway). Nick's wife Cora (Turner) is sexy, young, and dissatisfied with her older husband and their frugal, boring life. She falls for the bad boy Frank and they decide to run off together. When Cora realizes that they'll have no money if they flee, they come back. They hatch a plot to kill Nick and take over the business. Things go wrong, leading to mistrust between the lovers, betrayal and tragedy.

The Cast

Lana Turner
Cora Smith

John Garfield
Frank Chambers

Cecil Kellaway
Nick Smith

Hume Cronyn
Arthur Keats

Leon Ames
Kyle Sackett

Alan Reed
Ezra Liam Kennedy

Audrey Totter
Madge Gorland

Jeff York
Blair

Director
Tay Garnett

Producer
Carey Wilson

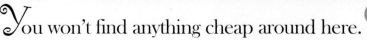

"You won't find anything cheap around here." *--Cora*

The Stars

Lana Turner
Cora

HOLLYWOOD'S original "Sweater Girl" got her nickname thanks to a form-fitting pullover that showed her off to great advantage in **They Won't Forget** (1937). Within five years, she became M-G-M's No. 1 glamour girl, gracing such productions as **Ziegfeld Girl** (1941) and **Johnny Eager** (1942). Though **Postman** presented Lana with her strongest screen role, she shined nearly as bright in **The Bad and the Beautiful** (1952) and **Peyton Place** (1957).

John Garfield
Frank

THE WORLD seemed out to get John Garfield in nearly every film he made, starting with his first, **Four Daughters** (1938), in which he played a sullen musician hopelessly in love with Priscilla Lane, to his last, **He Ran All the Way** (1951), as a killer holding Shelley Winters and her family hostage. Sadly, the fates seemed out to get Garfield in real life — by the early '50s he was blacklisted in Hollywood and died in 1952 at age 39.

Cecil Kellaway
Nick

THE LOVABLE character actor brought a tenderness to the role of Nick that was missing in Cain's novel, and as such, made Nick's screen murder seem all the more brutal. With his cherub-like cheeks, mile-wide smile and lilting voice, it's no wonder that Kellaway was originally considered to play Kris Kringle in **Miracle on 34th Street** (1947). He turned it down, but received an Oscar nomination for his magical performance as a fun-loving leprechaun in **Luck of the Irish** (1948).

❝We got off to a wrong start. Somehow or other, we never got back on the right track.❞
— *Frank*

Screen Team

Turner and Kellaway also worked together in **The Prodigal** (1955).

SELZNICK-LONDON FILMS

1950

THE THIRD MAN

OUT-OF-WORK American writer Holly Martins (Cotten) arrives in post-war Vienna to meet his friend Harry Lime (Welles). When he gets there, he learns Harry is dead. Holly meets Maj. Calloway (Howard), a British police official who describes Harry as a racketeer. Holly suspects foul play. During his investigation he falls for the enigmatic, displaced Czech actress Anna Schmidt (Valli), who was in love with Harry. Officially, Harry was hit by a truck, but Holly learns that he was involved in the Black Market.

The Cast

Joseph Cotten
Holly Martins

Alida Valli
Anna Schmidt

Orson Welles
Harry Lime

Trevor Howard
Maj. Calloway

Bernard Lee
Sgt. Paine

Paul Hoerbiger
Porter

Annie Rosar
Mrs. Porter

Ernst Deutsch
"Baron" Kurtz

Director and Producer
Carol Reed

DAVID O. SELZNICK and ALEXANDER KORDA
present

THE 3RD MAN
by GRAHAM GREENE

JOSEPH COTTEN   VALLI
ORSON WELLES   TREVOR HOWARD
PRODUCED AND DIRECTED BY CAROL REED

"Next time we'll use a foolproof coffin.
—*Calloway*

Academy Awards

3 NOMINATIONS 1 OSCAR ✱

Director (Reed)
✱ **Cinematography, Black and White**
(Robert Krasker)
Film Editing (Oswald Hafenrichter)

THE BUZZ

Reed also received two other best director nominations. The first was for **The Fallen Idol** (1949) and the third time was the charm when he won for **Oliver!** (1968).

' *Holly:* Have you ever seen any of your victims?
Harry: Victims? Don't be melodramatic. Tell me. Would you really feel any pity if one of those dots stopped moving forever? '

Screen Team

Cotten and Valli also co-starred in **Walk Softly, Stranger** (1950).

The Stars

Alida Valli
Anna

THE Italian-born beauty somehow never quite clicked in Hollywood, despite getting to work with Hitchcock in her first American effort. Unfortunately, **The Paradine Case** (1947) was not one of the master's best efforts, nor did her next U.S. film, **Miracle of the Bells** (1948), ring true with audiences. But she was radiant in **The Third Man** and then stayed on in Europe where she gained a reputation as one of the best international actresses in films such as **Senso** (1954).

Joseph Cotten
Holly

THOUGH Cotten was never a film icon along the lines of Bogart or Gable, he was fortunate in landing choice material in the 1940s and collaborating with some of the cinema's true artists. He once boasted, "Orson Welles lists **Citizen Kane** as his best film, Alfred Hitchcock opts for **Shadow of a Doubt** and Sir Carol Reed chose **The Third Man**—and I'm in all of them."

Orson Welles
Harry

WELLES' gift for character acting is often overshadowed by his renown as a filmmaker par excellence. Harry Lime is his most memorable character role, though he's also hard to forget as the Clarence Darrow-ish lawyer in **Compulsion** (1959) and the corrupt police captain in his own **Touch of Evil** (1958).

Gossip

Reed discovered zither player Anton Karas during a visit to a Viennese wine cellar with Cotten and Valli. Upon hearing Karas' music, Reed decided he wanted to only use a zither for the background music. The film launched a craze for zither music in Europe and the United States.

Welles didn't want to play the small role of Harry Lime and supposedly came to see Reed in Vienna, where the film was being shot, to personally decline. Reed somehow convinced Welles to film one scene—the chase through the city's sewers. Welles got so caught up in the scene that he came up with new ideas for filming it, which resulted in shooting it ten times.

Noel Coward was David O. Selznick's choice to play Harry Lime, but Reed insisted on Welles.

' Leave death to the professionals. '
—*Calloway*

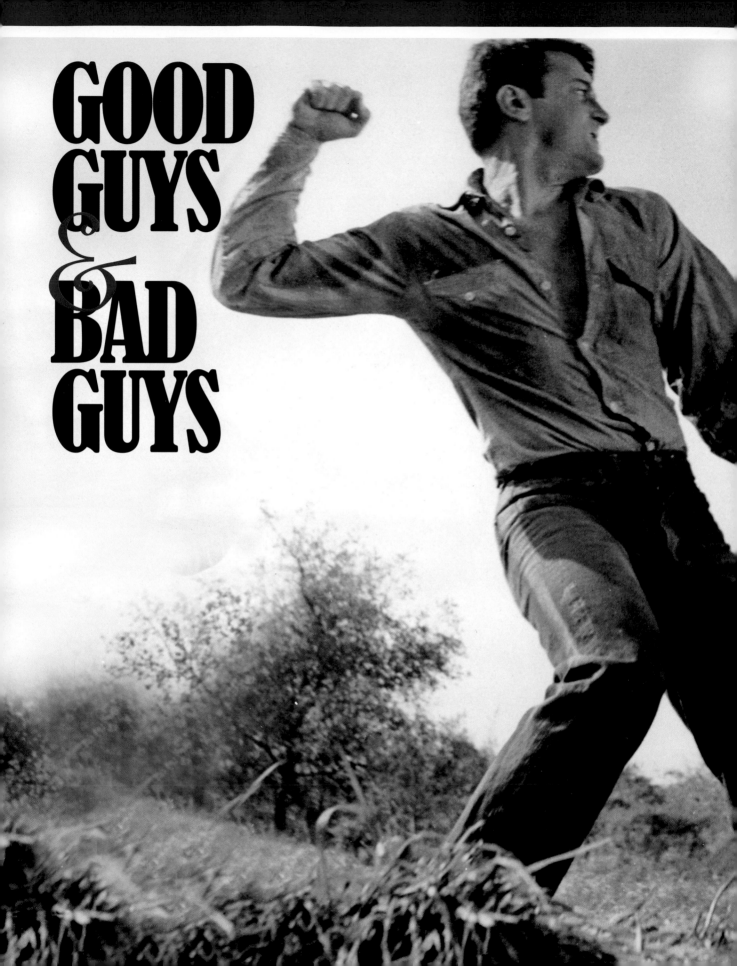

GOOD GUYS & BAD GUYS

GOOD GUYS & BAD GUYS

Heroic Errol Flynn, Lew Ayres, Kirk Douglas —you gotta love these guys. For that matter, you gotta love bad guys like Cagney, too. And then there's Tony Curtis and Sidney Poitier, who fall somewhere in between. The leading men in these five movies are victims of circumstance or products of their time, forces of good and evil played out in larger-than-life roles. We root for the hero, but sometimes we can't help but love the villain, who acts out our secret rebellious side.

Of course, who says the good guys can't be rebels, too? In **The Adventures of Robin Hood**, our hero gives up his title and his estate to live in Sherwood Forest as an outlaw, to plunder and rob with swords and guile. But he does it all to fight oppression and help the poor.

Two antiwar films show the dehumanizing effects of both World Wars. Boys are forced to become men in **All Quiet on the Western Front**, which spares nothing in showing us the

REBELS WITH A CAUSE

brutal fighting up close. Lew Ayres starts out as a gung-ho German soldier, but gradually grows more vulnerable and sympathetic as we are plunged into the pathos of World War I. Through his eyes, we grow disillusioned. War is also hell in **Paths of Glory**, which depicts realistic battle scenes, bad leaders, and frustrated, condemned soldiers. Brave, honorable Kirk Douglas fights for right.

Tony Curtis and Sidney Poitier are about as close as you can get in **The Defiant Ones**. A white, racist bad boy is chained to an angry black man as they try to escape from prison. They hate each other, but as they get to know each other they find a grudging respect.

James Cagney is a psychotic gangster in **White Heat**, but he's not your typical cold-blooded killer. He's also smart, occasionally funny, and boy, does he love his Ma. Just think of tortured Cagney with a crippling migraine headache, sitting on his domineering mother's lap while she soothes him. Even manly men can have their soft side.

PATHS OF GLORY

UNITED ARTISTS
1957

D URING World War I, General Broulard (Menjou) orders his men to go on an impossible mission. They refuse and retreat, suffering losses. Three soldiers are picked out to be court-martialed. An outraged Colonel Dax (Douglas) defends his men, but in vain.

The Stars

Kirk Douglas
Col. Dax

D OUGLAS loved taking risks, whether it was playing an unlikable character, such as the ruthless boxer in **Champion** (1949), or making a film like **Paths of Glory** that he suspected wouldn't make a dime. On the last count, he was correct, but the movie's message and enduring impact are priceless. Douglas and Kubrick more than recouped their losses with their next collaboration, the blockbuster **Spartacus** (1960).

The Cast

Kirk Douglas
Col. Dax

Adolphe Menjou
Gen. George Broulard

Ralph Meeker
Cpl. Philip Paris

George Macready
Gen. Paul Mireau

Wayne Morris
Lt. Roget

Richard Anderson
Maj. Saint-Auban

Joe Turkel
Pvt. Pierre Arnaud

Susanne Christian
German singer

Jerry Hausner
Café owner

Emile Meyer
Father Dupree

Director
Stanley Kubrick

Producers
Kirk Douglas
Stanley Kubrick
James B. Harris

Screen Team

Douglas and Macready worked together again in **The Detective Story** (1951) and **Two Weeks in Another Town** (1962).

Gossip

K ubrick could not get any studio interested in making **Paths of Glory**. Douglas ultimately cornered United Artists into financing the movie by telling them he already had a deal in place with M-G-M, even though he didn't.

France and Switzerland considered **Paths of Glory** subversive propaganda that took shots at the French; it wasn't shown in either country until the 1970s.

Adolphe Menjou
Gen. Broulard

T HE DAPPER, mustachioed bon vivant dressed up nearly 150 films, working for everyone from Chaplin to Disney. He was charm personified as the skirt-chasing producer in **Stage Door** (1937), the most dignified movie mogul you'd ever want to meet in **A Star Is Born** (1937), and outrageously over the top as lawyer Billy Flynn in **Roxie Hart** (1942).

" I apologize, sir, for not telling you sooner that you're a degenerate, sadistic old man. — *Col. Dax* "

THE ADVENTURES OF ROBIN HOOD

WARNER BROS. 1938 -COLOR-

KIND, MEDIEVAL King Richard the Lion Heart (Hunter) is captured. While he is gone, Prince John (Rains) taxes his people, making them live in poverty. Dashing, romantic Robin of Locksley, aka Robin Hood (Flynn), and his Merry Men of Sherwood Forest rebel, stealing from the rich and giving to the poor. Robin woos Maid Marian (de Havilland), and fights villainous Sir Guy of Gisbourne (Rathbone) to help King Richard regain the throne.

The Cast

Errol Flynn
Robin
of Locksley

Olivia de Havilland
Maid Marian

Basil Rathbone
Sir Guy
of Gisbourne

Claude Rains
Prince John

Patric Knowles
Will Scarlett

Alan Hale
Little John

Ian Hunter
King Richard
the Lion Heart

Eugene Pallette
Friar Tuck

Melville Cooper
The Sheriff of
Nottingham

Una O'Connor
Bess

Herbert Mundin
Much
the Miller's son

Directors
Michael Curtiz
William Keighley

Producer
Hal B. Wallis

'I'll never rest until every Saxon in this shire can stand up free men, and strike a blow for Richard and England. -- *Robin*

Warner Bros. began preparation for **Robin Hood** in 1935 with James Cagney in the title role, but when Flynn caused a sensation in **Captain Blood**, Warners realized he was the ideal choice for Robin.

At a cost of roughly $2 million, **Robin Hood** was Warners' most expensive movie to date.

The horse ridden by Olivia de Havilland's Marian was Trigger, Roy Rogers' palomino.

It was twenty years after filming before de Havilland finally saw **Robin Hood.** Afterward, she wrote to Flynn telling him how much she enjoyed it, but hesitated mailing the letter. She finally sent it, but he died before getting to read it.

Olivia de Havilland
Maid Marian

Errol Flynn
Robin

De Havilland never relished playing the angelic damsel in distress at Warners, and the studio rarely offered her parts of dramatic consequence. She eventually showed up her old studio with best actress Oscars for Paramount's **To Each His Own** (1946) and **The Heiress** (1949), but she's proudest of her other victory— a 1945 legal win against Warners for trying to extend her seven-year contract by tacking on time from when she had gone on suspension.

When Robert Donat turned down the swashbuckler **Captain Blood** (1935), Warners took a chance on Flynn, a handsome unknown from Tasmania. Flynn handled a sword and leading lady de Havilland with gusto, and was launched as Warners' top action star. **Robin Hood** was his definitive film, but Flynn's favorite role, which showed him throwing punches and punch lines with style, was as boxer James J. Corbett in **Gentleman Jim** (1942).

Screen Team

Flynn and de Havilland had one of the longest and most successful screen partnerships in movie history, and made seven other films together: **Captain Blood, The Charge of the Light Brigade** (1936), **Four's a Crowd** (1938), **Dodge City** (1939), **The Private Lives of Elizabeth and Essex** (1939), **Santa Fe Trail** (1940), and **They Died with Their Boots On** (1941).

Academy Awards

Best Picture
✱ Interior Decoration (Carl J. Weyl)
✱ Music, Original Score
(Erich Wolfgang Korngold)
✱ Film Editing (Ralph Dawson)

4 NOMINATIONS 3 OSCARS ✱

THE BUZZ
Curtiz didn't get a best director nod for **Robin Hood** but he wasn't complaining— he was nominated for both **Angels with Dirty Faces** (1938) and **Four Daughters** (1938). Frank Capra ended up winning the Oscar for **You Can't Take It With You** (1938).

ALL QUIET ON THE WESTERN FRONT

UNIVERSAL
1930

GERMAN college student Paul Baumer (Ayres) thinks World War I will be adventuresome after his patriotic teacher Kantorek (Lucy) incites his class to enlist. Strict disciplinarian Himmelstoss (Wray) trains the boys for war. Their commander Katczinsky (Wolheim) befriends them. At the front, the reality of war is gruesome amid the explosions and bullets. Paul is given leave to visit his sick mother, grudgingly returns to grim adventures at the front and watches all his friends die. Sorely disillusioned with his earlier ideals, Paul sees that his sacrifices were for nought.

The Cast

Lew Ayres
Paul Baumer

Slim Summerville
Tjaden

Louis Wolheim
Katczinsky

John Wray
Himmelstoss

Arnold Lucy
Kantorek

Russell Gleason
Muller

Raymond Griffith
Gerard Duval

Ben Alexander
Kemmerick

Owen Davis Jr.
Peter

Beryl Mercer
Mrs. Baumer

William Bakewell
Albert

Joan Marsh
Poster Girl

Scott Kolk
Leer

Director
Lewis Milestone

Producer
Carl Laemmle Jr.

Gossip

Preview audiences saw the original print of the movie with comedienne ZaSu Pitts as Ayres' mother and, to Universal's horror, laughed at her dramatic scenes. The studio withdrew all prints and reshot the film with Beryl Mercer.

Nazis released rats and snakes into Berlin theaters that showed **All Quiet on the Western Front.** The movie was eventually banned in Germany for its "demoralizing effect" on the country's youth.

The film's antiwar sentiments stayed with Ayres, who became a vocal objector to American involvement in World War II. His stance made him unpopular in Hollywood, but all was forgiven when he joined the Medical Corps as a noncombatant serving overseas.

All Quiet on the Western Front cost a then-enormous $1.25 million, and employed acres of California farmland for the battle scenes and more than 2,000 extras.

The Stars

Slim Summerville
Tjaden

TALL, skinny, and sad-sacked, Summerville is remembered only slightly today thanks to appearances in a few of Fox's Shirley Temple and Charlie Chan movies of the '30s. His other, more dubious claim to fame is as the punch line to Carl Laemmle's comment upon first meeting Bette Davis: 'She has about as much sex appeal as Slim Summerville.'

Lew Ayres
Paul

AYRES rocketed to stardom after his powerful performance as Baumer, then crash-landed in a series of forgettable movies. His rave reviews as Katharine Hepburn's tipsy brother in **Holiday** (1938) led to his most famous role as Dr. Kildare, which he played in nine films. Deeply religious, Ayres' most personal works were two documentaries he directed —**Altars of the East** (1955) and **Altars of the World** (1976)— espousing his beliefs.

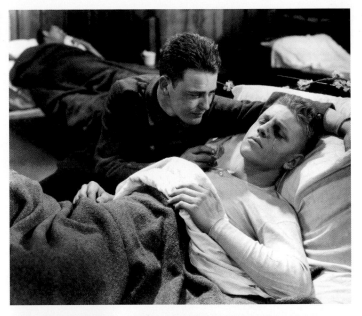

Academy Awards

✳ Best Picture
✳ Director (Milestone)
Writing (George Abbott, Maxwell Anderson and Dell Andrews)
Cinematography, Black and White (Arthur Edeson)

4 NOMINATIONS 2 OSCARS ✳

THE BUZZ

Universal had the longest stretch between best picture winners out of any major studio. It wouldn't win Hollywood's top prize again until **The Sting** (1973).

'I'll take the mother's milk out of you. I'll make you hard-boiled. I'll make soldiers out of you, or kill you!

— *Himmelstoss*

UNITED ARTISTS

1958

THE DEFIANT ONES

Racist, white mechanic "Joker" Jackson (Curtis) and resentful, black Noah Cullen (Poitier) escape from a southern farm prison. They are linked by a chain. They hate each other, but must work together to survive and escape the police. Trying to steal food, they are almost hanged. They meet a lonely woman (Williams), whom they think will help them. Once they're untethered, they must decide if their paths will cross again, or if they want to go it alone.

One of the great ones!

STANLEY KRAMER presents

TONY CURTIS and SIDNEY POITIER

THE DEFIANT ONES

with Theodore Bikel · Charles McGraw
Lon Chaney · King Donovan · Kevin Coughlin and Cara Williams
Written by NATHAN E. DOUGLAS and HAROLD JACOB SMITH
Produced and Directed by STANLEY KRAMER · UNITED ARTISTS

> ❝I ain't gettin' mad, Joker. I been mad all my natural life.❞
> —*Noah*

The Cast

Tony Curtis
John "Joker" Jackson

Sidney Poitier
Noah Cullen

Theodore Bikel
Sheriff Max Muller

Cara Williams
The Woman

Charles McGraw
Capt. Frank Gibbons

Lon Chaney Jr.
Big Sam

King Donovan
Solly

Claude Akins
Mack

Lawrence Dobkin
Editor

Whit Bissell
Lou Gans

Carl Switzer
Angus

Kevin Coughlin
Billy

Director and Producer
Stanley Kramer

> '*They'll kill each other in five miles.* —Muller'

Gossip

Kramer originally planned to have Poitier listed among the supporting players in the opening credits, but at Curtis' insistence, Poitier was given top billing with him.

The script was co-written by Harold Jacob Smith and blacklisted Ned Young, who used the pseudonym Nathan E. Douglas. When the screenplay received an Oscar nomination, a swirl of controversy ensued because of a recent ruling that now permitted blacklisted writers' names to be included on the ballot.

Kramer thought Curtis was too handsome to play Joker and hoped to get Marlon Brando instead. But Curtis was determined to win the part and even donned a fake nose to lose his pretty-boy image.

The Stars

Tony Curtis
Joker

Sidney Poitier
Noah

IN HIS autobiography, Curtis called **The Defiant Ones** a physically exhausting picture. At the same time, it was one of his most rewarding experiences as the second leg of his triple crown of the late '50s, along with **Sweet Smell of Success** (1957) and **Some Like It Hot** (1959).

POITIER shattered the black screen stereotype in his first film, **No Way Out** (1950), playing a brilliant doctor threatened by racist killer Richard Widmark, and has been doing it ever since. He's earned praise from actors of all races for helping black actors to be taken seriously in Hollywood through his thought-provoking performances in **A Raisin in the Sun** (1961), **Lilies of the Field** (1963), and **In the Heat of the Night** (1967).

Academy Awards

Best Picture
Director (Kramer)
Actor (Curtis)
Actor (Poitier)
Supporting Actor (Bikel)
Supporting Actress (Williams)
✻ Writing, Story and Screenplay (directly for the screen)
(Nathan E. Douglas and Harold Jacob Smith)
✻ Cinematography (black and white) (Sam Leavitt)
Film Editing (Frederick Knudtson)

9 NOMINATIONS 2 OSCARS ✻

THE BUZZ

Poitier became the first black performer to ever be nominated for best actor. Five years later, with **Lilies of the Field**, he made history again as the first black actor to win in the category.

The Cast

James Cagney
Cody Jarrett

Virginia Mayo
Verna Jarrett

Edmond O'Brien
Vic Pardo,
Hank Fallon

Margaret Wycherly
Ma Jarrett

Steve Cochran
Big Ed Somers

John Archer
Philip Evans

Wallys Cassell
Giovanni "Cotton"
Valletti

Fred Clark
Daniel Winston

Director
Raoul Walsh

Producer
Louis F. Edelman

WHITE HEAT

WARNER BROS.

1949

CODY JARRETT (Cagney) is a dangerous, psychotic killer with an Oedipus complex, a hot temper, and a deep mistrust of anyone except his manipulative mother (Wycherly). His wife (Mayo) deserves his mistrust. She lusts after Big Ed Somers (Cochran), Jarrett's henchman. Jarrett goes to jail where he meets Hank Fallon (O'Brien), an undercover Treasury agent who gains his trust. Jarrett needs a

friend, especially after he flips out when he learns his beloved ma is dead. The two men escape from jail, and once on the outside Jarrett begins planning a robbery. But his plans go awry, which leads to the film's climax, a nasty gun battle in an oil refinery.

> "Ya know somethin', Verna? If I turned my back long enough for Big Ed to put a hole in it, there'd be a hole in it."
> — *Cody*

Gossip

IT WAS Cagney's idea to play up the psychotic aspects of Jarrett, in particular, his mother fixation. Cagney suggested to Walsh that the actor sit on Ma Jarrett's lap for consolation in the scene when Cody gets a migraine headache.

For his famous breakdown in prison upon hearing the news of Ma Jarrett's death, Cagney recalled two personal experiences—a visit he made to an insane asylum on Ward's Island to see his buddy's uncle, and the shrieks his alcoholic father made.

Cody Jarrett was Cagney's first gangster role since **The Roaring Twenties** (1939).

Ma Jarrett was modeled after gang leader Ma Barker.

Academy Awards

Writing, Motion Picture Story
Virginia Kellogg

THE BUZZ

Academy voters rarely acknowledged gangster films, which could be why Cagney did not receive a best actor nomination for his dynamic performance. Mayo always thought he should have won. As she told Cagney biographer John McCabe, "Who was better?"

1 NOMINATION

The Stars

Edmond O'Brien
Vic/Hank

James Cagney
Cody

Virginia Mayo
Verna

O'BRIEN was a burly character actor who had one of his rare starring roles as a dying man frantically searching for the man who poisoned him in **D.O.A.**, released the same year as **White Heat**.

CAGNEY had created a rogues gallery at Warners since his breakthrough in **Public Enemy** (1931). Still, his only Oscar came for a change of pace role as song-and-dance man George M. Cohan in **Yankee Doodle Dandy** (1942).

MAYO was one of the few Goldwyn Girls who made it out of the chorus line and into the spotlight, most frequently as Danny Kaye's leading lady. She left Goldwyn in 1948 for Warner Bros.

Screen Team

Cagney and Mayo were paired again in much lighter fare, the musicals **The West Point Story** (1950) and **Starlift** (1951). Mayo and O'Brien co-starred once more in **Backfire** (1950).

COMEDY

Eric Idle
Actor, Comedian
(b. 1943)

Citizen Kane
Kind Hearts and Coronets
The Lady Vanishes
The Ladykillers (1955)
The Maltese Falcon
Some Like It Hot
The Third Man
The Thirty-Nine Steps
The Wizard of Oz

Hugh Jackman
Actor (b. 1968)

All About Eve
Casablanca
Citizen Kane
Roman Holiday
Scaramouche (1952)
Singin' in the Rain
Witness for the Prosecution
The Wizard of Oz

Anthony LaPaglia
Actor (b. 1959)

The Best Years of Our Lives
The Great McGinty
The Magnificent Ambersons
The Palm Beach Story

Piper Laurie
Actress (b. 1932)

The 400 Blows
Dark Victory
Dodsworth
Notorious
Now, Voyager
Public Enemy
Spellbound
Sullivan's Travels
The Treasure of the Sierra Madre

Good comedies not only make us laugh, they make us think. And it's hard not to think of your favorite comedy—whether it's screwball, slapstick, sophisticated, romantic, witty, or silly—and not want to quote your favorite lines.

Duck Soup, a political satire, pokes fun at war and so-called leaders. Its biting sarcasm against dictators caused Hitler to ban it in Germany. In their movies, the Marx Brothers surrounded themselves with straight men who never acknowledged the brothers' hysterical zany slapstick humor. Groucho: "If you run out of gas, get ethyl. If Ethel runs out, get Mabel."

The western spoof **My Little Chickadee** is the only film to pair the sly, cynical comic legends W.C. Fields and Mae West. Their ridiculous character names (Cuthbert J. Twillie, Flower Belle Lee) and witty repartee set the tone. Cuthbert: "Will you take me?" Flower Belle: "I'll take you—and how!"

My Man Godfrey skewers the rich and pretentious, and though set against the backdrop of the Depression, this William Powell—Carole Lombard screwball classic is anything but depressing. Godfrey: "The only difference between a derelict and a man is a job."

Dinner at Eight has it all: romance, adultery, alcoholism, aging, economics, social climbing, and suicide—not to mention the creme de la creme of M-G-M, from Wallace Beery and Jean Harlow to everyone's favorite scatterbrain, Billie Burke. Millicent: "You're joking! Ask that common little woman to the house with that noisy, vulgar man? He smells like Oklahoma!"

The affectionate **Harvey** has feel-good charm and the endearing Jimmy Stewart as Elwood, a likeable drunk with an imaginary friend. Wilson: "Who's Harvey?" Miss Kelly: "A white rabbit, six feet tall." Wilson: "Six feet?" Elwood: "Six feet three and a half inches. Now let's stick to the facts." Much of the subtle humor comes from his long-suffering sister Veta: "Myrtle Mae, you have a lot to learn, and I hope you never learn it."

Bringing Up Baby, a screwball romantic comedy, pairs Cary Grant and Katharine Hepburn as an absent-minded professor and a ditsy dame. When Grant first sees the leopard (named Baby) in Hepburn's bathroom, he yells: "Susan, you have to get out of this apartment!" Susan: "I can't, I have a lease."

Grant appears again in **His Girl Friday**, a fast-talking romantic comedy. In fact, he and Rosalind Russell talk so fast they often speak over each other, instead of waiting for the other to finish. Walter Burns: "There's been a lamp burning in the window for ya, honey." Hildy Johnson: "No thanks—I jumped out that window a long time ago."

The battle of the sexes continues in **It Happened One Night**, with Clark Gable and Claudette Colbert. Peter: "Why didn't you take off all your clothes? You could've stopped forty cars!" Ellen: "I'll remember that when we need forty cars." An early favorite, it was the first film to win Oscars in the five major categories.

It was also the only one of our comedies to receive any Oscars except for **Harvey**, which featured supporting actress winner Josephine Hull, and **Born Yesterday**, for which Judy Holliday was named best actress. Her not-so-dumb blonde pulls off a squeaky voice with perfect timing. Harry Brock: "Shut up! You ain't gonna be tellin' nobody nothin' pretty soon!" Billie Dawn: "Double negative! Right?" Paul Verrall: "Right."

In **Sullivan's Travels**, director John L. Sullivan wants to get away from the fluff movies he's making, and do something serious and important, but when he gets to know the real people, he sees that his audience needs comedy. Sullivan: "There's a lot to be said for making people laugh. Did you know that that's all some people have?"

These ten movies not only make us laugh, they also send a message, told either sympathetically or maliciously, with wit or irony, slapstick or deadpan. Still, they make us feel better; they elevate our mood, whether we roar with snorting whoops, chuckle with contented cheer, or serenely grin with gentle amusement.

MAKE 'EM LAUGH

BORN YESTERDAY

BILLIE Dawn (Holliday), the uneducated, vulgar, dumb-blonde mistress of corrupt, boorish millionaire Harry Brock (Broderick), is an embarassment to him. Although she screeches in a high-pitched voice and acts like a wise-assed, stupid floozy, she fronts for him by signing his checks. Harry hires Paul Verrall (Holden), a suave, bookish Washington, D.C. reporter who's writing a story about Brock, to teach her how to fit in with the local swells and politicians who can help Harry. Billie spends time with Paul, who teaches her about government as well as love. Her sophistication, knowledge, and conscience develop, and she starts to see Brock for what he is—a two-bit crook. Eventually she must choose between her old and new self.

COLUMBIA 1950

The Cast

Judy Holliday
Billie Dawn

William Holden
Paul Verrall

Broderick Crawford
Harry Brock

Howard St. John
Jim Devery

Frank Otto
Eddie

Larry Oliver
Congressman
Norval Hedges

Barbara Brown
Mrs. Hedges

Grandon Rhodes
Sanborn

Claire Carleton
Helen

Director
George Cukor

Producer
S. Sylvan Simon

Academy Awards

Best Picture
Director (Cukor)
✳ Actress (Holliday)
Writing, Screenplay
(Albert Mannheimer)
Costume Design, Black and White
(Jean Louis)

5 NOMINATIONS 1 OSCAR ✳

THE BUZZ

Holliday's win over Bette Davis
(**All About Eve**) and
Gloria Swanson (**Sunset Boulevard**)
is still considered one of the great
Oscar upsets in movie history.
On Oscar night, Holliday and
Swanson attended a party hosted
by Jose Ferrer at La Zambra
restaurant in New York.
From the moment her name was
announced as the best actress winner,
Holliday spent most of the time
in tears, feeling guilty that she
had won over Swanson.

‘ A world full of ignorant people is too dangerous to live in. *— Paul* **’**

Gossip

Columbia boss Harry Cohn had purchased the rights to the stage version of **Born Yesterday** for Rita Hayworth.

Cohn didn't think Holliday was a bankable name for the movie version of **Born Yesterday**. He was finally persuaded to take a chance on her by Cukor, who had directed Holliday in **Adam's Rib**.

Jan Sterling, Evelyn Keyes, and Gloria Grahame all tested for Billie.

As a warm-up before going in front of the cameras, Cukor had his entire **Born Yesterday** cast perform the play in a theater on the Columbia lot in front of members of the film community whom he had personally invited.

Holliday was paid $750 a week for six weeks' work on **Born Yesterday**. After the film opened, her contract was renegotiated— she'd make one film a year for seven years and received $5,250 per week for the first.

The Stars

William Holden
Paul

HOLDEN had a banner year in 1950, showing his range in four diverse roles: a drifter who plays dad to five orphans in the family-friendly **Father Is a Bachelor**; a screenwriter/gigolo to an aging film actress in the star-making **Sunset Boulevard**; the intellectual Paul in **Born Yesterday**; and a hard-boiled police detective in **Union Station**.

Judy Holliday
Billie

HOLLIDAY played the part of the dumb blonde with intelligence in a series of sparkling comedies from **Adam's Rib** (1949) to **The Solid Gold Cadillac** (1956). But there was so much more to Holliday, who also touched our hearts in **The Marrying Kind** (1952), and stopped the show with her singing and dancing in **Bells Are Ringing** (1960).

Broderick Crawford
Harry

THE BURLY Crawford was born to play uncouth junk dealer Harry Brock. Having apprenticed for twelve years as a supporting player in a string of B movies, he became a star playing an unscrupulous politician modeled after Louisiana governor Huey Long in **All the King's Men** (1949). The role won him an Oscar.

> 'You an' your big numbers. You don' watch out, you'll be wearing one across yer chest!'
> —*Billie*

1938 RKO RADIO
BRINGING UP BABY

BOOKISH, distracted paleontologist David Huxley (Grant) is engaged to prim, frigid Alice Swallow (Walker). He meets beautiful, madcap, scatterbrained Susan Vance (Hepburn) in a series of mishaps on the golf course, while he is trying to get a million-dollar donation for his museum. Susan has a crush on David and plots to ensnare him, with the help of Baby, a tame leopard sent from Susan's

brother, a big-game hunter. David is lured to the Connecticut estate owned by Susan's aunt. A wild leopard escapes from the circus, just as Baby runs away, leading to much confusion and a stint in jail. All is resolved back at the museum, atop David's brontosaurus skeleton.

The Cast

Cary Grant
David Huxley

Katharine Hepburn
Susan Vance

May Robson
Aunt Elizabeth Random

Charlie Ruggles
Maj. Horace Applegate

Walter Catlett
Constable Slocum

Barry Fitzgerald
Gogarty

Fritz Feld
Dr. Fritz Lehman

Director and Producer
Howard Hawks

> Now, it isn't that I don't like you, Susan, because after all, in moments of quiet, I'm strangely drawn towards you. But— well, there haven't *been* any quiet moments.
> —David

unt Elizabeth's mischievous terrier George was played by Skippy, the lovable canine best known as Asta from the **Thin Man** movies.

Grant and Hepburn wore resin on the soles of their shoes so they wouldn't make any jerky movements and startle Nissa, the leopard.

Hawks recycled the gag in which Grant tears Hepburn's dress for two other films, **Monkey Business** (1952) and **Man's Favorite Sport** (1964).

' His name is Baby. He's three years old, gentle as a kitten, and likes dogs. I wonder whether Mark means that he eats dogs or is fond of them. *—Susan* '

The Stars

Cary Grant
David

Katharine Hepburn
Susan

GRANT proved he was an excellent farceur a year earlier in **The Awful Truth,** and then topped himself with an even funnier performance in **Baby.** Some of the credit also belongs to Hawks, who told Grant to emulate Harold Lloyd by playing David as a bespectacled innocent lost in a world of crazies.

BABY was Hepburn's first stab at screwball comedy after a string of dramas at RKO that ranged from the sublime (1935's **Alice Adams)** to the ridiculous (1934's **Spitfire,** in which she played a God-fearing mountain girl). Hepburn was happy to sever ties with RKO after **Baby** and take full control of her career.

M-G-M

1933

The Cast

Marie Dressler
Carlotta Vance

John Barrymore
Larry Rennault

Lionel Barrymore
Oliver Jordan

Jean Harlow
Kitty Packard

Wallace Beery
Dan Packard

Billie Burke
Millicent Jordan

Lee Tracy
Max Kane

Edmund Lowe
Dr. Wayne Talbot

Madge Evans
Paula Jordan

Director
George Cukor

Producer
David O. Selznick

DINNER AT EIGHT

SOCIAL-CLIMBING matron Millicent Jordan (Burke) is obsessed with planning a party for some swells. She's unaware that her easygoing husband Oliver (Barry-more) is not doing well in business. He needs unethical, rich Dan Packard (Beery) to help him, and wants Millicent to invite Dan and his spoiled wife Kitty (Harlow) to the dinner. Also there will be Oliver's old flame, flamboyant diva Carlotta Vance (Dressler); their nineteen-year-old daughter (Evans);

her boring fiance (Holmes); a drunken, over-the-hill actor (Barrymore); and others. The party showcases fast-talking repartee, pretentious ranting, young love, elegant guests, servant trouble, marital woes and the resolution of the story.

The Stars

> "If there's one thing I know, it's men. I ought to. It's been my life's work."
> —*Carlotta*

Lionel Barrymore
Oliver

Jean Harlow
Kitty

Gossip

Louis B. Mayer recruited his son-in-law David O. Selznick from RKO to produce **Dinner at Eight,** thus the gag 'the son-in-law also rises' was born. But Selznick got the last laugh: the film's success led to a full-time job at M-G-M, and within three years he formed his own production company.

Like his film character, John Barrymore also was drinking heavily, and he often had to rely on cue cards to remember his lines.

The art directors designed Kitty's boudoir using eleven shades of white so the room would match Harlow's hair and wardrobe.

Marie Dressler
Carlotta

NO ONE can call Dressler an overnight sensation—she was a seasoned veteran of vaudeville and silents before finally achieving stardom at age sixty-one as the drunken wharf rat Marthy in **Anna Christie** (1930). Neither glamorous nor youthful, she managed to become a marquee draw until her sudden death in 1934.

John Barrymore
Larry

THE DAPPER Barrymore built his reputation as a charming Lothario in romantic fare like **Don Juan** (1926) and **Arsene Lupin** (1932), and played out the role in real life as well.

FEW actors could rival Barrymore for diversity during his forty-two-year film career. Though sometimes prone to overplaying, it's hard to imagine anyone else as the evil Rasputin in **Rasputin and the Empress** (1932), the miserly Mr. Potter in **It's a Wonderful Life** (1946), or the grandfatherly Dr. Gillespie in M-G-M's **Dr. Kildare** series.

HOLLYWOOD'S favorite platinum blonde oozed sex and projected a wordly, tough-as-nails aura in racy comedies like **Red-Haired Woman** (1932) and **Hold Your Man** (1933). But the film that comes closest to capturing the childlike, down-to-earth nature of the real Harlow is **Bombshell,** in which she plays a film star who'd gladly chuck it all for romance and a little privacy.

Screen Team

Harlow worked again with Lionel Barrymore in **The Girl From Missouri** (1934) and **Saratoga** (1937), and with Wallace Beery in **The Secret Six** (1931) and **China Seas** (1935).

Dressler co-starred with Beery in **Min and Bill** (1930) and **Tugboat Annie** (1933) and with Lionel Barrymore in her last film, **The Late Christopher Bean** (1933).

DUCK SOUP

PARAMOUNT 1933

MANIPULATIVE, plotting Ambassador Trentino (Calhern), a diplomat from Sylvania, wants to take over neighboring, failing Freedonia. A rich benefactor, dowager Gloria Teasdale (Dumont), agrees to save Freedonia from bankruptcy by giving the small European country $20 million if scheming, madcap Rufus T. Firefly (Groucho), with whom she is smitten, becomes its leader. His insulting antics (to which Teasdale is oblivious) provoke Sylvania to declare war against Freedonia. Trentino has two spies, Chicolini and Pinky (Chico and Harpo), who try to get information and spread gossip, and a vamp (Torres) who tries to seduce Firefly so Mrs. Teasdale will abandon him. Chaos and mayhem ensue on and off the battlefield.

The Cast

Groucho Marx
Rufus T. Firefly

Harpo Marx
Pinky

Chico Marx
Chicolini

Zeppo Marx
Lt. Bob Roland

Margaret Dumont
Mrs. Gloria Teasdale

Raquel Torres
Vera Marcal

Louis Calhern
Ambassador
Trentino

Edmund Breese
Zander

Leonid Kinskey
Sylvanian agitator

Charles Middleton
Prosecutor

Edgar Kennedy
Lemonade vendor

Director
Leo McCarey

Producer
Herman J.
Mankiewicz

Chicolini: Now I ask you. What is it has a trunk, but no key, weighs 2,000 pounds, and lives in a circus.
Court official: That's irrelevant.
Chicolini: A relephant! Hey, that's the answer.

The Stars

Chico Marx
Chicolini

CHICO'S mastery of accents served him well as a youth pretending to be a foreigner to hustle takers at pool halls and crap games. He had better luck using a fake Italian accent on screen. Chico was also the team's business manager.

Zeppo Marx
Bob

EVERY comedy team needs a straight man, and Zeppo filled the bill nicely, but after five feature films, he got tired of playing the unfunny brother. Instead, he took on another role and became a highly successful talent agent.

Groucho Marx
Rufus

GROUCHO tossed off one-liners as easily as he flicked ashes from his cigars. His quips were irreverent without being profane, racy without being offensive. He had his greatest success hosting the quiz show **You Bet Your Life** on radio and television, where he took delight in embarrassing contestants at every opportunity.

Harpo Marx
Pinky

A FLOPPY blond wig, an oversized coat that held everything from axes to piping-hot cups of coffee, and a horn that served as his voice were all the tools Harpo needed to mine laughs without uttering a single word. His sweet nature also came through in his gentle harp solos, which were a highlight of the Marx Brothers' films.

Screen Team

Groucho called straight woman Margaret Dumont the brothers' "good luck charm." She also worked with them in **The Cocoanuts** (1929) and **Animal Crackers** (1930), and with Groucho, Harpo, and Chico in **A Night at the Opera** (1935), **A Day at the Races** (1937), **At the Circus** (1939), and **The Big Store** (1941).

> *Mrs. Teasdale:* This is a gala day for you. *Rufus:* That's plenty. I don't think I could handle more than a gal a day.

HARVEY

ECCENTRIC, genial innocent Elwood P. Dowd (Stewart) has an imaginary friend, a six-foot-tall white rabbit named Harvey. Elwood's snooty judgmental sister Veta (Hull) and her desperate spinster daughter Myrtle (Horne) live with Dowd and would like him to behave more conventionally. Veta commits her brother to an asylum,

UNIVERSAL-INTERNATIONAL 1950

manned by pedantic psychiatrist Dr. Sanderson (Drake), his nurse Miss Kelly (Dow), administrator Dr. Chumley (Kellaway), and gruff orderly Wilson (White), who falls for Myrtle. Lovable, tipsy Elwood introduces everyone to Harvey, and endearingly bumbles his way out of the asylum and on through life, with Harvey at his side.

The Cast

James Stewart
Elwood P. Dowd

Josephine Hull
Veta Louise Simmons

Peggy Dow
Miss Kelly

Charles Drake
Dr. Sanderson

Cecil Kellaway
Mr. Chumley

Jesse White
Wilson

Victoria Horne
Myrtle Mae

Director
Henry Koster

Producer
John Beck

The Stars

James Stewart
Elwood

THOUGH Stewart critiqued his performance in **Harvey** as "too nice," his naiveté suited the role and charmed audiences. He must have felt some affection for Elwood because he played the part on three more occasions—in a 1970 Broadway revival with Helen Hayes as Veta; in a 1972 television production (again with Hayes); and on the London stage in 1975.

Josephine Hull
Veta

HULL'S fluttery waddle was her comic calling-card in her other great role as Aunt Abby in the stage and screen versions of **Arsenic and Old Lace** (1944). **Harvey** would turn out to be the peak of her career—she retired in 1951, after making only one more film.

> "After this he'll be a perfectly normal human being. And you know what stinkers they are!"
> —*The Cab Driver*

Academy Awards

2 NOMINATIONS 1 OSCAR ✳

Actor (Stewart)
✳ Supporting Actress (Hull)

THE BUZZ

According to Universal publicity, Hull won her Academy Award the same day she was celebrating her golden anniversary in show business. The day after the awards, she was photographed with her Oscar and a giant anniversary cake surrounded by Universal contract players such as Tony Curtis, and a man dressed in a rabbit suit.

Screen Team

Drake and Dow co-starred in **You Never Can Tell** (1951).

> I've wrestled with reality for thirty-five years, doctor, and I'm happy to state I finally won out over it.
> —*Elwood*

Gossip

Universal wanted Bing Crosby to play Elwood, but the crooner didn't think his fans would accept him as a tippler.

Stewart, who had played Elwood on Broadway during the summers of 1947 and 1948, campaigned for the role. He got it, but Universal insisted he also make **Winchester '73** (1950), which surprisingly made even more money than **Harvey**.

Hull, Horne, and White had all originated their roles on stage.

Every day at the lunch table, the cast left an empty chair for Harvey.

Cary Grant
Walter Burns

Rosalind Russell
Hildy Johnson

Ralph Bellamy
Bruce Baldwin

Gene Lockhart
Sheriff Peter B.
Hartwell

Helen Mack
Molly

John Qualen
Earl Williams

Alma Kruger
Mrs. Baldwin

Billy Gilbert
Joe Pettibone

Edwin Maxwell
Dr. Egelhoffer

Abner Biberman
Louie

Director and Producer
Howard Hawks

HIS GIRL FRIDAY

COLUMBIA

1940

ELEGANT, flamboyant, fast-talking, city newspaper editor Walter Burns (Grant) is still in love with his star reporter and ex-wife Hildy Johnson (Russell), who is engaged to dull insurance salesman Bruce Baldwin (Bellamy). Burns has one day to win her back before she and Bruce embark on a train for their wedding. The next day is also scheduled to be the last one for convicted killer Earl Williams

(Qualen), who is to be hanged. Burns lures Hildy into interviewing the murderer, who has escaped. Hildy has access to him and sweet, desperate Molly Malloy (Mack), his paramour. Hildy follows the story, while we follow her down the path to her choice between the two men in her life.

Gossip

Ginger Rogers, Irene Dunne, and Jean Arthur all said no to playing Hildy.

Grant introduced Russell to Frederick Brisson, whom she married in 1941.

Much of the overlapping dialogue was ad-libbed by the actors.

The script features several in-jokes, including a reference to Archie Leach (Grant's real name) and cast member Ralph Bellamy.

The Stars

Cary Grant
Walter

GRANT made his comical highjinks seem effortless, and he was always even more amusing under Hawks' direction. In addition to his witty performance as Walter Burns, he got plenty of laughs in drag in **I Was a Male War Bride** (1949), and as the absent-minded professor in **Monkey Business** (1952).

Ralph Bellamy
Bruce

POOR Ralph Bellamy never seemed to get the girl. He lost Carole Lombard in **Hands Across the Table** (1935), Irene Dunne in **The Awful Truth** (1937), Ginger Rogers in **Carefree** (1938), and Russell in **His Girl Friday**. In 1960, however, he did end up with the first lady when he starred as Franklin D. Roosevelt in **Sunrise at Campobello**, which had also been a great stage success for him.

Rosalind Russell
Hildy

SOME actresses seemed made for shimmery gold lame. Russell seemed tailor-made for blue pinstripe business suits — and vice versa. It's hard to think of another actress from Hollywood's golden age who embodied the career woman with as much style and wit as she did in **His Girl Friday, Hired Wife** (1940), and **My Sister Eileen** (1942).

> *Walter:*
> I only acted like any husband that didn't want his home broken up.
> *Hildy:*
> What home?
> *Walter:*
> What home? Don't you remember the home I promised you?

Screen Team

Grant and Bellamy co-starred in another comedy classic **The Awful Truth** (1937).

IT HAPPENED ONE NIGHT

COLUMBIA 1934

The Cast

Clark Gable
Peter Warne

Claudette Colbert
Ellen Andrews

Walter Connolly
Alexander
Andrews

Roscoe Karns
Shapeley

Jameson Thomas
King Westley

Ward Bond
Bus driver
no. 1

Alan Hale
Danker

Wallis Clark
Lovington

Director
Frank Capra

Producer
Harry Cohn

SPOILED socialite Ellen Andrews (Colbert) runs away from her millionaire father Alexander Andrews (Connolly) after he foils her attempted elopement to playboy King Westley (Thomas). Suddenly penniless Ellen takes a bus, where she meets hard-edged, straight-talking reporter Peter Warne (Gable). He wants to write her tabloid love story and she needs help to get back to her fiance without getting caught by her father's detectives. Never having been out of her pampered environment, Ellen gets a real eye-opener about the Depression and life from her traveling companion. Peter falls for her even though he hates the rich. Ultimately, they both get what they want, although it's not what they thought they wanted.

Gossip

Robert Montgomery and Myrna Loy were originally requested for the leads, but neither one wanted to make the film.

Neither Gable nor Colbert wanted to make **It Happened One Night**. M-G-M loaned Gable to Columbia as punishment when the actor complained his home studio was overworking him. Colbert only agreed to make the movie when Columbia doubled her salary to $50,000.

It Happened One Night was remade two more times as the musicals **Eve Knew Her Apples** (1944) with Ann Miller and William Wright, and **You Can't Run Away From It** (1956) starring June Allyson and Jack Lemmon.

Gable caused a sensation when he disrobed in the "Walls of Jericho" scene and revealed he wasn't wearing an undershirt. As a result, men's undershirt sales took a nosedive.

The Stars

Clark Gable
Peter

Whenever Gable appeared on screen in the early '30s, sparks were sure to ignite, especially when he starred opposite such firecrackers as Jean Harlow and Joan Crawford in slightly naughty romps like **Red Dust** (1932) and **Possessed** (1931). With **It Happened One Night**, Gable's comic muscles were finally given a chance to stretch, and critics as well as audiences took notice.

Claudette Colbert
Ellen

If GABLE was Hollywood's "King," Colbert was screwball comedy's queen. The saucy comedienne sparkled in such delights as Ernst Lubitsch's **The Smiling Lieutenant** (1931), Wesley Ruggles' **The Gilded Lily** (1935), and Mitchell Leisen's **Midnight** (1939). Her infectious humor and coquettish behavior also brought enjoyment to her performances as sexy sirens in Cecil B. DeMille's **The Sign of the Cross** (1932) and **Cleopatra** (1934).

Academy Awards

✳ Best Picture
✳ Director (Capra)
✳ Actor (Gable)
✳ Actress (Colbert)
✳ Writing, Adaptation (Robert Riskin)

5 NOMINATIONS 5 OSCARS ✳

THE BUZZ

Colbert, who didn't expect to win, was boarding a New York-bound train when her name was announced as the best actress victor. One of the Academy's press VIPs tracked her down at the train station and dragged her to the Biltmore Hotel to accept her award. Immediately after thanking everyone, Colbert headed back to the station and boarded her train, which was held for her return.

It Happened One Night was the first film to ever win Oscars in all five major categories.

The Cast

Mae West
Flower Belle Lee

W.C. Fields
Cuthbert J. Twillie

Joseph Calleia
Jeff Badger
aka The Masked
Bandit

Dick Foran
Wayne Carter

Margaret Hamilton
Mrs. Gideon

Director
Edward Cline

Producer
Lester Cowan

MY LITTLE CHICKADEE

CYNICAL, curvaceous flirt Flower Belle Lee (West) is run out of town. She meets drunken, inept con man Cuthbert J. Twillie (Fields) and hatches a plan to gain credibility by marrying him so she can return to the Wild West town of Greasewood City as a proper lady. He falls for her. On their wedding night Flower Belle puts a goat in bed with Cuthbert and the marriage remains unconsummated. When they get back to town, Flower Belle is given the unlikely job of schoolmarm. Town gossip Mrs. Gideon (Hamilton) tries to make trouble. Cuthbert becomes sheriff, plays cards, tends bar, and ends up in a pickle, while Flower Belle looks for love.

UNIVERSAL 1940

Gossip

West asked producer Lester Cowan to cast Hamilton as Mrs. Gideon. Hamilton said of working with Fields and West, "I never laughed so hard in my life."

There was a clause in West's contract that if Fields drank during production, she wouldn't work until he sobered up or was sent home. Fields fell off the wagon only once, and as he was being ushered off the set, tipped his hat to his co-star.

By 1940, West's box-office strength had weakened, and she was only paid $40,000 for **My Little Chickadee**, about one-tenth of her salary during her heyday at Paramount five years earlier.

Though Fields and West each received credit for the final screenplay, West claimed that the bulk of it was hers and that Fields' contribution was only eight pages of a bar scene. To add to the confusion, Cowan claimed he adapted the script from Ferenc Molnar's play **The Guardsman**.

The Stars

Mae West
Flower Belle

NO ONE ever had as much fun with sex on the screen. Her implied sexcapades with the likes of Cary Grant in **She Done Him Wrong** and **I'm No Angel** saved Paramount from bankruptcy in 1933. Unfortunately, the wrong party got a rise out of Mae's racy double entendres— the Hays Office, which responded by enforcing the Production Code in 1934.

> " Come, my fox. . . I have some very definite pear-shaped ideas that I'd like to discuss with thee. "
> —*Cuthbert*

W. C. Fields
Cuthbert

THE bulbous-nosed comic played the hen-pecked husband to side-splitting perfection in **It's a Gift** (1934) and **The Man on the Flying Trapeze** (1935), and made conning a comic art in **The Old-Fashioned Way** (1934). For many Fields fans, his most endearing performance— and the one that demonstrated his potential as a dramatic actor— was as Mr. Micawber in **David Copperfield** (1935).

> " *Judge:* Are you trying to show contempt for this court? *Flower Belle:* No, your honor, I'm doin' my best to hide it! "

MY MAN GODFREY

ON A SOCIETY scavenger hunt, while looking for a "forgotten man," ditsy, self-absorbed, high society darling Irene Bullock (Lombard) finds unemployed, charming Godfrey Parke (Powell) with other bums. She hires him as a butler for her eccentric family: gruff patriarch Alexander (Pallette), his daffy wife Angelica (Brady), Mrs.

UNIVERSAL 1936

Bullock's protege Carlo (Auer), and Irene's scheming sister Cornelia (Patrick). Irene falls in love with Godfrey, whose true identity is hidden. He's lost everything in the Depression except his street smarts and his morality. He comes up with a scheme to get on his feet and also to help his old destitute companions, who live in a camp down by the river as Irene doggedly pursues him.

The Cast

William Powell
Godfrey Parke

Carole Lombard
Irene Bullock

Alice Brady
Angelica Bullock

Eugene Pallette
Alexander Bullock

Gail Patrick
Cornelia Bullock

Mischa Auer
Carlo

Jean Dixon
Molly

Alan Mowbray
Tommy Gray

Franklin Pangborn
Guthrie,
the scavenger hunt
emcee

Director and Producer
Gregory La Cava

"Can you butle?"
—*Irene*

Academy Awards

Director (La Cava)
Actor (Powell)
Actress (Lombard)
Supporting Actor (Auer)
Supporting Actress (Brady)
Writing, Screenplay
(Eric Hatch and Morris Ryskind)

6 NOMINATIONS

THE BUZZ

Though Powell and Lombard were divorced from each other, they remained friends and came to the Oscars on a double date. She was with Clark Gable and he was with his fiancée, Jean Harlow.

My Man Godfrey was the first film to earn Oscar nominations in all four acting categories.

The Stars

William Powell
Godfrey

Carole Lombard
Irene

WHEN it came to being witty, urbane, charming, and funny, Powell had no peers, except possibly Cary Grant. Though he began his career in silent films playing villains, Powell's star rose with the arrival of sound, and he sparkled in romances (1932's **One Way Passage**), screwball comedies (**Love Crazy** in 1941), and character roles (Clarence Day in 1947's **Life With Father**). He also made a crack screen detective playing Philo Vance five times and Nick Charles in six **Thin Man** films.

IT'S HARD to imagine '30s screwball comedies without the vivacious, irreverent Lombard. Her shouting matches with John Barrymore in **Twentieth Century** (1934) and her faux boxing antics with Fredric March in **Nothing Sacred** (1937) show her gift for mayhem—on-screen and off—in full force. It seemed as if her peak years were just beginning after her triumph in Ernst Lubitsch's **To Be or Not to Be** (1942) when she was killed in a plane crash. Her husband Clark Gable never recovered from her death. Neither did movie fans.

Gossip

Powell requested his ex-wife for **Godfrey**, feeling she'd be perfect as Irene.

The technical crew adored Lombard, and presented her with an enormous china egg, signed by each crew member. It was inscribed with the following: "To Carole, a Good Egg."

A stand-in was used for Powell in the scene when he must carry Lombard over his shoulder to her upstairs bedroom.

Lombard liked to keep audiences wondering what she'd wear next. Her favorite designer, Travis Banton, designed twenty-four gowns for her to wear in the film.

Jane Wyman can be spotted at the scavenger hunt.

My Man Godfrey was remade in 1957 with David Niven and June Allyson.

> **Godfrey:** May I be frank?
> **Molly:** Is that your name?
> **Godfrey:** No, My name is Godfrey.
> **Molly:** All right, be Frank.

Screen Team

Powell and Lombard made two other films together in 1931, **Man of the World** and **Ladies' Man**. A few weeks after **Ladies' Man** was released, they married, a union that ended in 1933 due to incompatibility and conflicting careers.

'You don't know anything about anything. You don't know how to get a meal. You don't know how to keep a secret. . . I know fifty times as much about trouble as you ever will. *—The Girl*'

PARAMOUNT
1941

The Cast

Joel McCrea
John Lloyd Sullivan

Veronica Lake
The Girl

Robert Warwick
Mr. Lebrand

William Demarest
Mr. Jones

Franklin Pangborn
Mr. Casalsis

Porter Hall
Mr. Hadrian

Byron Foulger
Mr. Johnny Valdelle

Margaret Hayes
Secretary

Eric Blore
Sullivan's valet

Robert Greig
Sullivan's butler

Torbin Meyer
Doctor

Victor Potel
Cameraman

Richard Webb
Radio man

Director
Preston Sturges

Producer
Paul Jones

SULLIVAN'S TRAVELS

WELL-MEANING, successful, dilettante director John Lloyd Sullivan (McCrea) makes musicals and comedies, but wants to make a serious film called **Oh Brother, Where Art Thou?** about the poor. His producers are upset when he tramps off across the country, without any money, to see what it's like among the hoboes. He meets a beautiful but unsuccessful actress (Lake), who's on her way home after giving up on Hollywood. Through a series of mishaps, Sullivan lands in jail, sentenced to six years doing hard labor. His only pleasure in the labor camp comes when a cartoon is shown, and he learns a lesson about the importance of fluff and fun as distractions for the downtrodden.

Gossip

Lake was pregnant at the time she made **Sullivan's Travels** but did her best to keep it a secret out of fear that she'd be fired from the film. When Sturges heard, he reassured her that something would be "worked out."

Lake nearly drowned when her petticoat became twisted over her head during a poolside scene. The quick-thinking McCrea released the petticoat from her head and carried her out of the water.

Screen Team

McCrea and Lake were partnered again for **Ramrod** (1947), a western directed by Lake's husband at the time, Andre de Toth.

The Stars

Joel McCrea
Sullivan

THE AFFABLE, cornfed McCrea was the embodiment of the red-blooded American male, with a gentle masculinity that appealed to men, and a boyish sex appeal that made women swoon in such confections as **The More the Merrier** (1943) and romances such as **These Three** (1936). But McCrea never felt happier than in a Stetson and chaps, and in the latter phase of his career carved a niche as one of the great screen cowboys in oaters such as **Four Faces West** (1948) and **Ride the High Country** (1962).

Veronica Lake
The Girl

AFTER scoring a hit as a sultry gold digger in **I Wanted Wings** (1941), Paramount saw Lake as its answer to Lana Turner. Lake, however, didn't relish being typecast as a blond mantrap and pounced on the chance to engage in Sturges' brand of eccentric comedy like a feline to catnip. She earned critical raves and was rarely sexier or funnier.

'There's a lot to be said for making people laugh. Did you know that that's all some people have? — *Sullivan*'

ROMANCE

ROMANCE

Get in the mood for love. You don't have to wait for Valentine's Day to watch these romances.

When Irene Dunne and Charles Boyer meet on an ocean cruise in **Love Affair**, we know that they are meant to be together, even if they must overcome the hurdles of circumstance.

In **Now, Voyager**, Bette Davis and Paul Henreid also meet on a cruise. (It must be something in those sea breezes!) She is transformed from spinster to swan. In her brief liaison she learns of the healing power of love, and that it is better to have loved and lost than never to have loved at all.

In **Sabrina**, it's Humphrey Bogart who's transformed from a workaholic to a man who can relax (and goes off to meet his love on a boat, I might add). Who can blame him? Doe-eyed gamine Audrey Hepburn made us all swoon. Her femininity and petite grace are riveting.

The most romantic leading man was Laurence Olivier, who appeared in both **Pride and Prejudice** and **Wuthering Heights** as a dashing, proud hero. He could be touchingly gentle or as tough as he needed to be.

He was also easy on the eyes. In both films, we know that his character was meant to be with the heroine, even if they didn't know it, and we hope fate will intervene.

Accidents, neurotic families, missed meetings, and miscommunication all conspire to keep our paramours apart. But even if they're doomed to live separate lives, we have the pleasure of their passion, the memory of an intense magical connection. These films make us fall in love all over again.

REEL LOVE

RKO RADIO 1939

LOVE AFFAIR

ELEGANT American Terry McKay (Dunne) meets charming Frenchman Michel Marnet (Boyer) on a cruise, and they fall in love. Unfortunately they are both committed to others and decide that they must part and spend six months ironing out their affairs, ending their romantic

entanglements, and seeing if they still feel the same about each other. They plan to meet at the Empire State Building. An accident prevents Terry from making the date, and the lovers seem doomed to lead separate lives.

The Stars

Irene Dunne
Terry

WITH her talents both as an actress and a soprano, Dunne sparkled as a tragedienne in weepies such as **Back Street** (1932), a comedienne in **The Awful Truth** (1937), and a musical ingenue in **Show Boat** (1936). She retired following the delightful **It Grows on Trees** (1952).

Charles Boyer
Michel

BOYER listed **Love Affair** as the favorite of his films, largely because of his rapport with Dunne and McCarey and the craftsmanship of the writing. Most important, McCarey wrote the part of Michel with Boyer in mind.

Academy Awards

6 NOMINATIONS

Best Picture
Actress (Dunne)
Supporting Actress (Ouspenskaya)
Writing, Original Story
(McCarey and Mildred Cram)
Interior Decoration
(Van Nest Polglase and Al Herman)
Music, Song ("Wishing" by Buddy De Sylva)

THE BUZZ

Dunne was nominated four other times for best actress—**Cimarron** (1931), **Theodora Goes Wild** (1936), **The Awful Truth** (1937), and **I Remember Mama** (1948)—but never won.

The Cast

Irene Dunne
Terry McKay

Charles Boyer
Michel Marnet

Maria Ouspenskaya
Grandmother Janou

Lee Bowman
Kenneth Bradley

Astrid Allwyn
Lois Clarke

Director and Producer
Leo McCarey

Gossip

McCarey dusted off the story for his 1957 hit, **An Affair to Remember**. Warren Beatty filmed it again in 1994 using the original title.

"If you can paint, I can walk.
—*Terry*"

Screen Team

Dunne and Boyer began a lifelong friendship on **Love Affair**. Professionally, they also worked harmoniously on **When Tomorrow Comes** (1939) and the aptly titled **Together Again** (1944).

WARNER BROS.

1942

The Cast

Bette Davis
Charlotte Vale

Paul Henreid
Jerry Durrance

Claude Rains
Dr. Jaquith

Gladys Cooper
Mrs. Vale

John Loder
Elliot Livingston

Ilka Chase
Lisa Vale

Bonita Granville
June Vale

Lee Patrick
Deb McIntyre

Janis Wilson
Tina

Franklin Pangborn
Mr. Thompson

Katherine Alexander
Miss Trask

James Rennie
Frank McIntyre

Mary Wickes
Dora

Director
Irving Rapper

Producer
Hal B. Wallis

NOW, VOYAGER

MOUSY, frustrated Boston spinster Charlotte Vale (Davis) suffers a nervous breakdown under her mother's domination. Understanding psychiatrist Dr. Jaquith (Rains) helps Charlotte to recover. She emerges from his sanitarium as a changed, glamorous, sophisticated woman. On her first exciting sea voyage to South America, she falls in love with charming but married Jerry Durrance (Henreid). He has a daughter Tina (Wilson) who has similar problems to Charlotte, also caused by an unfeeling mother. After the trip, self-confident Charlotte rebels against her mother, whereupon Mrs. Vale dies of a heart attack. Charlotte's guilt drives her back to the sanitarium and Dr. Jaquith. Coincidentally, Jerry's daughter is there and Charlotte nurtures her back to health.

' Oh Jerry, don't let's ask for the moon. We have the stars. ' — *Charlotte*

Screen Team

Davis, Henreid, and Rains all worked together on another Rapper soap opera, **Deception** (1946). Rains also co-starred with Davis in **Juarez** (1939) and **Mr. Skeffington** (1944), and with Henreid in **Casablanca** (1942) and **Rope of Sand** (1949).

Academy Awards

Actress (Davis)
Supporting Actress (Cooper)
✱ Music, Scoring of a Dramatic or Comedy Picture (Max Steiner)

3 NOMINATIONS 1 OSCAR ✱

THE BUZZ

Davis earned a best actress nomination for the fifth year in a row, a feat accomplished by one other person—Greer Garson, who took the prize that year for **Mrs. Miniver.**

Gossip

Upon learning that Warners intended to make **Now, Voyager** with Irene Dunne in the lead, Davis went after Jack Warner and Hal Wallis and convinced them to give the part to her.

Davis wanted the film to retain the flavor of the novel upon which it was based, and had the screenwriters restore portions of the book.

Norma Shearer and Ginger Rogers both turned down the part of Charlotte.

The film's title was taken from a line in Walt Whitman's *Leaves of Grass.*

> ‘These are only tears of gratitude —an old maid's gratitude for the crumbs offered.’
> —*Charlotte*

The Stars

Paul Henreid
Jerry

LIKE most of Davis' leading men, Henreid was a vanilla type who was overshadowed by his dominant co-star. Still, whenever he lit cigarettes for two, the sparks that appeared weren't only from the lighter. Though Henreid continued to play romantic heroes, he later moved behind the camera, and even directed Davis in a dual role in **Dead Ringer** (1964).

Bette Davis
Charlotte

THE screen's premier actress was in the midst of her glory years in Hollywood, though reaching and maintaining that position took all of Davis' determination. "I always had to fight to get anything good," she said of landing **Now, Voyager.** She also had the box-office muscle to make her studio bosses back down, and from 1937 to 1945 excelled in a string of "woman's pictures" that have never been equaled.

PRIDE AND PREJUDICE

The Cast

Greer Garson
Elizabeth Bennet

Laurence Olivier
Mr. Darcy

Maureen O'Sullivan
Jane Bennet

Mary Boland
Mrs. Bennet

Edmund Gwenn
Mr. Bennet

Edna May Oliver
Lady Catherine
de Bourgh

Ann Rutherford
Lydia Bennet

Marsha Hunt
Mary Bennet

Heather Angel
Kitty Bennet

Melville Cooper
Mr. Collins

Director
Robert Z. Leonard

Producer
Hunt Stromberg

PLOTTING to make good matches for her daughters takes all of distracted Mrs. Bennet's (Boland) time. Wise Mr. Bennet (Gwenn) is bemused by her machinations, and engaged only by his favorite daughter Elizabeth (Garson). Wealthy, young Mr. Bingley (Bruce Lester) moves next door with his sister. His friend, the dashing Mr. Darcy (Olivier), is a frequent visitor. Bingley falls in love with Jane (O'Sullivan), Elizabeth's older sister. Elizabeth dislikes Darcy's proud, condescending ways and they fight whenever they meet, yet there is an underlying attraction between them. Elizabeth's younger sister Kitty (Angel) is involved in a scandal, bringing potential shame upon the family. A hero surprises all and saves the day, helping Elizabeth to decide upon her fate.

M-G-M
1940

Gossip

Although the story took place during the 1820s, designer Adrian decided to update the women's costumes to the Victorian era of hoopskirts and corsets.

Each day at 4 p.m. sharp, Garson held afternoon tea in her dressing room for the largely British cast.

Screen Team

Hunt appeared with Garson in **Blossoms in the Dust** (1941), with Rutherford in **These Glamour Girls** (1939) and with Gwenn in **Cheers for Miss Bishop** (1941).

Academy Awards

* Interior Decoration, Black and White (Cedric Gibbons and Paul Groesse)

1 NOMINATION
1 OSCAR
*

THE BUZZ

Gibbons' win was one of eleven Oscars he got for interior decoration, and he earned a total of thirty-nine nominations between 1929 and 1956.

The Stars

Greer Garson
Elizabeth

PRIDE and Prejudice was a pivotal film for Garson. Having scored in her film debut, **Goodbye, Mr. Chips**, M-G-M needed another strong movie to enhance her star luster. Director Leonard did his best to favor Garson in each shot, even those with Olivier, and delivered an immediate hit. More important, Garson was now poised as M-G-M's likely successor to Norma Shearer and Greta Garbo, both of whom were on the fringe of retirement.

Laurence Olivier
Mr. Darcy

WITH an Oscar nomination for **Wuthering Heights** (1939) to his credit, and another one for **Rebecca** (1940) imminent, Olivier's rising star and commanding presence made him the ideal choice for Mr. Darcy. Though he wanted his lady love Vivien Leigh to play Elizabeth, he got on famously with Garson, whom he had worked with on the London stage five years earlier in a West End production of **Golden Arrow**.

PARAMOUNT
1954

SABRINA

GRACEFUL, luminous Sabrina (Hepburn) is the daughter of the chauffeur (Williams) on an estate owned by distracted patriarch Oliver Larrabee (Hampden). Sabrina has always been in love with Oliver's charming playboy son David (Holden), who wants nothing to do with the family business run by his workaholic brother Linus (Bogart). Linus wants David to marry the daughter of a potential business partner. Sabrina is sent to Paris to forget David, and returns transformed into a sophisticated, enchanting, fashionable lady who catches David's eye. Linus is upset that his plans for David's marriage may be thwarted, so he tries to woo Sabrina away from David, and falls in love with her.

Screen Team

Hepburn and Holden starred once more in the comedy **Paris When It Sizzles** (1964). Holden appeared previously with Bogart in **Invisible Stripes** (1940).

Academy Awards

6 NOMINATIONS 1 OSCAR ✱

Director (Wilder)
Actress (Hepburn)
Writing, Screenplay (Wilder, Samuel A. Taylor, and Ernest Lehman)
Cinematography, Black and White (Charles Lang Jr.)
Art Direction-Set Decoration (Hal Pereira and Walter Tyler; Sam Comer and Ray Moyer)
✱ **Costume Design, Black and White** (Edith Head)

THE BUZZ

Hepburn was pregnant and was ordered by doctors not to make the trip from London, where she was living at the time, to Los Angeles for the ceremony. In addition to being a nominee, she was to present the best actor award. Bette Davis was her replacement.

The Stars

❝A woman happily in love, she burns the souffle. A woman unhappily in love, she forgets to turn on the oven.❞
—*Baron St. Fontanel*

Audrey Hepburn
Sabrina

EVERYONE fell in love with the delectable waif after her Oscar-winning performance as the most royal of royals in **Roman Holiday** a year earlier. And it's a love affair that intensified after her divine **Sabrina**. She also made a nimble partner for Astaire in **Funny Face** (1957) and a stylish one for Cary Grant in **Charade** (1963). But her most important and heartfelt role was as special ambassador to UNICEF, helping children in Latin America and the Third World.

Humphrey Bogart
Linus

BOGART was thirty years older than his leading lady and felt somewhat uncomfortable chasing after her in **Sabrina,** but still made us hope Sabrina would choose his Linus in the end. **Sabrina** was also a rare opportunity for Bogart to shed his tough guy image, the second time he had done so in 1954, having recently completed the satiric **Beat the Devil.**

William Holden
David

FRESH from an Oscar in Wilder's **Stalag 17** (1953), Holden was now Hollywood's golden boy. After working with Hepburn, he teamed up twice with the screen's other regal beauty Grace Kelly in **The Country Girl** and **The Bridges at Toko-Ri** (1954), and finished the decade in blockbusters like **The Bridge on the River Kwai** (1957).

Gossip

Hepburn was torn between Bogart and Holden in the film, but there was no contest off the set. Bogart was barely cordial to Hepburn, but she and Holden began a serious love affair.

Though Edith Head got screen credit for the costumes, it was Hepburn's favorite designer, Hubert de Givenchy, who created them. Hepburn was furious that Head got the costume design Oscar rather than Givenchy. The day after the ceremony, Hepburn apologized to him and vowed he'd receive screen credit on each of her films that he worked on.

The white organdy ball gown and the black Capri pants worn by Hepburn caused a sensation, and Givenchy established a fashion trend called *décolleté Sabrina.*

Linus was written specifically for Cary Grant, who bowed out of the movie at the last minute.

Holden dyed his hair blonde for the movie.

WUTHERING HEIGHTS

GOLDWYN-UNITED ARTISTS

1939

ETHEREAL Catherine Earnshaw (Oberon) lives on the English moors in a nineteenth-century estate. Her gentleman-farmer father (Kellaway) adopts a poor Liverpool orphan, Heathcliff (Olivier). Her supercilious brother Hindley (Williams) hates and envies Heathcliff and taunts him. Brooding Heathcliff falls in love with material-istic Cathy, as they grow up wandering the moors and their favorite place, Penstone Crag. When Earnshaw dies, Hindley inherits the estate and abuses Heathcliff, who runs away to make his fortune. Cathy marries the wealthy, cultured neighbor Edgar Linton (Niven). Heathcliff returns and exacts revenge on all who spurned him.

The Cast

Merle Oberon
Catherine Earnshaw

Laurence Olivier
Heathcliff

David Niven
Edgar Linton

Geraldine Fitzgerald
Isabella Linton

Flora Robson
Ellen Dean

Donald Crisp
Dr. Kenneth

Hugh Williams
Hindley

Leo G. Carroll
Joseph

Miles Mander
Mr. Lockwood

Cecil Kellaway
Mr. Earnshaw

Cecil Humphreys
Judge Linton

Sarita Wooton
Cathy, as a child

Rex Downing
Heathcliff, as a child

Douglas Scott
Hindley, as a child

Director
William Wyler

Producer
Samuel Goldwyn

"If he loved you with all the power of his soul for a whole lifetime, he couldn't love you as much as I do in a single day. —*Heathcliff*"

Gossip

Producer Walter Wanger had planned to make **Wuthering Heights** in 1937 with Charles Boyer and Sylvia Sidney. Eventually both actors bowed out, but Sidney had shown the script to Wyler while they were making **Dead End**. When Wyler heard Wanger's project was scrapped, he urged Goldwyn to buy the script.

Goldwyn wanted Vivien Leigh for Isabella, but the actress refused to play a supporting role.

Olivier wanted Leigh to play Cathy, and therefore had little patience or respect for Oberon. During one scene, Oberon complained that Olivier spat at her while saying his lines. An enraged Olivier responded by calling her "an amateur little bitch."

Oberon's nerves were also strained by Wyler, who berated her so much to get the desired reaction from her in the storm sequence that she had to be admitted to a hospital afterward.

The Stars

Laurence Olivier
Heathcliff

OLIVIER'S first love was the London stage, and when Goldwyn wooed him to Hollywood, he did so reluctantly. His feelings didn't waver when he began work on **Wuthering Heights,** but by the time it wrapped, he and Wyler had become good friends and Olivier had been somewhat humbled. For the next fifty years, he'd continue to split his time between stage and screen, and gain a reputation as a consummate actor in both media.

Merle Oberon
Cathy

OBERON worked on both sides of the Atlantic throughout the '30s. British producer Alexander Korda showcased her in **The Private Life of Don Juan** (1934) and **The Scarlet Pimpernel** (1935), and for Goldwyn, she did her best work in **The Dark Angel** (1935) and **These Three** (1936). Her nightmarish experience on **Wuthering Heights** ended her ties to Goldwyn, and she headed back to England where she married Korda in June 1939.

Screen Team

Olivier and Oberon worked together more amicably in **The Divorce of Lady X** (1938).

> 'Ellen, I *am* Heathcliff. — *Cathy*'

Academy Awards

Best Picture
Director (Wyler)
Actor (Olivier)
Supporting Actress (Fitzgerald)
Writing, Screenplay
(Ben Hecht and Charles MacArthur)
✻ Cinematography, Black and White
(Gregg Toland)
Interior Decoration, Black and White
(James Basevi)
Music, Original Score (Alfred Newman)

8 NOMINATIONS 1 OSCAR ✻

THE BUZZ

This was the first of Olivier's ten best actor nominations. He did win acting and directing Oscars for **Hamlet** (1948) and received two honorary awards.

TEARJERKERS

TEARJERKERS

$\mathcal{S}$ome might accuse me of being overly sentimental. I admit, I have cried occasionally during commercials for long-distance telephone service. But these movies really start the waterworks.

A Tree Grows in Brooklyn is the story of the impoverished Nolan family, in particular, starry-eyed Francie, who longs to know everything about the world. Scene that had me sobbing: at her graduation, Francie finds the flowers that her Aunt Sissy bought with the money that Francie's beloved papa had given to Sissy just before his death.

In Stella Dallas, Barbara Stanwyck is a garish, low-class mother who sacrifices all to give her daughter Laurel a better life. Stella fears that her crass ways will embarrass her daughter, and gives her up. The final scene is shattering.

There are so many touching moments in the poignant, sentimental epic How Green Was My Valley, about coal miners in a small Welsh village at the turn of the century. It is impossible not to be touched by the scene following an explosion in the mine. As the women wait, the elevator comes up each time from the depths without any survivors.

BOO HOO

In Goodbye Mr. Chips, the gentle schoolteacher Mr. Chips finds a deep love, cut tragically short, with Greer Garson. This love transforms him from an awkward, inept disciplinarian to a giving, understanding mentor.

Jimmy Stewart learns that his life is valuable from the angel Clarence in It's a Wonderful Life. The final scene around the Christmas tree, when the whole town comes through for him, moves me every time.

The emotions depicted in these films are deep and universal. You'll relate to them. Just remember to have plenty of tissues handy.

GOLDWYN-UNITED ARTISTS

1937

STELLA DALLAS

$\mathcal{S}$TELLA MARTIN (Stanwyck) marries upper-cruster Stephen Dallas (Boles). They have a daughter Laurel (Shirley), whom they love dearly. As Laurel grows up, Stella's vulgarity becomes embarrassing. Stella thinks her behavior will stand in her daughter's way, and sacrifices their relationship to the point of ostracizing herself, so that Laurel can have a good life.

Gossip

A tearful Shirley complained to Goldwyn that Vidor wasn't giving her any direction. Goldwyn phoned Vidor and shouted, "Tell her she's lousy if she's great or great if she's lousy. Tell her any damn thing you please. I just can't cope with hysterical females."

The Cast

Barbara Stanwyck
Stella Dallas

John Boles
Stephen Dallas

Anne Shirley
Laurel Dallas

Barbara O'Neil
Helen Morrison Dallas

Alan Hale
Ed Munn

Marjorie Main
Mrs. Martin

George Walcott
Charlie Martin

Director
King Vidor

Producer
Samuel Goldwyn

Academy Awards

2 NOMINATIONS

Actress (Stanwyck)
Supporting Actress (Shirley)

THE BUZZ

Stanwyck also earned best actress nominations for **Ball of Fire** (1941), **Double Indemnity** (1944), and **Sorry, Wrong Number** (1948), but never won.

Barbara Stanwyck
Stella

$\mathcal{T}$HE hard-working Stanwyck had made nearly thirty movies since 1927, most of them forgotten. In **Stella Dallas**, she had her first real tour de force filled with tearful and joyful moments, and the type of heartbreaking finale every actress dreams of playing.

John Boles
Stephen

$\mathcal{A}$CTRESSES loved working with Boles because they never had to worry about him stealing their thunder. Throughout the '30s, he was the cause of suffering for tragic heroines like Irene Dunne in **Back Street** (1932) and Margaret Sullavan in **Only Yesterday** (1933).

Anne Shirley
Laurel

$\mathcal{S}$WEET Dawn O'Day was rechristened for the title character she played in **Anne of Green Gables** (1934). She then became RKO's favorite girl next door in family fare like **Mother Carey's Chickens** (1938).

M-G-M

1939

"The Best Picture of Any Year"

The Cast

Robert Donat
Chipping
aka "Mr. Chips"

Greer Garson
Katherine Chipping

Terry Kilburn
John Colley, Peter Colley, Peter Colley II, Peter Colley III

Paul von Hernreid (Paul Henreid)
Staefel

Judith Furse
Flora

Lyn Harding
Wetherby

Milton Rosmer
Chatteris

Frederick Leister
Marsham

Louise Hampton
Mrs. Wickett

Austin Trevor
Ralston

David Tree
Jackson

Scott Sunderland
Sir John Colley

Director
Sam Wood

Producer
Victor Saville

GOODBYE MR. CHIPS

LATIN schoolmaster, gentle Charles "Chips" Chipping (Donat) remembers his fifty-eight years at Brookfield, an English private school. He couldn't control his students when he began teaching, and the boys didn't like him. On holiday with German teacher Herr Staefel (Henreid), Chipping falls in love with charming Katherine Ellis (Garson). They marry and she helps him to be an inspirational and popular teacher. He also is promoted to housemaster. When she dies during childbirth, Chips continues his teaching with morals, ethics and friendship for the boys. He grows old, spending his whole life in devoted service.

"Modern methods! Poppycock! Give a boy a sense of humor and a sense of proportion and he'll stand up to anything! --*Chips*

Gossip

Producer Irving Thalberg originally proposed turning James Hilton's novel into a film in 1936 with Charles Laughton or Lionel Barrymore in the title role. (Hilton made his own suggestion—Wallace Beery!)

Garson was unhappy about getting what she considered a "small" role.

Donat and Garson had a warm relationship. Nervous about working before the cameras for the first time, Garson frequently turned to Donat for advice and reassurance.

England's historic Repton College, which was founded in 1557, doubled for Brookfield School. More than 200 Repton students gave up their Christmas holiday to work as extras.

Academy Awards

7 NOMINATIONS 1 OSCAR ✱

Best Picture
Director (Wood)
✱ **Actor** (Donat)
Actress (Garson)
Writing, Screenplay (Eric Maschwitz, R.C. Sherriff and Claudine West)
Sound Recording (A.W. Watkins)
Film Editing (Charles Frend)

THE BUZZ
Several newspapers wrote after the awards that Garson would have likely taken home a statuette had the Academy placed her in the supporting actress category.

> *Doctor:*
> Pity he had no children.
> *Chips:*
> You're wrong. I have . . . thousands of them . . . and all boys.

The Stars

Greer Garson
Katherine

GARSON had been under contract to M-G-M for eighteen months without ever setting foot on a soundstage before her assignment as Mrs. Chips. She was taken aback by the warm response to her performance, and for the next six years, had plum roles in box-office bonanzas such as **Random Harvest** (1942) and **Madame Curie** (1943), and won an Oscar for her biggest hit, **Mrs. Miniver** (1942).

Robert Donat
Chips

HAVING built his reputation on adventure yarns such as **The Count of Monte Cristo** (1934) and Hitchcock's suspenseful **The 39 Steps** (1935), friends warned Donat not to accept the role of Chips because it would hurt his heroic image. Wisely, he ignored them, or else we would have been denied one of the most moving performances ever delivered by an actor.

Screen Team

McDowall and Pidgeon also starred in **Man Hunt** and **Holiday in Mexico** (1946).

Academy Awards

* Best Picture
* Director (Ford)
* Supporting Actor (Crisp)
Supporting Actress (Allgood)
Writing, Screenplay (Philip Dunne)
* Cinematography, Black and White (Arthur Miller)
* Interior Decoration, Black and White (Richard Day and Nathan Juran; Thomas Little)
Sound Recording (E.H. Hansen)
Music, Scoring of a Dramatic Picture (Alfred Newman)
Film Editing (James B. Clark)

10 NOMINATIONS 5 OSCARS *

THE BUZZ

Ford received the third of his four best director Oscars for this movie. He also won for **The Informer** (1935), **The Grapes of Wrath** (1940), and **The Quiet Man** (1952), but he was only on hand to accept the first. "I didn't show up at the ceremony to collect my Oscars," he said. "Once I went fishing, another time there was a war on, and on another occasion, I remember, I was suddenly taken drunk."

HOW GREEN WAS MY VALLEY

IN A PICTURESQUE Welsh mining village, the Morgans raise their six sons and a lovely daughter, Angharad (O'Hara). The men are all coal miners. The youngest, earnest ten-year-old Huw (McDowall), falls ill and is unable to walk. He convalesces and studies with the minister, Mr. Gruffydd (Pidgeon).

20th CENTURY-FOX 1941

Even though Angharad is in love with the minister, she is pressured by her parents to marry the mine owner's snooty son. There are accidents and tragedies in the mine, and the older sons want to leave. Huw grows from a naive innocent to a wise adult.

The Cast

Walter Pidgeon
Mr. Gruffydd

Maureen O'Hara
Angharad Morgan

Roddy McDowall
Huw Morgan

Donald Crisp
Mr. Gwilym Morgan

Sara Allgood
Mrs. Beth Morgan

Barry Fitzgerald
Cyfartha

Patric Knowles
Ivor Morgan

Morton Lowry
Mr. Jonas

Rhys Williams
Dai Bando

Director
John Ford

Producer
Darryl F. Zanuck

"*For you cannot conquer injustice with more injustice —only with justice and the help of God.* —*Mr. Gruffydd*"

Gossip

Zanuck wanted to shoot the film on location in the coal-mining district of South Wales, but the outbreak of World War II put an end to those plans. Instead, Fox built a coal mine and a Welsh village in the San Fernando Valley.

The eighty-member chorus of the Welsh Presbyterian Church of Los Angeles performed the songs.

❝Men like my father cannot die. They are with me still, real in memory as they were real in flesh, loving and beloved forever.**❞**

—Huw,
as an adult

The Stars

Walter Pidgeon
Mr. Gruffydd

IT TOOK a pair of loanouts to Fox for **How Green Was My Valley** and **Man Hunt** (1941) to make Pidgeon's home studio, M-G-M, take notice of his star potential. Pidgeon became one of the most reliable leading men in the '40s, romancing Ginger Rogers in **Weekend at the Waldorf** (1945), Claudette Colbert in **The Secret Heart** (1946), and his favorite co-star, Greer Garson, in eight movies.

Roddy McDowall
Huw

ELEVEN-year-old Roddy left London in 1940, and came to Hollywood with his mother. Many of McDowall's co-stars after that were of the four-legged kind, including Lassie, Flicka, and Thunderhead— Son of Flicka. McDowall's star waned a bit as he matured, but he constantly worked, and developed a second career as a photographer.

Maureen O'Hara
Angharad

RAVISHING, red-haired O'Hara hailed from the Emerald Isle, and got her start with Dublin's Abbey Players before making **Jamaica Inn** (1939) for Hitchcock. A friendship blossomed with co-star Charles Laughton, and he brought her to Hollywood to play the fiery gypsy Esmeralda opposite him in **The Hunchback of Notre Dame** (1939).

IT'S A WONDERFUL LIFE

GEORGE Bailey (Stewart) dreams of someday leaving Bedford Falls for adventure. Instead he is stuck running the family business, a savings and loan, while his younger brother gets to move away. Staying in his small town is more bearable with Mary (Reed) as his wife. They have a bunch of kids. Mr. Potter (Barrymore), a millionaire miser, facilitates the financial trouble that puts George on the brink of bankruptcy. George decides to end it all, when angel Clarence (Travers) rescues him, showing George how bad the town would be without him.

LIBERTY FILMS-RKO RADIO

1946

The Cast

James Stewart
George Bailey

Donna Reed
Mary Hatch Bailey

Lionel Barrymore
Mr. Potter

Thomas Mitchell
Uncle Billy Bailey

Henry Travers
Clarence Oddbody

Beulah Bondi
Mrs. Bailey

Frank Faylen
Ernie Bishop

Ward Bond
Officer Bert

Gloria Grahame
Violet Bick

H.B. Warner
Mr. Gower

Frank Albertson
Sam Wainwright

Todd Karns
Harry Bailey

Samuel S. Hinds
Peter Bailey

Mary Treen
Cousin Tilly

Virginia Patton
Ruth Dakin Bailey

Sheldon Leonard
Nick

Director and Producer
Frank Capra

'Do you want the moon? If you want it, I'll throw a lasso around it and pull it down for you. *--George*'

Gossip

The film was based on a short story called **The Greatest Gift**, which was originally mailed as a Christmas card to friends of author Philip Van Doren Stern.

RKO planned **It's a Wonderful Life** for Cary Grant, but Capra loved the story and bought the rights as the first production for Liberty Films, the new company he created with William Wyler and George Stevens.

It's a Wonderful Life was a flop when it came out, and RKO lost $525,000. In the 1970s, someone forgot to renew the copyright and the movie fell into public domain. Its popularity skyrocketed after airings on television.

> *One man's life touches so many others, when he's not there it leaves an awfully big hole.*
> —*Clarence*

Screen Team

Bondi played Stewart's mother in three other films—**Of Human Hearts** (1938), **Vivacious Lady** (1938), and **Mr. Smith Goes to Washington** (1939).

> *Teacher says, every time a bell rings, an angel gets his wings.* –*Zuzu*

The Stars

James Stewart
George

Donna Reed
Mary

It's a Wonderful Life was Stewart's first movie since returning from his stint in the Air Force, and critics welcomed him back with some of the best reviews of his career. Stewart foundered for the next couple of years, but hit a home run in 1949 with **The Stratton Story,** and was unstoppable in the '50s thanks to Hitchcock and horse operas.

GIRL-next-door Reed starred in dozens of movies for M-G-M in the '40s, but her film career was highlighted by just two movies—**It's a Wonderful Life** and **From Here to Eternity** (1953)—neither of which was for Metro. The fact that she played a small-town wife and mother in one and a parboiled dance hostess in the other points to her versatility.

Academy Awards

Best Picture
Director (Capra)
Actor (Stewart)
Sound Recording (John Aalberg)
Film Editing (William Hornbeck)

5 NOMINATIONS

THE BUZZ

This was Capra's last of his six nominations for best director. He'd previously won for directing **It Happened One Night** (1934) and **Mr. Deeds Goes to Town** (1936), and with **You Can't Take It With You** (1938) he became the first person to win Oscars for directing and producing in the same year.

"Bend down, Papa. My cup runneth over." —*Francie*

A TREE GROWS IN BROOKLYN

Dorothy McGuire
Katie Nolan

Peggy Ann Garner
Francie Nolan

Joan Blondell
Aunt Sissy

James Dunn
Johnny Nolan

Lloyd Nolan
Officer McShane

Ted Donaldson
Neely Nolan

Director
Elia Kazan

Producer
Louis D. Lighton

FRANCIE Nolan (Garner) is an eleven-year-old living in dire poverty in Williamsburg, Brooklyn, with her charming alcoholic father Johnny (Dunn), her long-suffering mother Katie (McGuire), and her younger brother Neely (Donaldson). Francie studies, runs errands and adores her daddy, who has a hard time making ends meet as a singing waiter. His drinking accelerates.

Katie's brassy older sister, Aunt Sissy (Blondell), is an embarassment to Katie, but a support to Francie. The family struggles to survive their harsh circumstances, just like the tree growing from the cement behind their tenement apartment.

20th CENTURY-FOX 1945

Gossip

Kazan thought Dunn would be perfect as the alcoholic Johnny because he knew the actor had experience with the bottle, and he was good at playing a drunk.

At the time **Tree** was being made, Garner's father was in the Air Force, and she feared he might be killed. For one scene, Kazan played on her fears to get the desired emotion.

Gene Tierney was supposed to portray Katie, but she had to drop out when she became pregnant.

The Stars

Dorothy McGuire
Katie

IN ONLY her second film, McGuire, right, showed her chameleon-like ability as an actress. Her embittered Katie is a far cry from the child bride she played in **Claudia** (1943). She continued showing her range in such diverse roles as a shy, homely maid in **The Enchanted Cottage** (1945), a mute girl marked for murder in **The Spiral Staircase** (1946), and a New York sophisticate in **Gentleman's Agreement** (1947).

Peggy Ann Garner
Francie

ON SCREEN since she was six, Garner was an unusually talented child actress whose performance as the young title heroine of **Jane Eyre** (1944) showed the dramatic promise that would be fulfilled in **Tree.**

Joan Blondell
Aunt Sissy

THE hard-working Blondell made twenty-nine films from 1930 to 1933 while under contract to Warner Bros. She cited Sissy as her finest role and Kazan as one of her favorite directors. "**Tree** came along and let me have a moment or two of tenderness, of maturity that nobody had ever given me before," she told Life in 1971.

James Dunn
Johnny

THOUGH **Tree** ensured Dunn a place in movie history, film buffs also remember him opposite Shirley Temple in three 1934 movies —**Stand Up and Cheer, Bright Eyes,** and **Baby Take a Bow.**

> ❝**M**y kids are gonna make something of themselves, even if I gotta turn into granite rock to do it. —*Katie*❞

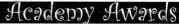

Academy Awards

✳ Supporting Actor (Dunn)
Writing, Screenplay
(Frank Davis and Tess Slesinger)

2 NOMINATIONS 1 OSCAR ✳

THE BUZZ

Peggy Ann Garner received a special juvenile Oscar for her beautiful performance as Francie, beating out Elizabeth Taylor for **National Velvet.**

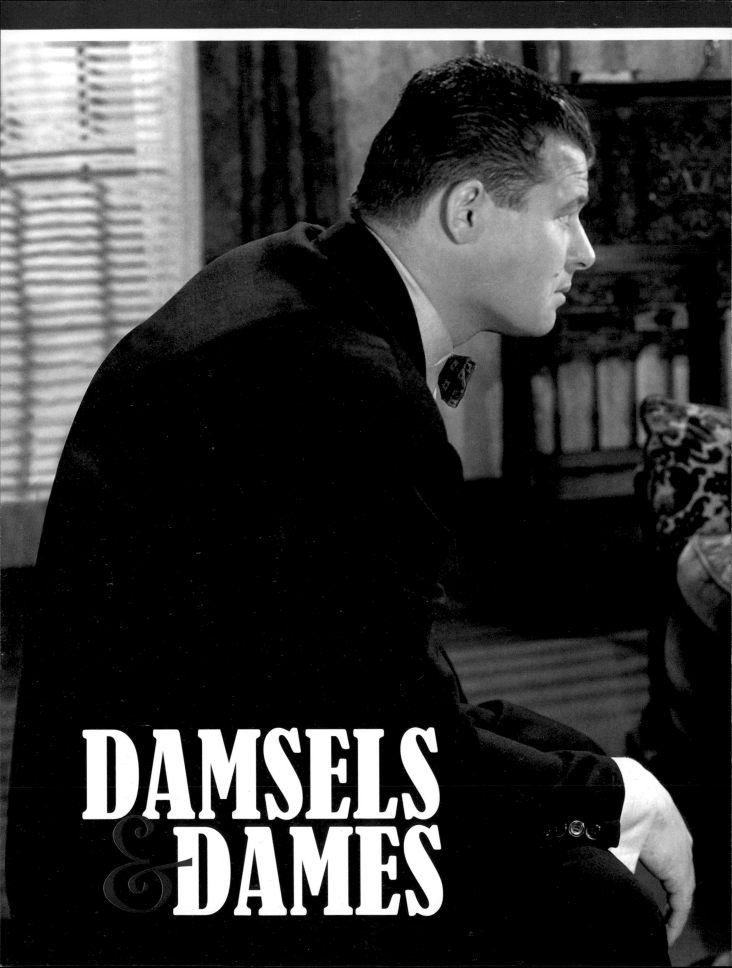

DAMSELS
& DAMES

DAMSELS & DAMES

Joan Crawford, Doris Day, Susan Hayward, Norma Shearer, Katharine Hepburn—they ruled!

In movies of the '30s, '40s, and '50s, these actresses were every bit as strong as their male counterparts. In fact, the guys often got stuck playing second fiddle to these powerhouses. And audiences loved these damsels and dames, whether they were weak or haughty or both.

In **Love Me or Leave Me**, Doris Day plays a torch singer that will do anything to succeed, and she does. First she uses her gangster boyfriend and later takes abuse from him, but her ambition pays off.

As selfless **Mildred Pierce**, Joan Crawford is intense, strong, and independent, but still allows herself to be bullied by her ungrateful daughter.

Gutsy survivor Susan Hayward tries to have a normal life in **I'll Cry Tomorrow**. Jostled by the slings and arrows of fate, she ends up in the clutches of alcohol, and then claws her way back from the gutter.

SUGAR AND SPICE

We root for Norma Shearer to get her husband back from venomous Joan Crawford in **The Women**. Peppered with catty bitches and sweet naives, castrating and devoted wives, all are having a fun ride.

Equally cool and clever are the wisecracking tough cookies in **Stage Door**. Who wouldn't want to be their friend and hang out at the Footlights Club, dishing about men, making it on Broadway, and—did we say men?

These women loomed larger than life. Watch them strut their stuff.

STAGE DOOR

RKO RADIO 1937

Katharine Hepburn
Terry Randall

Ginger Rogers
Jean Maitland

Adolphe Menjou
Anthony Powell

Lucille Ball
Judy Canfield

Eve Arden
Eve

Ann Miller
Ann

Andrea Leeds
Kay Hamilton

Director
Gregory La Cava

Producer
Pandro S. Berman

SPOILED, wealthy Terry (Hepburn) lives in a New York boarding house with other aspiring actresses. Her roommate Jean (Rogers) is a sassy dancer. The residents hope to make it on Broadway, but it's Terry who gets her big break after catching the eye of a lecherous producer (Menjou).

Screen Team

Rogers, Arden, Ball, and Carson were all featured in **Having Wonderful Time** (1938).

Menjou worked with Hepburn in **Morning Glory** (1933) and **State of the Union** (1948), with Rogers in **Roxie Hart** (1942) and **Heartbeat** (1946), and with Arden in **My Dream Is Yours** (1949).

The Stars

Ginger Rogers
Jean

THOUGH Rogers had proven her comedic skill in pictures such as **42nd Street** (1933) and **Star of Midnight** (1935), her identification as Fred Astaire's dance partner overshadowed her other work. With **Stage Door,** she supplanted Hepburn as queen of the RKO lot, and became the studio's top moneymaker with gems such as **Bachelor Mother** (1939) and **The Primrose Path** (1940).

Katharine Hepburn
Terry

STAGE DOOR was a much-needed hit for Hepburn, after mega-flops such as **Sylvia Scarlett** (1935), **Mary of Scotland** (1936), **A Woman Rebels** (1936), and **Quality Street** (1937).

This was Miller's film debut. Miller claimed she was only fourteen at the time, and changed her birth certificate so that producers would think she was seventeen.

Arden became friendly with a cat she saw on the RKO lot, and La Cava decided to use the feline as a prop for her character.

"The calla lilies are in bloom again. —*Terry*

Academy Awards

Best Picture
Director (La Cava)
Supporting Actress (Leeds)
Writing, Screenplay
(Morrie Ryskind and Anthony Veiller)

4 NOMINATIONS

THE BUZZ
The ceremony had to be postponed one week because of severe floods in the Los Angeles area.

M-G-M
1955

The Cast

Susan Hayward
Lillian Roth

Richard Conte
Tony Bardeman

Eddie Albert
Burt McGuire

Jo Van Fleet
Katie Roth

Don Taylor
Wallie

Ray Danton
David Tredman

Margo
Selma

Virginia Gregg
Ellen

Don "Red" Barry
Jerry

Carole Ann Campbell
Lillian (as a child)

Director
Daniel Mann

Producer
Lawrence Weingarten

I'LL CRY TOMORROW

THE TRUE story of singer Lillian Roth (Hayword) begins with her traumatic childhood. The manipulations of her ambitious stage mother Katie (Van Fleet) make her a child star, and she grows to become the toast of Broadway and Hollywood. Lillian plans to marry her first love, David Tredman (Danton). When he dies before their marriage, she

starts drinking. She has two bad marriages, one to a soldier (Taylor) and the second to abusive Tony Bardeman (Conte). She descends into wretched alcoholism. After she tries to kill herself, Burt McGuire (Albert) helps her regain her dignity and her life.

Academy Awards

Actress (Hayward)
Cinematography, Black and White
(Arthur E. Arling)
Art Direction–Set Decoration, Black and White
(Cedric Gibbons and Malcolm Brown;
Edwin B. Willis and Hugh B. Hunt)
✱ **Costume Design, Black and White**
(Helen Rose)

4 NOMINATIONS 1 OSCAR ✱

THE BUZZ

This was Hayward's third nomination
for playing an alcoholic, following
Smash-Up (1947) and **My Foolish Heart**.
It was her second nomination
for a biography of a singer, the last
time being **With a Song in My Heart**
(1952) about Jane Froman. Her only win
was for **I Want to Live** as death row
dame Barbara Graham.

Screen Team

Hayward worked previously with Albert in
Smash-Up and with Conte in **House of Strangers**.

The Stars

Eddie Albert
Burt

ALBERT has run
the show-biz gamut
from boy juvenile (his
stage and screen role
in **Brother Rat**) to
sturdy supporting
player (**Roman Holiday**
and **Attack!**) to
beloved TV star
(**Green Acres** and
Switch). Although he
rarely got the recogni-
tion he deserved for
his screen work,
he was awarded the
Bronze Star for
rescuing seventy
Marines at Tarawa
during World War
II, and has been
honored as a
champion of environ-
mental causes.

Susan Hayward
Lillian

HAYWARD'S
idol was fellow
Brooklynite
Barbara Stanwyck,
and the similarities
between the
roles they tackled
is apparent.
Like Stanwyck,
Hayward could
be tough as
nails in
Deadline at Dawn
(1946), **I Can
Get It for You
Wholesale** (1951),
and **I Want to Live**
(1958), and
deeply moving in
tearjerkers like
My Foolish Heart
(1949) and **Back
Street** (1961).

Richard Conte
Tony

NEVER a major
marquee name,
Conte's no-nonsense
style served him
well at Fox playing
social losers in his
best films **Call
Northside 777** and
Cry of the City in
1948, and Joseph L.
Mankiewicz's **House
of Strangers** (1949).

Gossip

Hayward was
in the midst
of a messy
divorce from actor
Jess Barker, and
took an overdose
of sleeping pills
prior to the onset
of production.

Hayward took dance
and voice lessons
for dubbing by
Roth. But M-G-M
thought Hayward's
voice was good
enough to do her
own singing.

Mann and Hayward
visited jails and
alcoholic wards
and attended AA
meetings as part of
their research.

Hayward had an
affair with actor Don
Barry, who had a
small part in an AA
sequence. They
made headlines
when Barry's jealous
girlfriend caught the
two of them together
at his home.

"You don't need a husband,
you need a keeper. —*Tony*"

LOVE ME OR LEAVE ME

The Cast

Doris Day
Ruth Etting

James Cagney
Marty "the Gimp"
Snyder

Cameron Mitchell
Johnny Alderman

Robert Keith
Bernard V.
Loomis

Tom Tully
Frobisher

Harry Bellaver
Georgie

Director
Charles Vidor

Producer
Joe Pasternak

THIS IS the true story of ambitious torch singer Ruth Etting (Day), married to obnoxious mobster Marty "The Gimp" Snyder (Cagney). He is intense, abusive, and full of rage, but propels her to stardom. Ruth falls for her

M-G-M 1955 -COLOR-

piano player, songwriter Johnny Alderman (Mitchell), and wants to leave Snyder, but, seeing him about to lose his club, she comes back to repay him for making her a star.

Screen Team

Day and Cagney appeared together once before in **The West Point Story** (1950).

*"*Gotta give her credit. The girl can sing. About that, I was never wrong.*"*
—*Marty*

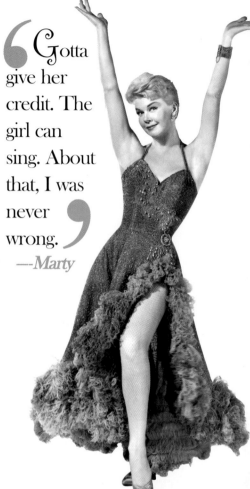

The Stars

Doris Day
Ruth

James Cagney
Marty

DAY was a liberated woman in 1955. She had just severed ties with Warner Bros., who made her America's singing sweetheart in a series of tuneful if familiar musicals, though the rollicking **Calamity Jane** (1953) was a standout. As Ruth Etting, she was anything but sweet and virginal, attacking the part intensely—vocally and dramatically. For the next ten years, Day was a box-office favorite and even scored an Oscar nomination for **Pillow Talk** (1959), her first of three battle-of-the-sexes romps with Rock Hudson.

CAGNEY recalled some of the gangland figures from the tough section of New York City where he grew up in creating his gripping portrait of Marty Snyder. His childhood experiences also served as invaluable research for the other hoods and hooligans he played to perfection at Warner Bros. in **The Roaring Twenties** (1939), **The Strawberry Blonde** (1941), and others.

Gossip

Day was proud of her work in a physically demanding scene in which Cagney attacked and abused her, and was disappointed when she saw the film and found that most of the scene was cut to get by the censors.

Vidor wanted Cagney to wear an iron clamp on his leg to copy Snyder's gimp, but Cagney said the device would hinder his performance so he created his own limp.

Day hesitated to play Etting because she feared fans might not accept her as a somewhat unethical character. Critics raved, but some fans did write attacking her for drinking and wearing scanty costumes. Day responded to every letter.

Ava Gardner was the original choice to play Etting.

Etting denied that she ever worked as a dance hall girl and claimed that element was added to the film just so the song "Ten Cents a Dance" could be used.

Academy Awards

Actor (Cagney)
✱ **Writing, Motion Picture Story** (Daniel Fuchs)
Writing, Screenplay
(Daniel Fuchs and Isobel Lennart)
Sound Recording (Wesley C. Miller)
Music, Song ("I'll Never Stop Loving You"
by Nicholas Brodszky and Sammy Cahn)
Music, Scoring of a Musical Picture
(Percy Faith and George Stoll)

6 NOMINATIONS 1 OSCAR ✱

THE BUZZ

This was Cagney's third best actor nomination. His first was for **Angels With Dirty Faces** (1938) and he won for his brilliant portrayal of entertainer George M. Cohan in **Yankee Doodle Dandy** (1942).

WARNER BROS. 1945

MILDRED PIERCE

MILDRED Pierce (Crawford) spoils her selfish daughter Veda (Blyth) at the expense of her husband Bert (Bennett), who leaves. Mildred needs money and takes a job as a waitress which gives her the idea to open her own restaurant. Her sarcastic pal Ida (Arden) and amorous business associate Wally Fay (Carson) give Mildred support. She falls for and marries slick playboy Monte Beragon (Scott) and ends up supporting his expensive tastes. Behind Mildred's back, Veda carries on with Monte while he cheats Mildred, causing her to lose the restaurant. He is killed in a suspenseful finale.

The Cast

Joan Crawford
Mildred Pierce

Zachary Scott
Monte Beragon

Ann Blyth
Veda Pierce

Jack Carson
Wally Fay

Eve Arden
Ida Corwin

Bruce Bennett
Bert Pierce

Lee Patrick
Maggie Biederhof

Jo Ann Marlowe
Kay Pierce

Moroni Olsen
Inspector Peterson

Veda Ann Borg
Miriam Ellis

Butterfly McQueen
Lottie

Director
Michael Curtiz

Producer
Jerry Wald

Personally, Veda's convinced me that alligators have the right idea. They eat their young. —Ida

Academy Awards

Best Picture
✱ Actress (Crawford)
Supporting Actress (Arden)
Supporting Actress (Blyth)
Writing, Screenplay (Ranald MacDougall)
Cinematography, Black and White (Ernest Haller)

6 NOMINATIONS 1 OSCAR ✱

THE BUZZ

Crawford claimed to have a fever of 104 the day of the ceremony. That night, when photographers arrived at her sickbed to snap Curtiz handing her the award, Crawford was neatly coiffed, decked out in a chic negligee and all smiles. And she had plenty to smile about — her photo kept the other winners off the front page the next morning.

Screen Team

Crawford worked once more with Scott in **Flamingo Road**, with Arden in **Goodbye, My Fancy** (1951), and with Bennett in **Sudden Fear**.

Carson and Arden paired up for **The Doughgirls** (1944) and **My Dream Is Yours** (1949).

Gossip

Bette Davis turned down the title role, and it was then considered for Ann Sheridan and Barbara Stanwyck.

Except for a cameo as herself in **Hollywood Canteen** (1944), Crawford spent most of her first two years at Warners rejecting scripts until Wald offered her **Mildred Pierce.**

Curtiz didn't relish working with Crawford and her "goddamn shoulder pads," but she was determined to play Mildred and even submitted to testing for the part. When the film wrapped, Crawford gave the director a pair of Adrian shoulder pads as a parting gift.

Monte's murder was one of many touches from screenwriter Ranald MacDougall that never occurred in James M. Cain's novel **Mildred Pierce.**

❝I've never denied you anything— anything money could buy I've given you. But that wasn't enough, was it?❞

—Mildred

The Stars

Ann Blyth
Veda

UNIVERSAL saw Blyth as a junior Deanna Durbin when she was signed in 1944. She made four forgettable musicals before her breakthrough as the bitchy Veda on loan to Warners. The studio was so impressed that they requested her for Faye Emerson's sister in **Danger Signal**, but she hurt her back and didn't make it. In 1951 she was signed by M-G-M, where she made a great impression opposite Mario Lanza in **The Great Caruso** (1951).

Zachary Scott
Monte

HOW SLEEK, sophisticated Zachary Scott never became a major star is a mystery. One answer could be that he played scoundrels so well in his first two major films, **The Mask of Dimitrios** (1944) and **Mildred Pierce** (1945), that he was forever typecast. He was earnest and touching in Jean Renoir's **The Southerner** (1945), but Warners preferred him nasty in **Her Kind of Man** (1946) or spineless in **Flamingo Road** (1949).

Joan Crawford
Mildred

HOLLYWOOD considered Crawford a has-been by 1945. Her last few movies at M-G-M were duds and her new studio seemed in no rush to star her in anything. With **Mildred Pierce**, a different Crawford emerged from the dewy-eyed heroines she'd played at Metro. She was strong, making it in a man's world and as a grown woman with two daughters. With solid follow-ups such as **Humoresque** (1946), **Possessed** (1947), and **Sudden Fear** (1952), Crawford was at her peak.

THE WOMEN

M-G-M
1939
B&W/COLOR

CLASSY socialite, devoted mother, and trophy wife Mary Haines (Shearer) is spurned by her husband for sexy, ambitious shopgirl and homewrecker Crystal Allen (Crawford). Mary overhears talk of her husband's infidelity at the spa. Her two-faced, fast-talking, catty cousin Sylvia Fowler (Russell) gossips incessantly about Mary's marital woes. Their naive, sweet friend Peggy Day (Fontaine) is supportive. Mary goes to Reno and stays at a ranch for divorcing women run by Lucy (Main). The social circle of fashionable gossips destroys lives, but her "Reno-vated" friends help Mary get her husband back.

The Cast

Norma Shearer
Mary Haines

Joan Crawford
Crystal Allen

Rosalind Russell
Sylvia Fowler

Mary Boland
The Countess
de Lave

Paulette Goddard
Miriam Aarons

Phyllis Povah
Edith Potter

Joan Fontaine
Peggy Day

Virginia Weidler
Young Mary

Lucile Watson
Mrs. Moorehead

Marjorie Main
Lucy

Virginia Grey
Pat

Ruth Hussey
Miss Watts

Muriel Hutchison
Jane

Hedda Hopper
Dolly Dupuyster

Florence Nash
Nancy Blake

Director
George Cukor

Producer
Hunt Stromberg

Gossip

Shearer's contract stipulated that she would only share top billing with a male co-star, but she agreed to having Crawford's name with hers above the title on **The Women**. When Shearer refused to grant Russell the same request, Russell staged a sickout and didn't come back until Shearer finally gave in.

Fifth-billed Goddard, who insisted on looking every bit as glamorous as Shearer and Crawford, revolted when she was assigned an assistant hairstylist. M-G-M agreed to have Sydney Guilaroff, hairdresser to Shearer and Crawford, style her hair as well.

Cukor was called the "lion tamer" for keeping clashes among the cast to a minimum. He accomplished this by keeping the actresses busy during breaks with fittings and hair and makeup sessions.

No males appeared in **The Women** — even the animals were female.

The Stars

Norma Shearer
Mary

"WHAT do you expect? She sleeps with the boss," was Crawford's envious assessment of how Shearer got the cream from M-G-M's script department. But Shearer had more going for her than being married to studio production head Irving Thalberg. Audiences couldn't get enough of her noble suffering in sudsers such as **The Divorcee** (1930) and **Marie Antoinette** (1938). After **The Women**, good scripts became scarce, and after Thalberg's death, she didn't care much about working, and retired in 1941.

Rosalind Russell
Sylvia

CRITICAL praise for melodramatic roles in **Craig's Wife** (1936) and **Night Must Fall** (1937) almost cost Russell her part in **The Women**. Cukor almost refused to test her because she was a "serious" actress, but Roz was persistent, and he relented. She not only stole **The Women** from M-G-M's two queen bees, but was cast almost exclusively in comedies for the next six years.

Joan Crawford
Crystal

CRAWFORD hadn't scored a hit in three years, and the "shopgirl in search of Prince Charming" formula of her previous M-G-M films had gotten moldy. She was anxious to sink her claws into the bitchy Crystal, though neither Stromberg nor Cukor were fully convinced she was up to it. Crawford proved them wrong, and **The Women** would be the first of several comebacks for her.

Screen Team

Crawford and Main worked together in two more Cukor films, **Susan and God** (1940) and **A Woman's Face** (1941).

"I've had two years to grow claws mother. Jungle red! --*Mary*

CHAPTER 10

ONE OF A KIND

HOLLYWOOD PICKS

Fayard Nicholas
Dancer (b. 1914)

Casablanca
Citizen Kane
Gone with the Wind
The Great Dictator
High Society
It Happened
One Night
Lost Horizon
Singin' in the Rain
Stagecoach
Stormy Weather

Margaret O'Brien
Actress (b. 1937)

Duel in the Sun
Gaslight (1944)
Gone with the Wind
Leave Her to Heaven
The Letter
Marie Antoinette
Meet Me in St. Louis
Mr. Skeffington
That Hamilton Woman
Waterloo Bridge
(1940)

Ryan O'Neal
Actor (b. 1941)

Birth of a Nation
Bringing Up Baby
Dodsworth
The Kid
The Ladykillers (1955)
On the Waterfront
A Place in the Sun
Red River
The Steel Helmet
The Yearling

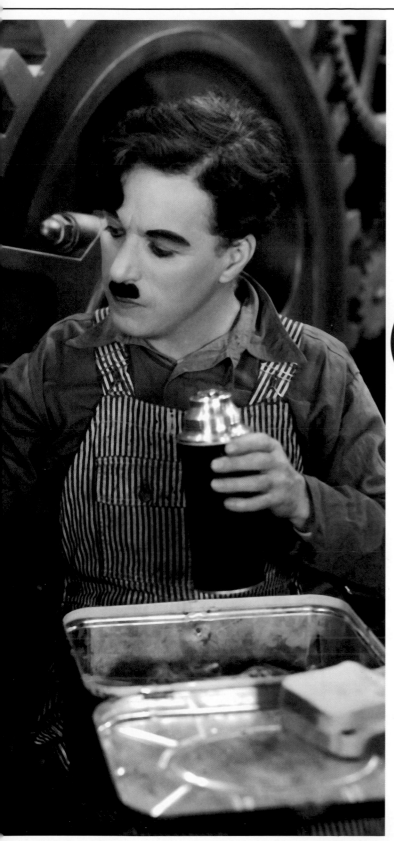

Y

ou can probably make a convincing argument that all of the actors in this book are one of a kind. Take Montgomery Clift, Vivien Leigh, Judy Garland—all unique talents with strong individual character traits.

Yet it's hard to envision first choice Clift giving a more powerful performance than William Holden as gigolo Joe Gillis in **Sunset Boulevard** (1950). Laurence Olivier wanted his paramour Leigh as his co-star in **Rebecca** (1940), but talented as she was, how could she have topped Joan Fontaine as the second Mrs. De Winter? And great as Garland could be, her replacement Betty Hutton seemed to be doing what comes naturally in **Annie Get Your Gun** (1950).

THEY HAD TO BE THEM

But no matter how deep you delve into the talent pool, absolutely no one could have replaced Esther Williams in **Million Dollar Mermaid**. She acts and sings *and* swims in stunning water ballet spectacles, a singular sensation.

Speaking of true originals, was there anyone who could replicate the spastic comedy or the nasal, squeaky voice and loony physicality of Jerry Lewis? His self-styled brand of clowning has made him an American favorite and a European institution.

Curly-topped moppet Shirley Temple was more than just a box-office champ, she was a symbol of optimism during the Depression. Her precocious tapping, adorable singing and charmingly coy delivery made her the best child actor of her day—or any day since. And those dimples!

Latina Carmen Miranda, in her fruity hats and platform shoes, belted out South American ditties like "I-Yi-Yi-Yi-Yi (I Like You Very Much)" in inimitable style, spoke her own fractured brand of English, and led unrivaled musical extravaganzas.

Charlie Chaplin, the brilliant comic genius, showed pathos, joy, curiosity, and love in his expressive, speechless, wonderful face. His films were all his own, with a visual style, pacing and plots that came from his immensely creative mind.

These films were showcases for the special talents and skills of their stars. Unparalleled, these actors were truly individual, irreplaceable, and one of a kind.

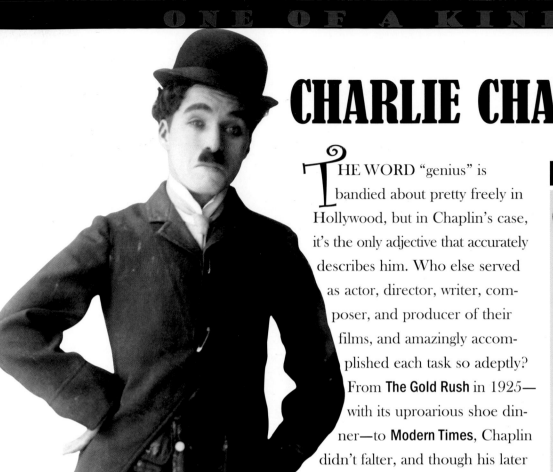

CHARLIE CHAPLIN

THE WORD "genius" is bandied about pretty freely in Hollywood, but in Chaplin's case, it's the only adjective that accurately describes him. Who else served as actor, director, writer, composer, and producer of their films, and amazingly accomplished each task so adeptly? From **The Gold Rush** in 1925— with its uproarious shoe dinner—to **Modern Times**, Chaplin didn't falter, and though his later works **Monsieur Verdoux** (1947) and **Limelight** (1952) are flawed, they are still more interesting than most lesser directors' successes. As Paulette Goddard said of her ex-husband shortly after his death in 1977, he was "not only the greatest creator of films but the most charming of men. Nobody was his equal."

> **All I need to make a comedy is a park, a policeman, and a pretty girl.**
> —*Charlie Chaplin*

The Cast

Charlie Chaplin
The Tramp

Paulette Goddard
The Gamine

Henry Bergman
Café proprietor

Tiny Sandford
Big Bill

Chester Conklin
The Mechanic

Hank Mann
Burglar

Stanley Blystone
The Gamine's
father

Allan Garcia
President of Electro
Steel Corp.

Director and Producer
Charlie Chaplin

SIGNATURE MOVIE
MODERN TIMES

UNITED ARTISTS
1936

THE TRAMP (Chaplin) works in a factory, where he is losing the battle between man and machine. His nerves frayed, the Tramp throws himself down a chute and gets caught up in the gears operating the machines. His boss sends him to a mental hospital, but upon his release the Tramp is arrested for being a Communist when he's caught waving a red flag. He's sent to jail where he thwarts an escape, then gradually begins to enjoy the peace and solitude of prison life. The Tramp gets pardoned and befriends the orphaned Gamine (Goddard).

Screen Team

Chaplin and
Goddard made one
other film together,
The Great Dictator
(1940).

JERRY LEWIS

IN FRANCE he's revered as "Le Roi du Crazy" (the King of the Crazy). In Italy, he's affectionately called "Picchiatello" (the Crazy One). Ironically, Americans have yet to crown Lewis with their own moniker of adoration, but no one can deny that his movies made a ton of money and brought smiles to millions here as well. As half of the duo Martin and Lewis, Dean always got the girl, but Jerry got the laughs. As a solo after the pair's 1956 breakup, Lewis sharpened his comedic skills in **The Geisha Boy** (1958) and the Jekyll-Hyde gem **The Nutty Professor** (1963). Lewis reached his peak in the mid-'60s, but his popularity mushroomed in Europe. His skillful dramatic performances in **The King of Comedy** (1983) and **Funny Bones** (1995) ensure it will continue to flourish.

Gossip

Lewis made his stage debut at age five, singing "Brother, Can You Spare A Dime?" at a resort in the Catskills, where his parents performed.

During the '50s and '60s, Lewis played first base with numerous professional baseball teams and trained every year with the Dodgers.

Lewis received the French Legion of Honor and was nominated for the Nobel Peace Prize.

Since 1960, Lewis has won eight best director awards in Europe—three in France, and one each in Italy, Germany, Belgium, Spain, and the Netherlands.

> **'** I've had great success being a total idiot. **'**
> —*Jerry Lewis*

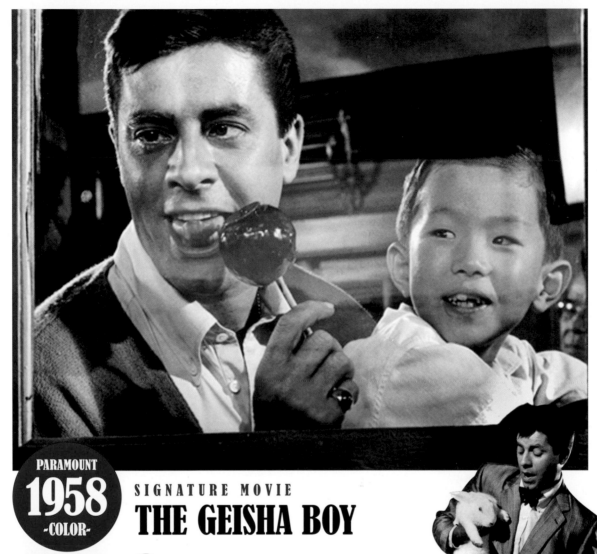

PARAMOUNT
1958
-COLOR-

SIGNATURE MOVIE
THE GEISHA BOY

The Cast

Jerry Lewis
Gilbert Woolley

Marie McDonald
Lola Livingston

Sessue Hayakawa
Mr. Sikita

Suzanne Pleshette
Sgt. Betty Pearson

Nobu McCarthy
Kimi Sikita

Robert Hirano
Mitsuo Watanabe

Director
Frank Tashlin

Producer
Jerry Lewis

SECOND-RATE magician Gilbert Woolley (Lewis) is in the Far East entertaining the troops—at least, he's trying to. He's nearly fired for humiliating stuck-up movie star Lola Livingston (McDonald). The only person amused by Gilbert is little Mitsuo (Hirano), the lonely nephew of aristocratic Mr. Sikita (Hayakawa). Mitsuo's hero worship leads to a disastrous attempt to follow Gilbert back to the United States and lots of laughs.

163

CARMEN MIRANDA

THE VIVACIOUS "Brazilian Bombshell" sang, Samba-ed and hilariously butchered the English language in a series of vivid Technicolor musicals for Fox that were short on plot, long on rhythm, and high on bananas. Miranda's flamboyance, often overshadowed her contribution as a Latin-music trendsetter during the war years. Her defining moment on screen was the phallic fantasia "The Lady in the Tutti-Frutti Hat" from **The Gang's All Here**. As she danced among bare-midriffed chorus girls raising and lowering gigantic bananas, Miranda entered cult status.

Gossip

Though she lived most of her early life in Brazil, Miranda was actually born in Portugal.

Miranda worked as a hatmaker before she was invited to attend a Brazilian music academy.

In 1998, the intersection of Hollywood Boulevard and Orange Drive in Los Angeles was renamed Carmen Miranda Square.

Miranda didn't realize she was having a heart attack after performing a number on Jimmy Durante's television show on August 4, 1955. She died the following morning.

> ❝Bananas is my business.❞
> -- *Carmen Miranda*

Academy Awards

Interior Decoration, Color (James Basevi, Joseph C. Wright, and Thomas Little)

1 NOMINATION

THE BUZZ
Phantom of the Opera also beat out contenders For Whom the Bells, This Is the Army, and Thousands Cheer.

20th CENTURY-FOX 1943 -COLOR-

SIGNATURE MOVIE

THE GANG'S ALL HERE

SOLDIER Andy Mason (Ellison) gets a weekend pass and meets attractive entertainer Eadie Allen (Faye). Andy neglects to mention that he's engaged to socialite Vivian Potter (Ryan). By the time he heads back to camp, Andy and Eadie have feelings for each other. Several months later Andy returns as a hero, and his proud pop (Pallette) gets Eadie and her pals Dorita (Miranda), Phil (Baker), and Goodman to stage a benefit show as a homecoming. Also on the bill is Vivian. Amid lavish, kaleidoscopic numbers, the romantic entanglements all have to be unsnarled.

The Cast

Alice Faye
Eadie Allen

Carmen Miranda
Dorita

Phil Baker
Himself

Benny Goodman and His Orchestra
Themselves

James Ellison
Andy Mason

Sheila Ryan
Vivian Potter

Eugene Pallette
Mr. Mason

Edward Everett Horton
Peyton Potter

Charlotte Greenwood
Mrs. Potter

Director
Busby Berkeley

Producer
William Le Baron

Screen Team

Miranda made two 1941 musicals with Faye, **That Night in Rio** and **Weekend in Havana**.

Horton and Greenwood worked with Miranda again in **Springtime in the Rockies** (1942).

SHIRLEY TEMPLE

DIMPLE for dimple, no child star has ever equaled Shirley Temple. The curly-topped moppet was the box-office champ of the mid-'30s thanks to some great emoting in heart-tuggers such as **Bright Eyes** (1934) and **Heidi** (1937). More important, she was a beacon of hope to Depression-era audiences as she sang the sunny anthem "On the Good Ship Lollipop" and tapped up and down stairs alongside Bill "Bojangles" Robinson with all the seasoned professionalism of a show-biz veteran. Though her star luster dimmed with adolescence, she had excellent roles in David O. Selznick's flag-waver **Since You Went Away** (1944) and the riotous **The Bachelor and the Bobby-Soxer** (1947). Since then, she's enjoyed a long, happy marriage and served in many government positions.

> "I also still get hundreds of letters from fans every week. All these years it hasn't stopped. Incredible."
> -- *Shirley Temple*

Gossip

Temple received a special Oscar in 1934 for her outstanding contribution to screen entertainment.

She was the number-one box-office star in 1936, 1937, and 1938.

Temple divorced her **Fort Apache** co-star John Agar in 1949 after three years of marriage. She is still married to businessman Charles Black, whom she wed in 1951.

The former child star served as ambassador to Ghana under the Nixon administration, and was appointed ambassador to Czechoslovakia by President George Bush in 1989.

SIGNATURE MOVIE
HEIDI

20th CENTURY-FOX
1937

SWISS orphan Heidi (Temple) is taken by her selfish Aunt Dete (Christians) to live in the mountains with the girl's grumpy grandfather (Hersholt). Heidi melts his icy disposition. Dete returns and tricks Heidi into coming to Frankfurt, where the girl becomes a paid com- panion for lame Klara Sesemann (Jones), the daughter of a prominent official. Heidi misses her grandfather, who begins a frantic search for her.

The Cast

Shirley Temple
Heidi

Jean Hersholt
Adolph Kramer, the Grandfather

Arthur Treacher
Andrews

Sidney Blackmer
Herr Sesemann

Mady Christians
Aunt Dete

Marcia Mae Jones
Klara Sesemann

Delmar Watson
Peter, the Goat Boy

Director
Allan Dwan

Producer
Darryl F. Zanuck

Screen Team

Temple was reunited with Treacher, Jones, and Nash in **The Little Princess** (1939).

ESTHER WILLIAMS

"AMERICA'S Mermaid" was spotted by an M-G-M talent scout while appearing in "Billy Rose's Aquacade" in 1941. Following a couple of nonmusical film roles, Williams made her first big splash in **Bathing Beauty** (1944) and for the next eleven years was one of M-G-M's top box-office draws. "All they ever did for me at M-G-M was change my leading man and the water in my pool," she once joked. Still, audiences couldn't get enough of the glorious Technicolor water ballets that were the center-pieces of her films, and Williams was instrumental in popularizing competitive and synchronized swimming.

> "I was called "America's Mermaid," because it appeared that I could stay underwater indefinitely."
> --*Esther Williams*

Gossip

As a teenage swimming champion, Williams dreamed of competing in the 1940 Olympics, and was disappointed when the games were canceled after the outbreak of World War II.

Her M-G-M screen test was made with Clark Gable for the female lead in his film **Somewhere I'll Find You** (1942).

Williams has had four husbands, including Latin lover Fernando Lamas.

SIGNATURE MOVIE
MILLION DOLLAR MERMAID

M-G-M
1952
-COLOR-

The Cast

Esther Williams
Annette Kellerman

Victor Mature
James Sullivan

Walter Pidgeon
Frederick Kellerman

Donna Corcoran
Annette, age 10

Director
Mervyn LeRoy

Producer
Arthur Hornblow Jr.

YOUNG Annette (Corcoran) lives in turn-of-the-century Australia with her musician father (Pidgeon). A birth defect weakens her legs, so she takes up swimming to strengthen them. Annette (now Williams) blossoms into a striking woman. Promoter James Sullivan (Mature), her manager, helps Annette to become famous after a swim in the Thames and a scandal over her "shocking" bathing suit.

Academy Awards

Cinematography, Color (George J. Folsey)

THE BUZZ
The Quiet Man took this prize, also beating out Hans Christian Andersen, Ivanhoe, and The Snows of Kilimanjaro.

1 NOMINATION

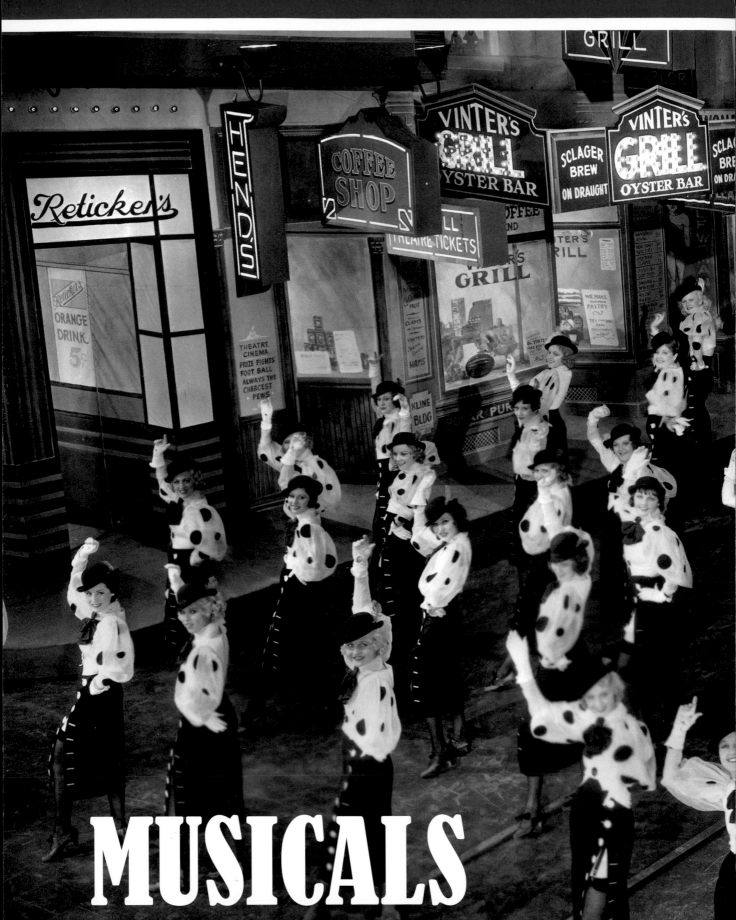

MUSICALS

MUSICALS

The M-G-M Technicolor musical marvels mark the heyday of the genre. They were extravagant, elegant, and entertaining. These movies could have just been plotless vehicles for some good singing and dancing, but no. They all spin a good yarn and the songs help move the stories along.

Both **42nd Street** and **Singin' in the Rain** are musicals about show business. They both explore the backstage workings of a set, the cast dynamics, and the final show-within-a-show. **42nd Street** was choreographed by the brilliant Busby Berkeley, and has been turned into a Broadway show, which is still playing. The undisputed movie musical champ of all time, **Singin' in the Rain**, boasts classic numbers and, of course, the glorious Kelly, gracefully stomping through the rain showers and straight into my heart.

Songs and plot blend perfectly in **Meet Me in St. Louis,** in which a grown-up, exuberant Judy Garland sings the zingy "Trolley Song" and comforts little Margaret O'Brien with the poignant

SINGIN' IN THE FRAME

"Have Yourself a Merry Little Christmas." It'll make you cry, but in a good way.

On the Town boasts a classic score by Leonard Bernstein, Betty Comden, and Adolph Green. The Big Apple anthem "New York, New York (It's a Wonderful Town)" is sung from the sparkling streets of 1940s Manhattan to the Statue of Liberty. Kelly and Sinatra light up the town.

In **Carmen Jones**, the exquisite sensuality of Dorothy Dandridge and Harry Belafonte alone is worth the price of admission.

Pearl Bailey is no slouch either. This unusual retelling of Bizet's opera *Carmen* is presented with an African-American cast. The brilliant rendition of "Stand Up and Fight" sung to the tune of "The March of the Toreadors" is unforgettable.

Although the studios essentially stopped making movie musicals after the '70s, a resurgence could be afoot with recent films such as **Moulin Rouge** and **Chicago.** But try the old musicals. They'll make you feel good. You might come away wanting to wave your arms around and to splash through the puddles, to swing on a lamppost, to sing in the rain.

42nd STREET

WARNER BROS. 1933

WEALTHY, lecherous producer Abner Dillon (Kibbee) invests his fortune in a Broadway musical to showcase the girl of his dreams—temperamental, scheming Dorothy Brock (Daniels), who is in love with Pat Denning (Brent). He, in turn, asks out talented, innocent chorus girl Peggy Sawyer (Keeler). Cantankerous ailing director Julian Marsh (Baxter) rehearses the show for five weeks with an iron fist. When Brock sprains her ankle and can't go on, understudy Sawyer steps in, becoming an overnight success.

The Cast

Warner Baxter
Julian Marsh

Ruby Keeler
Peggy Sawyer

Dick Powell
Billy Lawler

Bebe Daniels
Dorothy Brock

George Brent
Pat Denning

Ginger Rogers
Anytime Annie

Una Merkel
Lorraine Fleming

Guy Kibbee
Abner Dillon

Ned Sparks
Barry

Director
Lloyd Bacon

Producer
Darryl F. Zanuck

Academy Awards

2 NOMINATIONS

Best Picture
Sound Recording (Nathan Levinson)

THE BUZZ
The best song and musical scoring categories weren't established until the following year, so none of **42nd Street**'s musical numbers were recognized with a nomination.

The Stars

Ruby Keeler
Peggy

MRS. Al Jolson tapped her heart out in eight more Warner Bros. musicals. She divorced Jolson in 1940 and the following year retired from films after remarrying. In 1970, Keeler and Berkeley teamed up again for the nostalgic Broadway musical **No, No Nanette.**

Warner Baxter
Julian

THOUGH largely forgotten today, Baxter was Fox's top male star in the early '30s and was the second man to win a best actor Oscar (for originating the role of the Cisco Kid in 1929's **In Old Arizona**).

Dick Powell
Billy

42ND STREET began the first phase of Powell's screen career— as Warner's answer to Bing Crosby. But Powell preferred solving crimes to crooning in the '40s and donned a trench coat to play hard-boiled private eyes in **Murder, My Sweet** (1944) and **Johnny O'Clock** (1947).

Screen Team

Keeler and Powell were a popular romantic duo in **Gold Diggers of 1933**, **Footlight Parade** (1933), **Dames** (1934), **Flirtation Walk** (1934), **Shipmates Forever** (1935), and **Colleen** (1936).

‘Sawyer, you're going out a youngster, but you've got to come back a star. **’**
—*Julian*

CARMEN JONES

20th
CENTURY-FOX
1954
-COLOR-

BASED ON Bizet's tragic opera *Carmen*, **Carmen Jones** is set on a southern army base during World War II. Sultry Carmen (Dandridge) gets into a fight with a female co-worker at the parachute factory where they're employed and is put under arrest and placed in the charge of Army corporal Joe (Belafonte).

Deceitful Carmen seduces him and gets Joe involved in a murder. He's forced to desert the army and abandon his virginal fiancee (James). He follows Carmen to Chicago, where she takes up with hunky prizefighter Husky Miller (Adams). Joe gets jealous and his passion leads to the tragic ending.

The Cast

Dorothy Dandridge
Carmen Jones

Harry Belafonte
Joe

Olga James
Cindy Lou

Pearl Bailey
Frankie

Joe Adams
Husky Miller

Nick Stewart
Dink Franklin

Roy Glenn
Rum Daniels

Diahann Carroll
Myrt

Brock Peters
Sgt. Brown

**Madame
Sul-Te-Wan**
Carmen's grandma

Director and Producer
Otto Preminger

> '*S*cuse my dust, gentlemen. The air's gettin' mighty unconditioned 'round here. — *Carmen*

Gossip

Preminger at first thought Dandridge was "too sweet, too regal" to play Carmen. Dandridge met him again wearing a wig, a tight skirt and a low-cut, off-the-shoulder blouse and convinced Preminger that she understood Carmen's primitive nature.

Dandridge and Belafonte's voices weren't up to the film's operatic demands. They were dubbed by Marilyn Horne and Le Vern Hutcherson, respectively.

Preminger and Dandridge began a tempestuous affair that lasted several years.

The Stars

Harry Belafonte
Joe

BELAFONTE'S renown is greater for popularizing calypso music than for acting, though he's given some powerful performances in the ten films he's made. He was a sensuous partner for Dandridge in **Carmen Jones** and held his own histrionically in two 1959 films— the futuristic **The World, the Flesh and the Devil** and Robert Wise's heist drama **Odds Against Tomorrow.**

Screen Team

Dandridge and Belafonte also worked together in **Bright Road** (1953) and **Island in the Sun** (1957).

Dorothy Dandridge
Carmen

DANDRIDGE had bits in films like **A Day at the Races** (1937) and **Sun Valley Serenade** (1941) and then worked as a band singer before putting her career on hold after marrying dancer Harold Nicholas in 1945. Following their divorce in 1951, she was determined to make it in Hollywood even though good roles for black actors were scarce. **Carmen Jones** was her big break, but her follow-up films proved disappointing. In addition to her film work, Dandridge had a successful career in nightclubs.

Academy Awards

Actress (Dandridge)
Music, Scoring of a Musical Picture
(Herschel Burke Gilbert)

2 NOMINATIONS

THE BUZZ

Dandridge was the first black performer ever nominated for best actress. Forty-seven years later, HalleBerry became the first black actress to win in that category.

M-G-M
1944
-COLOR-

MEET ME IN ST. LOUIS

The Cast

Judy Garland
Esther Smith

Margaret O'Brien
Tootie Smith

Mary Astor
Anna Smith

Lucille Bremer
Rose Smith

Leon Ames
Alonzo Smith

Tom Drake
John Truett

Marjorie Main
Katie

Harry Davenport
Grandpa

Joan Carroll
Agnes Smith

Henry Daniels Jr.
Lon Smith

June Lockhart
Lucille Ballard

Hugh Marlowe
Col. Darly

Robert Sully
Warren Sheffield

Director
Vincente Minnelli

Producer
Arthur Freed

VIVACIOUS seventeen-year-old Esther Smith (Garland) likes the cute, clean-cut neighbor John Truett (Drake). She urges her sweet older sister Rose (Bremer) to invite him to a party for their college-bound brother Lon (Daniels). At the party their impish, youngest sister Tootie (O'Brien) joins Esther in an entertaining song and dance. After the festivities, John hangs around to help put out the lights and he and Esther fall in love. Rose has a beau also— eager Warren Sheffield (Sully). Meanwhile, the town is all abuzz because the 1904 World's Fair is coming to town. Then one day Mr. Smith (Ames) abruptly announces that the family will be moving to New York because he has a good job offer. Everyone is upset and hopes things will work out so they won't have to leave their beloved St. Louis.

> "Wasn't I lucky to be born in my favorite city?" —*Tootie*

The Stars

Judy Garland
Esther

Margaret O'Brien
Tootie

JUDY PINING for "The Boy Next Door" and telling O'Brien to "Have Yourself a Merry Little Christmas" are just two reasons Garland fans cherish her performance as Esther Smith. **Meet Me in St. Louis** also marked the beginning of Garland's golden period at M-G-M in smashes such as **Ziegfeld Follies** (1946), **The Harvey Girls** (1946), and **Easter Parade** (1948).

AUDIENCES wrung their hankies dry worrying if the precocious O'Brien could escape from the London Blitz in **Journey for Margaret** (1942). She did, and in the process became M-G-M's golden girl in a string of hits from **Music for Millions** (1944) to **The Secret Garden** (1949). But she was at her most captivating dressed as a drunken ghost and pelting the neighborhood grouch with flour on Halloween in **Meet Me in St. Louis.**

Academy Awards

Music, Song ("The Trolley Song" by Ralph Blane and Hugh Martin)
Music, Scoring of a Musical Picture (George E. Stoll)
Writing, Screenplay (Irving Brecher and Fred F. Finklehoffe)
Cinematography, Color (George F. Folsey)

4 NOMINATIONS

THE BUZZ
O'Brien received a special juvenile Oscar for her performance. The award was later stolen and wasn't returned for nearly fifty years when a pair of antique collectors discovered it in a shop.

Gossip

The song "Boys and Girls Together," written by Rodgers and Hammerstein for Garland, ended up on the cutting room floor because Freed thought it slowed down the movie.

Garland was tired of playing teenagers and argued with Freed about making this movie. By the time the movie previewed, Garland told Freed, "Arthur, remind me not to tell you what kind of pictures to make."

Meet Me in St. Louis became M-G-M's highest-grossing picture after **Gone With the Wind** (1939).

Garland and Minnelli developed an immediate rapport that blossomed into love by the time the movie wrapped. They married the following year.

Screen Team

O'Brien, Astor, and Ames were reunited for **Little Women** (1949).

Garland worked with Main in **The Harvey Girls** (1946) and **Summer Stock** (1950), and with Astor in **Listen, Darling** (1938)

O'Brien and Main co-starred again in **Bad Bascomb** (1946).

> *Rose:* Nice girls don't let men kiss them until after they're engaged. Men don't want the bloom rubbed off.
> *Esther:* Personally, I think I have too much bloom.

ON THE TOWN

M-G-M
1949
-COLOR-

THREE sailors—curious Chip (Sinatra), optimistic, romantic Gabey (Kelly) and likeable lug Ozzie (Munshin)—are on twenty-four hour leave in New York City. Sassy, irrepressible taxi driver Brunhilde (Garrett) is immediately smitten with Chip. Gabey falls for beautiful subway pin-up Miss Turnstiles nee Ivy Smith (Vera-Ellen), but they lose touch, and he spends the rest of the day looking for her. Ozzie has his eyes on museum anthropology researcher Claire (Miller). In one day, they sing and dance their way through the Big Apple.

The Cast

Gene Kelly
Gabey

Frank Sinatra
Chip

Ann Miller
Claire Huddesen

Betty Garrett
Brunhilde Esterhazy

Vera-Ellen
Ivy Smith aka Miss Turnstiles

Jules Munshin
Ozzie

Florence Bates
Madame Dilyovska

Alice Pearce
Lucy Shmeeler

George Meader
Professor

Directors
Stanley Donen and Gene Kelly

Producer
Arthur Freed

The Stars

Gene Kelly
Gabey

KELLY'S athletic prowess and inventive mind worked together to bring a masculinity to screen dancing in numbers such as "Mack the Black" from **The Pirate** (1948) and the opening sequence of **On the Town.** More than anyone else, he was responsible for expanding the borders of the movie musical with such risky undertakings as an eighteen-minute ballet for the finale of **An American in Paris** (1951).

Frank Sinatra
Chip

WHILE Kelly played the sea wolf, Sinatra played the bashful, small-town guy. It wasn't exactly inspired casting, given Sinatra's penchant for romancing many women around Hollywood, including his flame at the time, Ava Gardner, whom he married in 1951.

Ann Miller
Claire

"**I** MADE IT with my lucky legs, my mother, and a lot of backbreaking hard work," is how Miller once summed up her success. But no matter how hard she worked, Miller made it seem easy as she tapped with vigor—and stole the show—in **Easter Parade** (1948), **Lovely to Look At** (1952), and **Kiss Me Kate** (1953).

Screen Team

Kelly and Sinatra also co-starred in **Anchors Aweigh** (1945) and with Garrett and Munshin in **Take Me Out to the Ball Game** (1949).

Kelly had danced the "Slaughter on Tenth Avenue" ballet with Vera-Ellen in **Words and Music** (1948).

Academy Awards

✱ Music, Scoring of a Musical Picture
(Roger Edens and Lennie Hayton)

1 NOMINATION 1 OSCAR ✱

THE BUZZ
Edens and Hayton received their award from Cole Porter who was making a rare Oscar appearance.

Gossip

On the Town was the first musical to be shot on location in New York City.

To appease censors, the line "New York, New York, it's a helluva town" had to be changed to "New York, New York, it's a wonderful town."

Alice Pearce was the only member of the Broadway cast to repeat her role in the film.

Skinny Frank Sinatra wanted a little more bulk to his costume, so the backside of his sailor suit was padded. Garrett gave him a friendly tap on the rear and Sinatra wasn't too happy about having his secret revealed.

SINGIN' IN THE RAIN

HOLLYWOOD is about to go through a transition to talkies, which worries gorgeous, untalented diva Lina Lamont (Hagen) because of her screechy voice. Her smooth screen partner Don Lockwood (Kelly), on the other hand, has a strong, mellow voice and swooping grace. Lina is crazy about Don, but it's perky Hollywood hopeful Kathy Selden (Reynolds) that Don loves, so exuberantly that he's splashing through puddles after meeting her. Following the disastrous premiere of Don and Lina's first sound film, Don enlists Kathy and his friend Cosmo (O'Connor) to rework the movie as a musical. To correct Lina's problems, Kathy dubs her voice. Lina, who fears she'll be exposed, doesn't want Kathy to get any credit, but all is revealed in an uplifting climax.

The Cast

Gene Kelly
Don Lockwood

Donald O'Connor
Cosmo Brown

Debbie Reynolds
Kathy Selden

Jean Hagen
Lina Lamont

Millard Mitchell
R.F. Simpson

Cyd Charisse
Dancer

Douglas Fowley
Roscoe Dexter

Rita Moreno
Zelda Zanders

Madge Blake
Dora Bailey

Kathleen Freeman
Phoebe Dinsmore

Directors
Stanley Donen
and
Gene Kelly

Producer
Arthur Freed

The Stars

Gene Kelly
Don

Singin' in the Rain came hot on the heels of Kelly's Oscar-winning smash An American in Paris (1951). And the result was his masterpiece. Although Kelly had a reputation as a difficult taskmaster, the image of him gleefully clinging to a lamppost during a late-night shower is blissful simplicity.

Donald O'Connor
Cosmo

THOUGH he was only twenty-six when he taught Kelly how to "Make 'Em Laugh," O'Connor was a seasoned veteran of vaudeville, who had been dancing since he was a child. He made his film debut at age twelve, and by his teens was partnered with Peggy Ryan as Universal's answer to Mickey Rooney and Judy Garland. Singin' in the Rain was his career high point, but his greatest popularity came as the straight man to Francis the Talking Mule in six films.

Debbie Reynolds
Kathy

"I WASN'T nice to Debbie. It's a wonder she still speaks to me," Gene Kelly once said about the way he drove his co-star during dance rehearsals. To Reynolds, he was the teacher from whom she learned about discipline and perfectionism. That drive has made her one of the most durable and hardest-working performers in movies (an Oscar nomination in 1964 for The Unsinkable Molly Brown), Broadway (a '70s revival of Irene), and television (Will & Grace).

Gossip

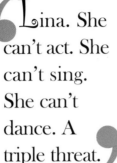

When the projectionist ran the Dueling Cavalier scene at the preview, he didn't realize the sound was supposed to be out of synchronization and decided to fix it.

The "speak into the bush" scene is based on actual incidents M-G-M sound department head Douglas Shearer related to screenwriters Betty Comden and Adolph Green about the studio's transition from silents to talkies.

Gossip columnist Dora Bailey was modeled after Louella Parsons.

"Lina. She can't act. She can't sing. She can't dance. A triple threat."
—*Cosmo*

Screen Team

O'Connor and Reynolds followed up Singin' in the Rain with I Love Melvin (1953).

Kelly and Charisse made two more films together, Brigadoon (1954) and It's Always Fair Weather (1955).

Academy Awards

Supporting Actress (Hagen)
Music, Scoring of a Musical Picture
(Lennie Hayton)

2 NOMINATIONS

THE BUZZ
Kelly and Singin' in the Rain were largely ignored in the nominations, but he did receive an honorary Oscar the year before for his "brilliant achievements in the art of choreography on film."

WESTERNS

WESTERNS

Branding these five movies with the label "western" is like calling **Casablanca** just another romance. Sure, these films deal with cowboys and Indians, and white hats vs. black hats, but at the center of those conflicts are important social issues such as prejudice or mob rule that are dealt with in a telling manner.

The Ox-Bow Incident is a strong statement against mob violence. Henry Fonda is the voice of good, trying to reason with the vigilante posse. The film is a searing indictment of how human fears and vengeful leaders can lead to witch hunts and injustice.

In **High Noon**, the hero is also a lone voice. In this case, the townsfolk, again prompted by fear, hide in their homes when evildoers threaten their peaceful existence. Gary Cooper must fight the bad guys alone, even though all he really wants to do is settle down.

A similar theme is found in **Shane**. Alan Ladd doesn't want to participate in gunfights anymore, but picks up his gun when rustlers threaten to push homesteaders off their land. He knows he's the only one who can beat the baddies.

In **Stagecoach**, a group of disparate passengers are on a journey in the title transport. The message: don't judge a book by its cover. An unrepentant drunk, a prostitute, and an escaped convict all behave with honor, whereas the venerable bank president is a crook.

The Searchers gave western icon John Wayne a chance to really act. He plays a prejudiced, angry cynic on a quest for his niece. He hates Indians, but his niece has become one. His dilemma is whether to kill her or change.

The myths of the Old West are explored, and the panoramic vistas, lovingly shot, transport us to a different world. But these five films also look at the myths of our nation and our collective unconscious. These westerns give us a lot to think about.

SHOOT THIS FILM

WARNER BROS.
1956
-COLOR-

THE SEARCHERS

CIVIL War veteran Ethan Edwards (Wayne) and his half-breed nephew Martin Pawley (Hunter) spend years in search of the Indians who killed Ethan's parents and kidnapped his niece Debbie (Wood). When they find her, she has assimilated and is like an Indian, forcing Ethan to confront his racism.

The Cast

John Wayne
Ethan Edwards

Natalie Wood
Debbie Edwards

Jeffrey Hunter
Martin Pawley

Vera Miles
Laurie Jorgensen

Ward Bond
Rev. Capt. Samuel
Johnston Clayton

John Qualen
Lars Jorgensen

Olive Carey
Mrs. Jorgensen

Henry Brandon
Chief Cicatrice

Director
John Ford

Producer
C.V. Whitney

Screen Team

Wayne and Miles worked together again in **The Man Who Shot Liberty Valance** (1962).

Gossip

Monument Valley in Utah, a frequent setting of Ford westerns, was a filming location for **The Searchers**.

Wood's younger sister, Lana, played Debbie as a child.

The Stars

Natalie Wood
Debbie

WOOD grew up right before our eyes, making her first real impression as Maureen O'Hara's precocious daughter in the Christmas charmer **Miracle on 34th Street** (1947). Like Elizabeth Taylor, Wood was that unusual child star whose popularity soared with maturity thanks to her natural beauty and brilliant performances in films such as **Rebel Without a Cause** (1955) and **Splendor in the Grass** (1961).

John Wayne
Ethan

THE SEARCHERS was one of fourteen films Wayne made with Ford, a partnership that started in 1939 with **Stagecoach**. Their collaborations on the flag-waver **They Were Expendable** (1945), the rough-and-tumble comedy **The Quiet Man** (1952), and scads of westerns such as **She Wore a Yellow Ribbon** established Wayne as an American institution.

The Cast

Gary Cooper
Will Kane

Grace Kelly
Amy Kane

Thomas Mitchell
Mayor Jonas
Henderson

Lloyd Bridges
Deputy Sheriff
Harvey Pell

Katy Jurado
Helen Ramirez

Otto Kruger
Judge
Percy Mettrick

Lon Chaney Jr.
Martin Howe

Harry Morgan
Sam Fuller

Ian MacDonald
Frank Miller

Eve McVeagh
Mildred Fuller

Morgan Farley
Dr. Mahin

Harry Shannon
Cooper

Lee Van Cleef
Jack Colby

Sheb Wooley
Ben Miller

Director
Fred Zinnemann

Producer
Stanley Kramer

UNITED ARTISTS
1952

HIGH NOON

RETIRING marshal Will Kane (Cooper) and his new wife Amy (Kelly) prepare to leave town. Outlaw Frank Miller (MacDonald), whom Will helped to convict, is arriving with his three henchmen on the noon train seeking revenge. The ungrateful, fearful citizens refuse to help Will defend the town. He is faced with a dilemma: Should he leave town before the train arrives, or stay and face the outlaws alone?

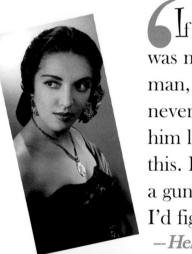

> ❛❛ If Kane was my man, I'd never leave him like this. I'd get a gun. I'd fight. ❜❜
> --*Helen*

7 NOMINATIONS 3 OSCARS ✻

Best Picture
Director (Zinnemann)
✻ **Actor** (Cooper)
Writing, Screenplay (Carl Foreman)
✻ **Music, Song** ("High Noon
[Do Not Forsake Me, Oh My Darlin']),"
Dimitri Tiomkin and Ned Washington)
✻ **Music, Scoring of a Dramatic or Comedy
Picture** (Tiomkin)
Film Editing
(Elmo Williams and Harry Gerstad)

THE BUZZ

Cooper couldn't attend the ceremony because he was in Mexico shooting **Blowing Wild** with Barbara Stanwyck. As a stand-in for his award, Stanwyck presented Cooper with an "Aztec Oscar"— a 4,000-year-old Mexican bust that she purchased.

The Stars

Grace Kelly
Amy

IN ONLY her second film, the gorgeous Philadelphia Main Liner seemed about as likely to be found in the Wild West as Greta Garbo. But Kelly's elegance and beauty did not go unnoticed, and the following year she caused a sensation as Ava Gardner's rival for big-game hunter Clark Gable in the jungle love triangle **Mogambo.**

Gary Cooper
Will

IN MOVIES such as **Sergeant York** (1941) and **Pride of the Yankees** (1942), Cooper was the definition of the strong, silent type, a quality perfect for the role of Will Kane. Some critics complained that Cooper could be stiff, but in **High Noon**, his ability to keep his emotions in tow— at least, on the surface—added an extra layer of tension as we wondered what his next move would be.

> ❛❛ Quit pushin' me, Harv. I'm tired of being pushed. —*Will* ❜❜

Gossip

Cooper and Kelly had a cordial relationship on the set that soon spilled over into an off-camera affair.

High Noon was made on a slim budget of $750,000. Cooper, who normally made $275,000 per movie, agreed to work for a paltry $60,000 plus a percentage of the profits.

Cooper had undergone a hernia operation shortly before making **High Noon**, and was not in prime physical condition. He threw his back out when he picked up Kelly in their post-wedding scene, and later on developed a bleeding ulcer. Despite his discomfort, he refused to use a double for his fight with Bridges.

Kramer first asked Gregory Peck to play Will, but the actor thought the part was too similar to his character in **The Gunfighter** (1950). He then wanted Marlon Brando or Montgomery Clift, but his backer— a lettuce grower— agreed to finance the movie on the condition that Cooper star in it.

The Cast

Henry Fonda
Gil Carter

Dana Andrews
Donald Martin

Mary Beth Hughes
Rose Mapen

Anthony Quinn
Juan Martinez

William Eythe
Gerald

Henry (Harry) Morgan
Art Croft

Jane Darwell
Ma Grier

Matt Briggs
Judge Daniel Tyler

Harry Davenport
Arthur Davies

Frank Conroy
Maj. Tetley

Marc Lawrence
Farnley

Paul Hurst
Monty Smith

Victor Kilian
Darby

Chris-Pin Martin
Pancho

Ted North
Joyce

Margaret Hamilton
Mrs. Larch

Francis Ford
Halva Harvey

Director
William A. Wellman

Producer
Lamar Trotti

THE OX-BOW INCIDENT

THERE'S been a cattle rustling in town, and drifters Gil Carter (Fonda) and Art Croft (Morgan) are suspects. The townsmen learn that a rancher is dead. To find the murderers, they form a posse, led by stony Maj. Tetley (Conroy) and bossy Ma Grier (Darwell). Carter and Croft join the posse, which

20th CENTURY-FOX 1943

finds three men in the woods: earnest Donald Martin (Andrews), tough Mexican Juan Martinez (Quinn), and addled, old Halva Harvey (Ford). The posse wants to hang them, while Arthur Davies (Davenport) and Carter try to dissuade them from making a rash judgment.

"Hangin' murderers is one thing, but to keep guys you don't know for sure did it standing around sweatin' while you shoot your mouth off, that's another."

—Carter

The Stars

Henry Fonda
Carter

Dana Andrews
Martin

FONDA played a genial all-American hero in his first film **The Farmer Takes a Wife** (1935), and over the next forty-six years he rarely veered from that persona. Instead, he became a master at adapting that image to fit each role, from his innocent boob tempted by Barbara Stanwyck in **The Lady Eve** (1941) to the moral **Mister Roberts** (1955) to Kate Hepburn's "knight in shining armor" in **On Golden Pond** (1981).

ANDREWS seemed to be a second-string player when he started out in Hollywood, often supporting top male stars such as Fonda, Tyrone Power, and Gary Cooper in A-list films. His yeoman work eventually paid off when male stars became in short supply during the war years and he was drafted to leads, most notably as the detective in **Laura** (1944).

Gossip

The Ox-Bow Incident was actually completed in 1941, but Fox, which had little faith in the movie because of its somber theme, kept it on the shelf for two years.

Wellman pushed Fox to make **The Ox-Bow Incident**, but in return he agreed to direct any two films the studio assigned him. He ended up making a good one (**Roxie Hart** with Ginger Rogers) and a not so good one (**Thunder Birds** with Gene Tierney).

As Fox predicted, wartime audiences stayed away from **The Ox-Bow Incident**. The studio didn't recoup its loss until the movie's international release and subsequent U.S. re-release.

Academy Awards

Best Picture

THE BUZZ

1 NOMINATION

Having just a single nomination, **The Ox-Bow Incident** went into the best picture race as the dark horse, losing to **Casablanca**.

Screen Team

Fonda and Andrews fought for the affections of Joan Crawford in **Daisy Kenyon** (1947) and against the axis powers in **Battle of the Bulge** (1965).

PARAMOUNT
1953
-COLOR-

SHANE

EX-GUNFIGHTER and loner Shane (Ladd) works on a homestead for beleaguered farmer Joe Starrett (Heflin), his wife Marian (Arthur) and their little son Joey (de Wilde), who idolizes Shane. Joe is battling ruthless cattleman Rufus Ryker (Meyer), and his hired gun Jack Wilson (Palance), who pick fights with the honest homesteaders. Shane is forced to fight one more time in the final showdown with Wilson.

The Cast

Alan Ladd
Shane

Jean Arthur
Marian Starrett

Van Heflin
Joe Starrett

Brandon de Wilde
Joey Starrett

Jack Palance
Jack Wilson

Ben Johnson
Chris Calloway

Director and Producer
George Stevens

"Shane! Come back!" —*Joey*

Gossip

Arthur had a three-picture deal with Paramount, but **Shane** was the only film she agreed to make. It was her last movie.

Shane was filmed on location in Jackson Hole, Wyoming; the Grand Tetons were used as a backdrop throughout the movie.

It took nearly two years to film **Shane**. By the time the 1953 Oscar nomination season came up, Ladd had left Paramount for Warner Bros. In retaliation, Paramount decided not to campaign for a best actor Oscar nomination for Ladd.

A romantic subplot involving Johnson's Chris Calloway was cut from the film.

The Stars

Alan Ladd
Shane

LADD was only 5 feet, 4 inches, but his portrayal of Shane made him seem larger than life. Shy and withdrawn, Ladd was a lot like the low-key screen characters he portrayed in films such as the star-making **This Gun for Hire** (1942). Shane would be his greatest role and his last major hit.

Jean Arthur
Marian

ARTHUR'S forte was screwball comedy, but occasionally she liked to saddle up for a western. In her previous oaters **The Plainsman** (1937) and **Arizona** (1940), she was tomboyish though romantic when it came to Gary Cooper and William Holden, respectively. In **Shane**, she plays a strong frontierswoman devoted to her husband and son, yet feels a kinship with the stranger who comes to her door.

Academy Awards

Best Picture
Director (Stevens)
Supporting Actor (de Wilde)
Supporting Actor (Palance)
Writing, Screenplay (A.B. Guthrie Jr.)
✱ **Cinematography, Color** (Loyal Griggs)

6 NOMINATIONS 1 OSCAR ✱

THE BUZZ

De Wilde's parents didn't tell their ten-year-old son that he was nominated for an Oscar. He found out four years later.

Stevens didn't get a best director Oscar that night, but he did receive the Irving G. Thalberg Memorial Award from the Academy.

❝A gun is as good or as bad as the man using it. Remember that.—*Shane*❞

Screen Team

Arthur and Edgar Buchanan were both in **Too Many Husbands** (1940), **Arizona** (1940), **Talk of the Town** (1942), and **The Impatient Years** (1944).

STAGECOACH

NINE people with diverse backgrounds are thrown together on a stagecoach trip through hostile Indian territory. Pretty prostitute Dallas (Trevor); gambler Hatfield (Carradine) who is the escort for haughty Lucy Mallory (Platt), an officer's wife;

alcoholic Dr. Josiah Boone (Mitchell); the notorious Ringo (Wayne), and the rest must learn to tolerate each other and stick together through adversity.

WANGER-UNITED ARTISTS

1939

The Cast

Claire Trevor
Dallas

John Wayne
The Ringo Kid

Andy Devine
Buck

John Carradine
Hatfield

Thomas Mitchell
Dr. Josiah Boone

Louise Platt
Lucy Mallory

George Bancroft
Sheriff Curly Wilcox

Donald Meek
Samuel Peacock

Berton Churchill
Henry Gatewood

Tim Holt
Lt. Blanchard

Tom Tyler
Luke Plummer

Director
John Ford

Producer
Walter Wanger

Gossip

Ford paid $7,500 for the rights to "Stage to Lordsburg," a short story published in Collier's magazine that was the source of **Stagecoach**.

Stagecoach had a small budget of $500,000. As a result, Ford worked for a reduced fee of $50,000, and the cast members all agreed to take salary cuts.

Ford taunted Wayne throughout the film, even calling him a "dumb bastard," to provoke his star into giving a stronger performance.

Stagecoach was remade in 1966 with the unlikely casting of Ann-Margret as Dallas, Alex Cord as Ringo, and Bing Crosby as Doc Boone.

The Stars

Claire Trevor
Dallas

STAGECOACH was one of the rare opportunities Trevor had to be the leading lady in an A picture. In a career of nearly seventy films, Trevor played her share of good girls (**Dante's Inferno** in 1935), bad girls (the 1944 noir **Murder, My Sweet**), and fallen women (**Dead End** in 1937). None had fallen lower than Trevor's boozy singer in **Key Largo** (1948); her pitiful rendition of "Moanin' Low" was the stuff that Oscars are made of.

John Wayne
Ringo

THE DUKE was saddled both literally and figuratively in more than fifty Z-grade western programmers throughout the '30s. Republic, which produced most of them, was reluctant to loan out Wayne for **Stagecoach**, but after heavy negotiations gave its OK. Wayne's success in **Stagecoach** led to considerably higher budgets on his subsequent Republic films such as **Dark Command** (1940) and **Flying Tigers** (1942), and he remained the studio's premiere star until they parted company in 1952.

> **W**ell, I guess you can't break out of prison and into society in the same week. —*Ringo*

Screen Team

Wayne and Trevor co-starred in **Allegheny Uprising** (1939), **Dark Command**, and **The High and the Mighty** (1954).

Academy Awards

Best Picture
Director (Ford)
✳ **Supporting Actor** (Mitchell)
Cinematography, Black and White (Bert Glennon)
Interior Decoration (Alexander Toluboff)
✳ **Music, Score** (Richard Hageman, Frank Harling, John Leipold and Leo Shuken)
Film Editing (Otho Lovering and Dorothy Spencer)

7 NOMINATIONS 2 OSCARS ✳

THE BUZZ

Mitchell seemed genuinely surprised by his win, as indicated in his acceptance: "I didn't think I was that good. I don't have a speech, I'm too incoherent."

SCI-FI
& HORROR

SCI-FI & HORROR

The science fiction and horror movies of the first half of the twentieth century promised chills and thrills, and they delivered. In many ways, filmmakers of the '30s, '40s, and '50s were way ahead of their modern successors in their approach to horror, inducing goose bumps by letting audiences use their imaginations rather than relying on gore for shock appeal.

James Whale directed **The Invisible Man** using innovative special effects and a witty screenplay. Claude Rains' invisibility was achieved by using traveling mattes, much like the blue screen today. The surprise ending is chilling.

Whale also directed Boris Karloff in **Frankenstein**, a haunting movie that scared me and also touched my heart. Frightening as the monster looked, Karloff made me feel sorry for him. None of the other characters seemed to understand that he didn't mean to commit murder and wreak havoc. All he really wanted was a friend.

The Day The Earth Stood Still is presented simply with minimalist spaceships and robots, but the film carries a strong message about the consequences of war and employing weapons of mass destruction on Earth.

Forbidden Planet is based on Shakespeare's **The Tempest** and is filled with Freudian undertones. I loved Anne Francis' futuristic outfits, but the bogeymen gave me nightmares.

Willis O'Brien, the father of stop-motion animation, started with a twenty-inch model of **King Kong** and amazingly detailed miniature sets. His designs were based on live animals, wrestlers, and other natural world references. The climax of **King Kong**, in which the great ape climbs to the top of the Empire State Building while holding Fay Wray, is a towering achievement of excitement and creative editing.

These creatures, monsters, and aliens capture our sympathies and our fears. And the technological innovations that the designers used served as a foundation for modern horror and science-fiction movies.

BE AFRAID

FORBIDDEN PLANET

M-G-M 1956 -COLOR-

ONLY two Earthlings survive on the planet Altair IV, crazy research scientist Dr. Edward Morbius (Pidgeon) and his innocent, lovely daughter Altaira (Francis), who live in isolation with their servant, Robby the Robot. The superior Krell race once shared the planet, but they are gone, along with the entire research team. A crew from Earth is sent to check it out, led by Capt. J.J. Adams (Nielsen). Altaira is fascinated with the crew, much to her father's consternation. After the spaceship and crew are attacked by a monster, Morbius urges them to leave.

The Cast

Walter Pidgeon
Dr. Edward Morbius

Anne Francis
Altaira Morbius

Leslie Nielsen
John J. Adams

Robby the Robot
Robot

Warren Stevens
Lt. "Doc" Ostrow

Jack Kelly
Lt. Jerry Farman

Richard Anderson
Chief Engineer Quinn

Director
Fred M. Wilcox

Producer
Nicholas Nayfack

Gossip

About ninety percent of the movie was made at M-G-M studios using a 10,000-foot circular painting as a backdrop.

Forbidden Planet was the first major studio release to use only electronic instruments for its score.

1 NOMINATION

Academy Awards

Special Effects (A. Arnold Gillespie, Irving Ries and Wesley C. Miller)

Walter Pidgeon
Dr. Morbius

PIDGEON was just two films away from wrapping up a nineteen-year tenure at M-G-M, where he made magic with Greer Garson in eight films, most notably the 1942 best picture winner **Mrs. Miniver.**

Anne Francis
Altaira

WITH silky blonde hair, a curvaceous figure, and a mole near her lower lip, Francis rose from a starlet at Fox to a leading lady at **M-G-M** in **The Blackboard Jungle** (1955) and **Forbidden Planet** (1956). Baby boomers remember her best as karate-chopping TV private eye **Honey West.**

Screen Team

Francis co-starred again with Pidgeon in **The Rack** (1956) and **Funny Girl** (1968), and with Holliman in **Don't Go Near the Water** (1957).

20th CENTURY-FOX

1951

FROM OUT OF SPACE....
A WARNING AND AN ULTIMATUM!

THE DAY THE EARTH STOOD STILL

MICHAEL RENNIE · PATRICIA NEAL · HUGH MARLOWE

The Cast

Michael Rennie
Klaatu/Mr. Carpenter

Patricia Neal
Helen Benson

Hugh Marlowe
Tom Stevens

Sam Jaffe
Professor Jacob Barnhardt

Billy Gray
Bobby Benson

Frances Bavier
Mrs. Barley

Lock Martin
Gort

Director
Robert Wise

Producer
Julian Blaustein

THE DAY THE EARTH STOOD STILL

A FLYING saucer lands in Washington, D.C., and is greeted by panic and troops. A soldier accidentally wounds the interplanetary visitor Klaatu (Rennie) dressed in a space suit. His robot Gort (Martin) saves him by melting the tanks and guns. Klaatu is taken to a hospital, but escapes and moves into a boarding house, where he befriends widowed Helen Benson (Neal) and her son, Bobby (Gray). Klaatu's mission is to speak to the world's leaders, but none will meet him. Fearing that his mission isn't being taken seriously, Klaatu scares everyone by making time stand still for a half hour.

Time resumes and Klaatu, realizing he has captured everyone's attention, puts forth his plan to address the world with his message to live in peace or be destroyed.

" *G*ort! Klaatu barada nikto! " —*Helen*

" *Mrs. Barley:* There's nothing strange about Washington, Mr. Carpenter. *Klaatu:* A person from another planet might disagree with you. "

Gossip

Wise wanted Claude Rains for Klaatu, but he was doing a play in New York. The studio also considered Spencer Tracy.

The Defense Department refused to loan Fox tanks for the film because they disliked the movie's message for peace. The producers then asked the National Guard, who graciously complied with their tank request.

Lock Martin, who played Gort, was seven feet, seven inches and worked as the doorman at Grauman's Chinese Theatre.

Neal found the script very silly and sometimes couldn't get through her scenes without breaking into laughter.

The Stars

Patricia Neal
Helen

THE DAY the Earth Stood Still was Neal's first film as a freelance after two less-than-stellar years at Warner Bros. She and Wise had worked together previously on one of her better Warner films, **Three Secrets** (1950). The director admired Neal's talents and asked for her again for the comedy **Something for the Birds** (1952). Neal's acting career was curtailed by a debilitating stroke in 1965, but she made an amazing comeback three years later in **The Subject Was Roses**.

Michael Rennie
Klaatu

RENNIE had been making films in England since the late '30s, but was a relative unknown when he came to the States in 1950. Klaatu became his signature role, and his performance has become a cult favorite in sci-fi circles. Rennie had other consequential assignments at Fox, notably Joan Valjean in **Les Miserables** (1952) and Peter in **The Robe** (1953), but none eclipsed Klaatu.

FRANKENSTEIN

DR. HENRY Frankenstein (Clive) and his hunchbacked assistant Fritz (Frye) create a gigantic creature out of dead body parts.

Fritz puts an abnormal brain in the monster, which causes problems. The doctor's fiancée, Elizabeth (Clarke), his colleague Dr. Waldman (Van Sloan), and his friend Victor (Boles) are all there at the awakening of the new life. The monster can obey elementary commands, but becomes uncontrollable, killing Waldman and terrorizing the villagers, who want to destroy him.

UNIVERSAL

1931

> ❝You have created a monster, and it will destroy you.❞
> —*Dr. Waldman*

The Cast

Colin Clive
Dr. Henry Frankenstein

Boris Karloff
The Monster

Mae Clarke
Elizabeth

John Boles
Victor

Edward Van Sloan
Dr. Waldman

Dwight Frye
Fritz

Frederick Kerr
The Baron

Frederick Leister
Marsham

Lionel Belmore
The Burgomaster

Michael Mark
Ludwig

Marilyn Harris
Maria

Director
James Whale

Producer
Carl Laemmle

Fresh from his success as Dracula, Bela Lugosi was Universal's first choice to play the Monster.

Bette Davis was supposed to play Elizabeth, but Whale thought she was too strong a personality for the role.

Karloff spent four hours in makeup each day, and especially disliked have putty applied to his eyes. His uncomfortable costume added eighteen inches to his height and made him sixty pounds heavier. By the time the movie wrapped six weeks later, Karloff had lost twenty pounds.

The scene in which the Monster drowns little Maria was considered too horrifying and was deleted upon its original release. It was later reinstated.

Frankenstein cost $250,000 to make and made $12 million.

Screen Team

Clive and Karloff were appropriately reteamed in 1935 for the first sequel, **Bride of Frankenstein.**

The Stars

Colin Clive
Dr. Frankenstein

CLIVE appeared in just twenty movies before his death in 1937, but made an indelible impression as the mad doctor in **Frankenstein.** He seemed to specialize in playing eccentrics, such as Mr. Rochester in a Poverty Row version of **Jane Eyre** (1934), a pianist with a reattached hand in **Mad Love** (1935), and Jean Arthur's jealous husband in **History Is Made at Night** (1937).

"It's alive. It's alive!"
—Dr. Frankenstein

Boris Karloff
The Monster

KARLOFF began his career in silents, but wasn't excited about his non-speaking role in **Frankenstein.** Little did he realize the impact his performance would have on his career and the horror genre. He played the Monster two more times, and in 1932 was wonderfully creepy as the Mummy and deliriously campy as Fu Man Chu. He kept scaring the daylights out of audiences for another three decades in everything from Robert Wise's excellent **The Body Snatcher** (1945) to Roger Corman's schlockfest **The Raven** (1963).

THE INVISIBLE MAN

SCIENTIST Jack Griffin's experiment to make himself invisible is a mixed success. It works at making him invisible, but his behavior becomes increasingly erratic. Griffin wreaks havoc at a country inn and then escapes to the home of his cowardly colleague Dr. Kemp (Harrigan). The Invisible Man cannot be seen except when he is dressed and his face is bandaged. He terrorizes the village and kills the police chief, all the while becoming alarmingly power mad, using Kemp as his pawn in a quest to rule the world. A fearful Kemp calls the police as well as fellow scientist Dr. Cranley (Travers), whose daughter, Flora (Stuart), is Griffin's former love. Flora tries to calm Griffin, but to no avail. Griffin goes on a crime spree and seeks revenge for Kemp's betrayal.

UNIVERSAL
1933

The Cast

Claude Rains
Jack Griffin

Gloria Stuart
Flora Cranley

William Harrigan
Dr. Kemp

Henry Travers
Dr. Cranley

Una O'Connor
Innkeeper's wife

Forrester Harvey
Innkeeper

Holmes Herbert
Chief of Police

E.E. Clive
Constable Jaffers

Dudley Digges
Chief detective

Harry Tubbs
Inspector Bird

Donald Stuart
Inspector Lane

Merle Tottenham
Millie

Director
James Whale

Producer
Carl Laemmle Jr.

Gossip

Universal's top horror star Boris Karloff was supposed to play Griffin, but when Laemmle asked Karloff to take a pay cut, the actor refused.

Whale wanted his friend Rains to play the lead, but Laemmle didn't want to risk his production on an unknown. Laemmle asked the director to approach Colin Clive about the part. Whale did speak to Clive— and begged him not to accept.

To make Rains seem invisible when he wasn't bandaged, Whale had Rains wear black velvet underneath his wrappings and clothes and filmed him against a black velvet background.

H.G. Wells, author of **The Invisible Man**, was highly amused by O'Connor's hysterical shrieks throughout the movie.

> **❝I** meddled in things that man must leave alone. *—Griffin* **❞**

> **❝T**he whole world's my hiding place! **❞** *—Griffin*

The Stars

Claude Rains
Griffin

FEW actors would be happy about getting just a few seconds of face time in their screen debut, but not many possessed Rains' distinguished, expressive voice, which he used to deliver a star-making performance. He soon moved over to Warner Bros., where he bolstered every film in which he appeared, whether as a dreamer (**Mr. Skeffington** in 1944), a schemer (**They Won't Forget** in 1937), or a scoundrel (**The Unsuspected** in 1947).

Gloria Stuart
Flora

PRETTY Gloria Stuart decorated a bevy of '30s films from Whale's 1932 thriller **The Old Dark House** to Busby Berkeley's **Gold Diggers of 1935**. Her best role of the decade was as the wife of the doctor who treated John Wilkes Booth in **The Prisoner of Shark Island** (1936). She was largely forgotten until James Cameron cast her as the aged Rose in **Titanic** (1997), a beautiful performance that earned her an Oscar nomination.

KING KONG

RKO RADIO
1933

FILMMAKER Carl Denham (Armstrong) and his crew arrive by boat to exotic, remote Skull Island, to make a film about a monster ape, Kong. Also on hand are Denham's beautiful blonde leading lady Ann Darrow (Wray) and his rough-hewn first mate Jack Driscoll (Cabot). The natives kidnap Ann from the ship and try to sacrifice her to Kong, whose animal attraction for Ann is clearly one-sided. Jack and Denham tackle all manner of prehis-toric beast before rescuing Ann. Denham also captures Kong and brings him to New York as a stage attraction. Still protective of Ann, Kong gets upset when photographers snap her picture. He escapes, kidnaps Ann, and goes on a rampage before climbing to the Empire State Building where a tragic battle ensues.

The Cast

Robert Armstrong
Carl Denham

Fay Wray
Ann Darrow

Bruce Cabot
Jack Driscoll

Frank Reicher
Capt. Englehorn

Sam Hardy
Charles Weston

Noble Johnson
Native chief

Steve Clemento
Witch king

James Flavin
Briggs

Directors and Producers
Merian C. Cooper
Ernest B. Schoedsack

Gossip

Cooper envisioned Jean Harlow as Ann, but when he couldn't get her from M-G-M, he cast Wray and had her wear a blonde wig.

A pair of twenty-inch Kong models was constructed and stop-motion animation was employed for his movements. A giant paw was also created for scenes in which Kong grabbed Wray.

San Pedro Harbor was the shipboard locale and L.A.'s Shrine Auditorium housed the theater scenes, but the remainder of the film was shot in the RKO lot.

In the famous finale atop the Empire State Building, Cooper and Schoedsack played the pilot and the gunner, respectively.

Several scenes were deleted after the movie's initial release for being too violent, such as close-ups of Kong sticking people in his mouth, and one was too sexy (Kong's disrobing of Wray). All of the scenes were restored in the '70s except for one in which the sailors fall into a ravine and are eaten by giant spiders.

'No, it wasn't the airplanes. It was beauty killed the beast.'
—*Denham*

Screen Team

Wray and Armstrong also made spines tingle in **The Most Dangerous Game** (1932).

The Stars

Robert Armstrong
Denham

ARMSTRONG falls into that category of actors whose face is more recognizable than his name, which is understandable, given that he made 128 movies, mostly second features, specializing in gangsters, killers, and adventurers. Armstrong's showy work in **King Kong** made such an impression that he engaged in more monkey business in **Son of Kong** (1933) and **Mighty Joe Young** (1949).

Fay Wray
Ann

COOPER promised Wray that she'd have "the tallest, darkest leading man in Hollywood." He forgot to tell Wray that her co-star was also the hairiest. Of the eighty-nine movies she made, **King Kong** is the one Wray will always be remembered for, though she screamed just as piercingly loud and clear in two other '30s horror gems— **Doctor X** (1932) and **Mystery of the Wax Museum** (1933).

Bruce Cabot
Jack

RUGGED, two-fisted Cabot took on the great ape Kong, and spent the rest of his film career taking on everyone from Randolph Scott's Hawkeye in **The Last of the Mohicans** (1936) to Bob Hope's buffoonish British valet in **Fancy Pants** (1950). As a drinking buddy of John Wayne, he became a frequent member of the Duke's stock company in films such as **Hatari!** (1962) and **McClintock!** (1963).

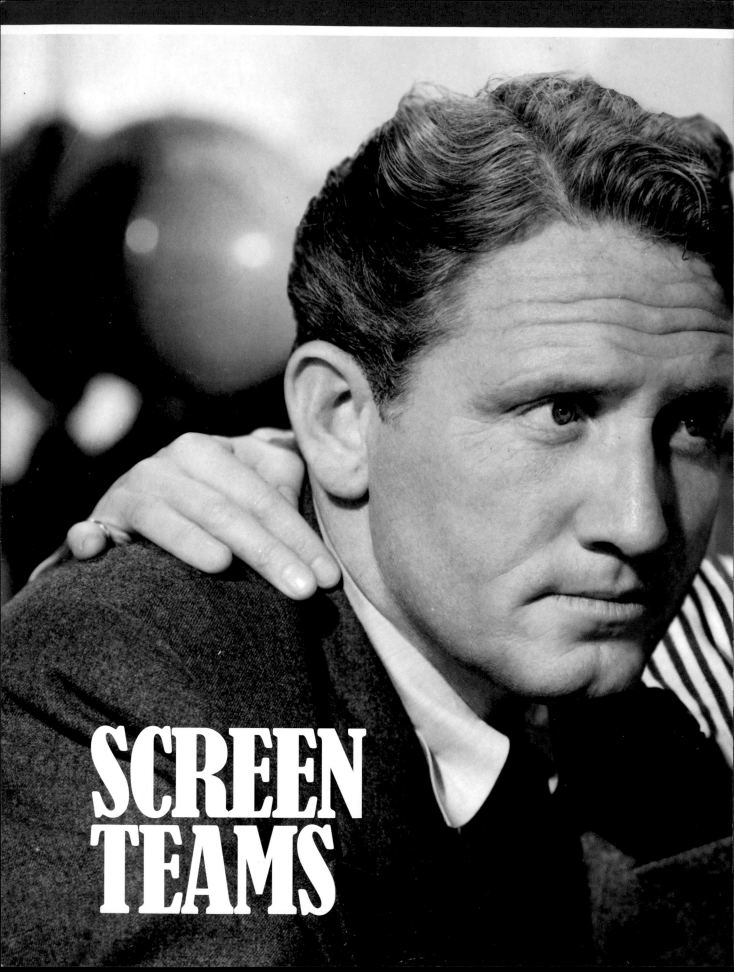

SCREEN TEAMS

CHAPTER 14

HOLLYWOOD PICKS

Barbara Walters
Anchorwoman (b. 1931)

All About Eve
Harvey
The Wizard of Oz

Esther Williams
Actress (b. 1922)

The African Queen
Camille
Gone with the Wind
The Great Ziegfeld
San Francisco
A Star Is Born (1954)

Rita Wilson
Actress (b. 1958)

All About Eve
Dark Victory
Gone with the Wind
It's a Wonderful Life
The Lady Eve
Mr. Skeffington
Notorious
Sullivan's Travels
The Wizard of Oz

John Woo
Director (b. 1946)

The 400 Blows
Ben-Hur (1959)
The Bicycle Thief
The Bridge on the River Kwai
On the Waterfront
Paths of Glory
Rear Window
The Seven Samurai
The Treasure of the Sierra Madre
The Wizard of Oz

Elijah Wood
Actor (b. 1981)

Harvey
Night of the Hunter

Evan Rachel Wood
Actress (b. 1987)

Auntie Mame
The King and I
Rebel Without a Cause
Sabrina
Some Like It Hot
The Wizard of Oz

Chemistry. Who knows what alchemy is needed to turn the pairing of two people who have never worked together into cinematic gold? Sometimes the right elements just come together, whether by accident or fate. Whatever chemistry is involved, these six screen teams had it, and the formulas they used to create movie magic were as winning as $E=mc^2$.

Sultry, smoky, cool Lauren Bacall and rough-hewn he-man Humphrey Bogart made a sizzling combo, on screen and off. Falling in love in real life can sometimes spell disaster for acting couples, but Bogey and Bacall managed to keep the sparks flying in each of their screen match-ups. Bacall was so nervous when shooting **To Have and Have Not**, her first film with Bogart, that she kept her chin to her collar, peering up and creating a style that was dubbed "The Look." She also taught Bogart to whistle.

Katharine Hepburn and Spencer Tracy were also in love in real life, though not as happily as Bogey and Bacall. Tracy was married and a devout Catholic whose wife would not divorce him, so he and Hepburn had to keep their romance a secret. Although the haughty Hepburn was always knocked down a peg or two by the down-to-earth Tracy, the love, devotion, and care they had for one another came through on screen. They triumphed in dramas such as **Guess Who's Coming to Dinner?** and excelled in comedies such as **Pat and Mike, Adam's Rib,** and their first teaming, **Woman of the Year.**

Mickey Rooney and Judy Garland had unbeatable energy and exuberance as they got into mischief, pined for their crushes, and put on shows in the barn. They were fresh-faced kids with huge talent to burn and made movies such as **Babes in Arms** and **Babes on Broadway** swing.

Playing fun-loving married couple Nick and Nora Charles, Myrna Loy and William Powell created a whole new genre: the sophisticated comedy caper. Their **Thin Man** series was witty, elegant, classy—a delight from beginning to end—as they searched for clues and swigged cocktails with equal ease. And their beloved terrier Asta earned more than a few dog biscuits as part of the team.

When it came to witty banter, Bob Hope and Bing Crosby were true masters. The smooth crooner and the ski-nosed comic sang, danced, and joked their way through seven **Road** pictures. The stories didn't vary much, only the locations: The boys would get themselves in a jam, they'd fall for the damsel in distress (almost always Dorothy Lamour) and play Pat-a-Cake to outwit their enemies. The big question was always who would get the girl.

No one ever had to ask whether Fred Astaire would wind up with Ginger Rogers in their musicals. The formula was always the same: Boy meets girl, boy loses girl or girl loses boy, boy gets girl. We knew they'd get together, but how they did made for a fun ride. They danced on air and on celluloid.

All of these talented individuals were strong on their own, but teamed with their other half, were dynamite. They solved mysteries, smoldered, romanced, sang, danced, laughed, and cried. These duos clicked.

IT TAKES TWO

FRED ASTAIRE & GINGER ROGERS

"HE GIVES her class, she gives him sex" was Katharine Hepburn's assessment of Astaire and Rogers. It was apparent from the moment Fred and Ginger did "The Carioca" in **Flying Down to Rio** and danced off with the movie from nominal stars Dolores Del Rio and Gene Raymond. The plots were never important in an Astaire-Rogers movie—they let their feet do the

SIGNATURE MOVIE
SWING TIME

RKO RADIO

1936

DANCER /gambler Lucky Garnett (Astaire) promises his fiancée Margaret (Furness) that they will be married as soon as he makes $25,000 in New York. He and his friend Pop (Moore) arrive in Manhattan, where Lucky meets pretty Penny Carrol (Rogers), a dance teacher. They fall in love after they dance for the first time. Effete band-leader Ricardo Romero (Metaxa) is determined to steal Penny from Lucky. Which one will sweep her off her feet?

talking, and their dances spoke volumes. Fred dressed in tails and Ginger dripping in ostrich feathers seemed as if they really were in heaven dancing "Cheek to Cheek" on the shiniest floor imaginable. But like so many relationships, theirs came to an end in 1939 after nine films, though they reunited ten years later. Fred would continue to dance with beauties from Rita Hayworth to Audrey Hepburn. Ginger would establish herself as a first-rate comedienne and win an Oscar for the drama **Kitty Foyle** (1940). But nothing they did can ever compare to the "la belle, la perfectly swell romance" of their magical musicals.

The Cast

2 NOMINATIONS 1 OSCAR ✱

Fred Astaire
John "Lucky" Garnett

Ginger Rogers
Penny Carrol

Victor Moore
Pop

Helen Broderick
Mabel

Eric Blore
Mr. Gordon

Georges Metaxa
Ricardo Romero

Betty Furness
Margaret Watson

Director
George Stevens

Producer
Pandro S. Berman

Academy Awards

✱ Music, Song
("The Way You Look Tonight," Jerome Kern and Dorothy Fields)
Dance Direction
("Bojangles of Harlem," Hermes Pan)

THE BUZZ

This was the second and last time an Astaire-Rogers film won a best song Oscar. "The Continental" from the duo's **The Gay Divorcee** won the first best song Oscar two years earlier.

Gossip

The difficult "Never Gonna Dance" number took more than forty takes. In the middle of filming, Rogers noticed her dance slippers were filled with blood. Trouper that she was, she finished the number.

Rogers' shampoo coif for "The Way You Look Tonight" was actually whipped cream. Before that, beaten egg whites were used for the lather, but the hot lights started cooking the eggs on her head.

THEIR OTHER MOVIES

Flying Down to Rio
(1933)
The Gay Divorcee
(1934)
Roberta
and
Top Hat
(1935)
Follow the Fleet
(1936)
Shall We Dance
(1937)
Carefree
(1938)
The Story of Vernon and Irene Castle
(1939)
The Barkleys of Broadway
(1949)

HUMPHREY BOGART & LAUREN BACALL

THE FIRST time Lauren Bacall met Humphrey Bogart was in 1944 right after she'd just gotten the lead in **To Have and Have Not.**

"I just saw your test. We'll have a lot of fun together," Bogart told her. He never could have guessed that what started out as the unlikely screen pairing of a nineteen-year-old newcomer and a middle-aged, box-office tough guy would blossom into one of the great romances of all time, both on screen and off. They married the following year, a union that would produce three more successful films and two handsome children. Their marriage lasted until Bogart's death in 1957.

SIGNATURE MOVIE
TO HAVE AND HAVE NOT

IN MARTINIQUE, Harry Morgan (Bogart) and his partner Eddie (Walter Brennan), a simple-minded drunk who tends to talk too much, have a small business renting out their fishing boat. Unfortunately, business has fallen off since the outbreak of World War II, and after a customer who owes them a large sum is killed before he can pay, they are forced to go to work for the Resistance transporting fugitives on the run from the Nazis. Along the way, Harry falls for Marie "Slim" Browning (Bacall), a stranded singer who, among other things, teaches him how to whistle.

WARNER BROS. 1944

The Cast

Humphrey Bogart
Harry "Steve" Morgan

Lauren Bacall
Marie "Slim" Browning

Walter Brennan
Eddie

Dolores Moran
Helene de Bursac

Hoagy Carmichael
Cricket

Sheldon Leonard
Lt. Coyo

Walter Sande
Johnson

Director and Producer
Howard Hawks

©1978 SID AVERY / MPTV

> **I'm hard to get, Steve. All you have to do is ask me.**
> —*Marie*

Gossip

Originally the script involved a flirtation between Bogart and Moran. In the middle of filming, Hawks ran some of the cut scenes for Bogart who convinced Hawks that no audience would believe anything would come between his character and Bacall's.

Bacall was nicknamed "The Look" after the film was released.

THEIR OTHER MOVIES

The Big Sleep (1946)
Dark Passage (1947)
Key Largo (1948)

BOB HOPE & BING CROSBY

PARAMOUNT
1942

THE HOPE-CROSBY films were a real trip, and not just because the boys were usually on the road to some exotic locale. It was impossible not to be tickled by the infectious camaraderie between the wise-cracking comic and the velvet-voiced crooner. Double-crossing each other, fighting for dames like Dorothy Lamour, trading gags with a sassy camel—they were just a few of the reasons Bob and Bing's movies were such a blast. Their **Road** adventures were the originally buddy movies, which made sense given that the two stars had the same sort of easygoing friendship in real life. The snappy song-and-dance routines in their films, with titles like "Put It There Pal" and "Harmony," reinforced that fact, and they were also breezy interludes among the zaniness. Hope and Crosby took us traveling over seven Roads, and we're glad for the rollicking time we had with them.

SIGNATURE MOVIE
ROAD TO MOROCCO

CASTAWAYS Jeff (Crosby) and Turkey (Hope) wash up on a desert shore and head to Morocco. While making their trek, Turkey is sold into slavery. Jeff wants to save his friend, and when he does, he

finds Turkey isn't in much danger. His owner is gorgeous Princess Shalmar (Lamour), and she and her slave girls treats Turkey like a king. Soon Jeff and Turkey are fighting for the princess' hand, and later trying to save their heads when her jealous suitor Mullay Kassim (Quinn) arrives.

The Cast

Bing Crosby
Jeff Peters

Bob Hope
Orville "Turkey"
Jackson/Aunt Lucy

Dorothy Lamour
Princess Shalmar

Anthony Quinn
Mullay Kassim

Dona Drake
Mihirmah

Director
David Butler

Producer
Paul Jones

Gossip

The camel spitting at Hope was completely candid.

The **Road** series had originally been intended for George Burns and Gracie Allen. Then Fred MacMurray and Jack Oakie were announced. Finally Paramount decided on Hope and Crosby.

"Like Webster's dictionary, we're Morocco bound."
—*Jeff and Turkey*

Academy Awards

Writing, Original Screenplay
(Frank Butler and Don Hartman)
Sound Recording (Loren Ryder)

2 NOMINATIONS

THE BUZZ

Hope served as host of the 1942 Oscar ceremony. It was his third time as master of ceremonies, an honor he held a record eighteen times.

THEIR OTHER MOVIES

Road to Singapore (1940)
Road to Zanzibar (1941)
Star Spangled Rhythm (1942)
Road to Utopia (1945)
Road to Rio (1947)
Variety Girl (1947)
Road to Bali (1952)
Road to Hong Kong (1962)

Crosby popped up
in Hope's comedies
My Favorite Blonde (1942)
The Princess and the Pirate
(1944)
My Favorite Brunette (1947)
Alias Jesse James (1959)

Hope and Crosby also
had cameos in
The Greatest Show on Earth
(1952).

WILLIAM POWELL & MYRNA LOY

EVERYONE thought Powell and Loy really were husband and wife. Loy herself joked that she made a better screen wife to Powell than she did to any of her four husbands. Fan letters flooded the M-G-M mailroom addressed to

M-G-M

1934

SIGNATURE MOVIE
THE THIN MAN

CONCERNED Dorothy Wynant (O'Sullivan) asks retired detective Nick Charles (Powell) to locate her missing father (Ellis). Nick's dizzy wife Nora (Loy), longs to join him and do some sleuthing of her own. When Mr. Wynant's mistress is found murdered, he becomes the prime suspect, until his dead body is also uncovered. As the plot thickens, so does the number of suspects, whom Nick and Nora gather for a suspenseful dinner party, where the murderer is revealed.

The Cast

William Powell
Nick Charles

Myrna Loy
Nora Charles

Maureen O'Sullivan
Dorothy Wynant

Edward Ellis
Clyde Wynant,
aka The Thin Man

Skippy
Asta

Director
W.S. Van Dyke

Producer

Nora: I read where you were shot five times in the tabloids.
Nick: It's not true. He didn't come anywhere near my tabloids.

the happy couple. It was an honest mistake: Powell and Loy seemed like a match made in movie heaven, and in thirteen films they showed that once two people tied the knot, they could still have plenty of fun. In their best roles as Nick and Nora Charles, they traded quips, solved murders, nursed each other's hangovers, and still couldn't wait to cozy up in the same upper berth at the fadeout.

Gossip

The trainer for Skippy, aka Asta, didn't want any of the actors to get friendly with the dog because it would break Skippy's concentration. Loy must not have listened because on one occasion the dog bit her.

The director was known as "one-take Van Dyke" because he got what he wanted from his cast on the first try. As a result, **The Thin Man** was shot in only sixteen days.

The popularity of wire-haired terriers rose after the release of **The Thin Man**.

Academy Awards

Best Picture
Director (Van Dyke)
Actor (Powell)
Writing, Adaptation
(Frances Goodrich and Albert Hackett)

4 NOMINATIONS

THE BUZZ

This was the first of Powell's three best actor nominations. He was also up for **My Man Godfrey** (1936) and **Life With Father** (1947), but never won.

THEIR OTHER MOVIES:

Manhattan Melodrama (1934)
Evelyn Prentice (1934)
The Great Ziegfeld (1936)
Libeled Lady (1936)
After the Thin Man (1936)
Double Wedding (1937)
Another Thin Man (1939)
I Love You Again (1940)
Love Crazy (1941)
Shadow of the Thin Man (1941)
The Thin Man Goes Home (1944)
Song of the Thin Man (1947)
Loy also made a cameo in Powell's 1947 comedy The Senator Was Indiscreet.

MICKEY ROONEY & JUDY GARLAND

IT WAS inevitable that someone would shout "Hey, let's put on a show!" in a Mickey and Judy musical. And conveniently, there was always a vacant barn that was the size of Iowa to accommodate the lavish Busby Berkeley numbers. It sounds corny, but thanks to the bubbly enthusiasm and natural showmanship Mickey and Judy had together, it was golden sweet corn, ripe for another helping. Romance was never in the forefront with Mickey and Judy. The buddy-buddy relationship both stars had off the set spilled over into **Babes in Arms, Babes on Broadway, Girl Crazy,** and their six other screen pairings. Both performers also brought plenty of personal baggage to the set, though no one would know it from their youthful exuberance. And they always put on one hell of a show in that barnyard.

SIGNATURE MOVIE
BABES ON BROADWAY

AMBITIOUS Tommy Williams (Rooney) and his friends are determined to make it on Broadway, but how to get there is the problem. An idea hits him after he meets singer Penny Morris (Garland) at a drugstore: he'll stage a show to send orphans on a trip to the country, and hopefully attract the attention of a producer. Along the way there are a few snags—the theater for the show is about to be condemned and Penny breaks up with Tommy after realizing that he's only out for himself. Tommy eventually realizes that being a star can be lonely.

M-G-M 1941

The Cast

Mickey Rooney
Tommy Williams

Judy Garland
Penny Morris

Fay Bainter
Jonesy Jones

Virginia Weidler
Jo Conway

Ray McDonald
Ray Lambert

Richard Quine
Hammy Hammond

Alexander Woollcott
Himself

Director
Busby Berkeley

Producer
Arthur Freed

Academy Awards

Music, Song ("How About You?" Burton Lane and Ralph Freed)

THE BUZZ

"How About You?" lost the Oscar to the yuletide classic "White Christmas" from **Holiday Inn**.

1 NOMINATION

Gossip

Garland eloped with producer David Rose during filming. An annoyed Louis B. Mayer wouldn't let her have time off for a honeymoon.

Rooney met future wife Ava Gardner when she visited the set during a studio tour. He was dressed as Carmen Miranda when he asked her for a date, and she said no.

SPENCER TRACY & KATHARINE HEPBURN

THEIR meeting was the stuff of legends. "I'm afraid I'm a little tall for you, Mr. Tracy," were supposedly Hepburn's first words to Tracy. His reply: "Don't worry, I'll cut you down to size." Even if that exchange has been embellished through the years, the sentiments permeated the nine films they made together. They shared a mutual respect for one another's work, contributed fifty-fifty in the romance department, and were a pair of equally matched heavyweights when it came to sparring in the battle of the sexes. Their off-screen love affair was far more complex, complicated by Tracy's marriage and his drinking problem. But the tenderness and devotion they shared in private came through vividly in all of their films. To rework a line from **Pat and Mike**, "There's a lot of meat to their films, and what there is, is cherce."

SIGNATURE MOVIE

WOMAN OF THE YEAR

M·G·M 1942

SPORTSWRITER Sam Craig (Tracy) is horrified when he hears outspoken political columnist Tess Harding (Hepburn) attack baseball in a radio interview.

Anxious to teach her a lesson, he invites her to a game, and they fall for each other. Sam and Tess elope and quickly discover they have different ideas of marriage. He objects to being neglected while Tess traipses all over the country. Even worse, she adopts a Greek orphan without first discussing it with Sam. On the night Tess is to be named Woman of the Year, Sam walks out on her. At her father's wedding Tess realizes what a flop she's been as a wife and tries to win back Sam.

The Cast

Spencer Tracy
Sam Craig

Katharine Hepburn
Tess Harding

Fay Bainter
Ellen Whitcomb

Reginald Owen
Clayton

Minor Watson
William Harding

William Bendix
Pinkie Peters

Gladys Blake
Flo Peters

Director
George Stevens

Producer
Joseph L. Mankiewicz

Gossip

Hepburn persuaded Louis B. Mayer to purchase the script for $211,000. Her demands included a $100,000 salary plus a ten percent commission as script agent, and her choice of director and leading man.

The original ending, which showed Tess more excited than Sam at a baseball game, was changed. Hepburn detested the existing ending in which Tess makes a mess of breakfast.

Sam: I love you.
Tess: You do?
Sam: Positive.
Tess: That's nice.

Academy

Actress (Hepburn)
* Writing, Original Screenplay (Michael Kanin and Ring Lardner Jr.)

THE BUZZ

This was Hepburn's fourth best actress nomination. She was up for best actress twelve times, an Academy record, and is the only performer to win four acting Oscars.

2 NOMINATIONS 1 OSCAR
*

THEIR OTHER MOVIES

Keeper of the Flame (1942)
Without Love (1945)
Sea of Grass (1947)
State of the Union (1948)
Adam's Rib (1949)
Pat and Mike (1952)
Desk Set (1957)
Guess Who's Coming to Dinner? (1967)

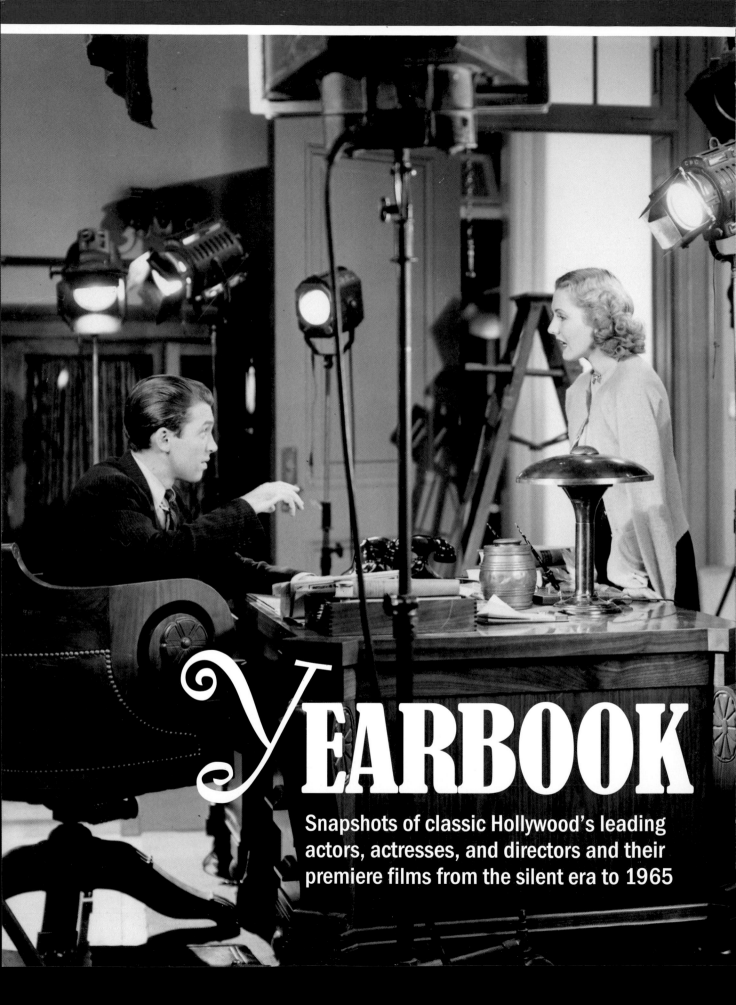

YEARBOOK

Snapshots of classic Hollywood's leading actors, actresses, and directors and their premiere films from the silent era to 1965

CHAPTER 15

Dana Andrews
1909-1992

The Westerner (1940)
Swamp Water (1941)
Ball of Fire (1941)
The Ox-Bow
Incident (1943)
Laura (1944)
State Fair (1945)
A Walk in the Sun (1945)
The Best Years of Our
Lives (1946)
Boomerang (1947)
Where the Sidewalk
Ends (1950)

Fred Astaire
1899-1987

The Gay Divorcee (1934)
Top Hat (1935)
Follow the Fleet (1936)
Swing Time (1936)
Shall We Dance (1937)
Holiday Inn (1942)
Easter Parade (1948)
The Band Wagon (1953)
Funny Face (1957)
Silk Stockings (1957)

John Barrymore
1882-1942

Dr. Jekyll and Mr.
Hyde (1920)
Don Juan (1926)
Svengali (1931)
Arsene Lupin (1932)
Grand Hotel (1932)
Dinner at Eight (1933)
Counsellor-at-Law
(1933)
Twentieth Century (1934)
The Great Man
Votes (1939)
Midnight (1939)

Lionel Barrymore
1878-1954

A Free Soul (1931) *
Grand Hotel (1932)
Dinner at Eight (1933)
Treasure Island (1934)
David Copperfield (1935)
The Little Colonel (1935)
The Devil Doll (1936)
You Can't Take It
With You (1938)
Since You Went
Away (1944)
It's a Wonderful
Life (1946)

Harry Belafonte
1927-

Bright Road (1953)
Carmen Jones (1954)
Island in the Sun (1957)
The World, the Flesh and
the Devil (1959)
Odds Against
Tomorrow (1959)

Humphrey Bogart
1899-1957

High Sierra (1941)
The Maltese
Falcon (1941)
Casablanca (1942) *
To Have and Have
Not (1944)
The Big Sleep (1946)
The Treasure of the Sierra
Madre (1948)
The African
Queen (1951) *
The Caine
Mutiny (1954) *

Charles Boyer
1897-1978

Mayerling (1936)
Algiers (1938) *
Love Affair (1939)
All This and Heaven,
Too (1940)
Back Street (1941)
Hold Back the Dawn (1941)
The Constant
Nymph (1943)
Gaslight (1944) *
Cluny Brown (1946)
The Earrings of
Madame De . . .(1953)

Marlon Brando
1924-

The Men (1950)
A Streetcar Named
Desire (1951) *
Viva Zapata! (1952) *
Julius Caesar (1953) *
The Wild One (1953)
On the
Waterfront (1954) *
Guys and Dolls (1955)
Sayonara (1957)

James Cagney
1899-1986

Public Enemy (1931)
Footlight Parade (1933)
Angels With Dirty
Faces (1938) *
The Roaring
Twenties (1939)
The Strawberry
Blonde (1941)
Yankee Doodle
Dandy (1942) *
White Heat (1949)
Love Me or Leave
Me (1955) *
Mister Roberts (1955)

Montgomery Clift
1920-1966

The Search (1948) *
Red River (1948)
The Heiress (1949) *
A Place in the
Sun (1951) *
From Here to
Eternity (1953) *
Suddenly, Last
Summer (1959)
Wild River (1960)
The Misfits (1960)
Judgment at
Nuremberg (1961) *

Gary Cooper
1901-1961

Mr. Deeds Goes to
Town (1936) *
The Plainsman (1937)
Beau Geste (1939)
The Westerner (1940)
Meet John Doe (1941)
Sergeant York
(1941) *
Ball of Fire (1941)
The Pride of the
Yankees (1942) *
High Noon (1952) *

Joseph Cotten
1905-1995

Citizen Kane (1941)
The Magnificent
Ambersons (1942)
Shadow of a
Doubt (1943)
Gaslight (1944)
Since You Went
Away (1944)
I'll Be Seeing You (1944)
The Farmer's
Daughter (1947)
Portrait of Jennie (1948)
Niagara (1953)

Bing Crosby
1903-1977

Pennies From
Heaven (1936)
Road to Zanzibar (1941)
Holiday Inn (1942)
Road to Morocco (1942)
Going My Way (1944) *
Road to Utopia (1945)
Blue Skies (1946)
A Connecticut Yankee in
King Arthur's
Court (1949)
The Country Girl
(1954) *

Tony Curtis
1925-

Houdini (1953)
Trapeze (1956)
Sweet Smell of
Success (1957)
The Defiant
Ones (1958) *
Some Like It Hot (1959)
The Rat Race (1960)
Spartacus (1960)
The Great
Impostor (1961)
Captain Newman, M.D.
(1964)

James Dean
1931-1955

East of Eden (1955) *
Rebel Without a
Cause (1955)
Giant (1956) *

* OSCARS
* ACADEMY
  AWARD
  NOMINATIONS

Kirk Douglas
1916-

Out of the Past (1947)
A Letter to Three
Wives (1949)
Champion (1949) ✳
The Big Carnival (1951)
The Detective
Story (1951)
The Bad and the
Beautiful (1952) ✳
Lust for Life (1956) ✳
Paths of Glory (1957)
Spartacus (1960)
Lonely Are the
Brave (1963)

W.C. Fields
1879-1946

If I Had a Million (1932)
Tillie and Gus (1933)
You're Telling Me (1934)
The Old-Fashioned
Way (1934)
It's a Gift (1934)
David
Copperfield (1935)
The Man on the Flying
Trapeze (1935)
My Little
Chickadee (1940)
The Bank Dick (1940)

Errol Flynn
1909-1959

Captain Blood (1935)
The Charge of the Light
Brigade (1936)
The Prince and the
Pauper (1937)
The Adventures of Robin
Hood (1938)
The Dawn Patrol (1938)
The Sea Hawk (1940)
They Died With Their
Boots On (1941)
Gentleman Jim (1942)
Objective Burma! (1945)

Henry Fonda
1905-1982

You Only Live Once (1937)
Young Mr.
Lincoln (1939)
The Grapes of
Wrath (1940) ✳
The Lady Eve (1941)
The Ox-Bow
Incident (1943)
My Darling
Clementine (1946)
Mister Roberts (1955)
The Wrong Man (1957)
12 Angry Men (1957)

Glenn Ford
1916-

Gilda (1946)
A Stolen Life (1946)
Lust for Gold (1949)
Convicted (1950)
The Big Heat (1953)
The Blackboard
Jungle (1955)
Interrupted
Melody (1955)
The Fastest Gun
Alive (1956)
3:10 to Yuma (1957)
The Gazebo (1959)

Clark Gable
1901-1960

Red Dust (1932)
It Happened One
Night (1934) ✳
Mutiny on the
Bounty (1935) ✳
Gone with the
Wind (1939) ✳
Strange Cargo (1940)
The Hucksters (1947)
Command
Decision (1948)
Mogambo (1953)
Teacher's Pet (1958)

John Garfield
1913-1952

Four Daughters (1938) ✳
Saturday's Children (1940)
The Sea Wolf (1941)
Pride of the
Marines (1945)
The Postman Always
Rings Twice (1946)
Humoresque (1946)
Body and Soul
(1947) ✳
Gentleman's
Agreement (1947)
The Breaking
Point (1950)

Cary Grant
1904-1986

Topper (1937)
The Awful Truth (1937)
Bringing Up
Baby (1938)
The Philadelphia
Story (1940)
His Girl Friday (1940)
My Favorite Wife (1940)
Notorious (1946)
I Was a Male War
Bride (1949)
North by
Northwest (1959)

Paul Henreid
1908-1992

Goodbye, Mr.
Chips (1939)
Night Train to
Munich (1940)
Joan of Paris (1942)
Now, Voyager (1942)
Casablanca (1942)
Between Two
Worlds (1944)
Of Human
Bondage (1946)
Deception (1946)
Rope of Sand (1949)

William Holden
1918-1981

Golden Boy (1939)
Dear Ruth (1947)
Sunset
Boulevard (1950) ✳
Born Yesterday (1950)
The Moon Is Blue (1953)
Stalag 17 (1953) ✳
Executive Suite (1954)
Sabrina (1954)
The Country Girl (1954)
The Bridge on the River
Kwai (1957) ✳

Bob Hope
1903-2003

The Cat and the
Canary (1939)
The Ghost Breakers (1940)
Road to Zanzibar (1941)
My Favorite Blonde (1942)
Road to Morocco (1942)
They Got Me
Covered (1943)
Road to Utopia (1945)
My Favorite
Brunette (1947)
The Paleface (1948)
The Seven Little
Foys (1955)

Boris Karloff
1887-1969

Frankenstein (1931)
The Mask of Fu Man
Chu (1932)
The Mummy (1932)
The Lost Patrol (1934)
Bride of
Frankenstein (1935)
The Black Room (1935)
Charlie Chan at the
Opera (1936)
The Body
Snatcher (1945)
Bedlam (1946)

Gene Kelly
1912-1996

For Me and My
Gal (1942)
Cover Girl (1944)
Anchors Aweigh
(1945) ✳
The Pirate (1948)
Take Me Out to the Ball
Game (1949)
On the Town (1949)
An American in
Paris (1951)
Singin' in the Rain (1952)
It's Always Fair
Weather (1955)

Alan Ladd
1913-1964

This Gun for Hire (1942)
The Glass Key (1942)
Lucky Jordan (1942)
Salty O'Rourke (1945)
O.S.S. (1946)
The Blue Dahlia (1946)
Two Years Before the
Mast (1946)
Calcutta (1947)
The Great
Gatsby (1949)
Shane (1953)

Burt Lancaster
1913-1994

The Killers (1946)
Sorry, Wrong
Number (1948)
Criss Cross (1949)
From Here to
Eternity (1953) ✳
Sweet Smell of
Success (1957)
Elmer Gantry (1960) ✳
Judgment at
Nuremberg (1961)
Birdman of
Alcatraz (1962) ✳

Jack Lemmon
1925-2002

It Should Happen to
You (1954)
Mister Roberts
(1955) *
Bell, Book and
Candle (1959)
Some Like It
Hot (1959) *
The Apartment
(1960) *
Days of Wine and
Roses (1962) *

Jerry Lewis
1926-

Sailor Beware (1952)
Jumping Jacks (1952)
Living It Up (1954)
You're Never Too
Young (1955)
Artists and Models (1955)
The Delicate
Delinquent (1957)
The Geisha Boy (1958)
The Nutty
Professor (1963)
The Family Jewels (1965)

Fred MacMurray
1908-1991

The Gilded Lily (1935)
Alice Adams (1935)
Hands Across the
Table (1935)
Swing High, Swing
Low (1937)
Remember the
Night (1940)
Double Indemnity (1944)
Murder, He Says (1945)
The Caine Mutiny (1954)
Pushover (1954)
The Apartment (1960)

Fredric March
1897-1975

Dr. Jekyll and
Mr. Hyde (1932) *
Death Takes a
Holiday (1934)
Les Miserables (1935)
Anna Karenina (1935)
A Star Is Born (1937) *
The Adventures of Mark
Twain (1944)
The Best Years of Our
Lives (1946) *
Death of a
Salesman (1951) *
Executive Suite (1954)

The Marx Brothers
Chico *1886-1961*
Groucho *1890-1977*
Harpo *1888-1964*
Zeppo *1901-1979*

The Cocoanuts (1929)
Animal Crackers (1930)
Monkey
Business (1931)
Horse Feathers (1932)
Duck Soup (1933)
A Night at the
Opera (1935)
A Day at the
Races (1937)

Joel McCrea
1905-1990

The Most Dangerous
Game (1932)
These Three (1936)
Dead End (1937)
The Primrose Path (1940)
Foreign
Correspondent (1940)
Sullivan's Travels (1941)
The Palm Beach
Story (1942)
The More the
Merrier (1943)
Ride the High
Country (1962)

Ray Milland
1907-1986

The Gilded Lily (1935)
Easy Living (1937)
Beau Geste (1939)
The Major and the
Minor (1942)
The Uninvited (1944)
Ministry of Fear (1944)
The Lost
Weekend (1945) *
The Big Clock (1948)
Alias Nick Beal (1949)
Dial M for
Murder (1954)

Robert Mitchum
1917-1997

Crossfire (1947)
Out of the Past (1947)
Blood on the
Moon (1948)
The Lusty Men (1952)
Track of the Cat (1954)
Night of the
Hunter (1955)
Heaven Knows Mr.
Allison (1957)
The Sundowners (1960)
Cape Fear (1962)

Laurence Olivier
1907-1989

Wuthering
Heights (1939) *
Rebecca (1940) *
Pride and
Prejudice (1940)
Henry V (1945) *
Hamlet (1948) *
Carrie (1952)
Richard III (1955) *
The Entertainer
(1960) *
Spartacus (1960)

Gregory Peck
1916-2003

Spellbound (1945)
The Yearling (1946) *
Gentleman's
Agreement (1947) *
Twelve O'Clock
High (1949) *
The Gunfighter (1950)
Roman Holiday (1953)
The Guns of
Navarone (1961)
To Kill a
Mockingbird (1962) *
Cape Fear (1962)

Walter Pidgeon
1897-1984

Man Hunt (1941)
Blossoms in the
Dust (1941)
How Green Was My
Valley (1941)
Mrs. Miniver (1942) *
Madame Curie (1943) *
Weekend at the
Waldorf (1945)
The Bad and the
Beautiful (1952)
Executive Suite (1954)
Forbidden Planet (1956)

Sidney Poitier
1924-

No Way Out (1950)
The Blackboard
Jungle (1955)
Something of
Value (1957)
The Defiant
Ones (1958) *
A Raisin in the
Sun (1961)
Lilies of the
Field (1963) *
The Bedford Incident
(1965)
A Patch of Blue (1965)

William Powell
1892-1984

The Thin Man (1934) *
The Great Ziegfeld (1936)
My Man
Godfrey (1936) *
Libeled Lady (1936)
After the Thin
Man (1936)
Love Crazy (1941)
Life With Father
(1947) *
How to Marry a
Millionaire (1953)
Mister Roberts (1955)

Tyrone Power
1913-1958

In Old Chicago (1938)
Alexander's Ragtime
Band (1938)
Jesse James (1939)
The Rains Came (1939)
The Mark of Zorro (1940)
Blood and Sand (1941)
The Razor's Edge (1946)
Nightmare Alley (1947)
The Long Gray
Line (1955)
Witness for the
Prosecution (1957)

Edward G. Robinson
1893-1973

Little Caesar (1930)
Five Star Final (1931)
The Whole Town's
Talking (1935)
A Slight Case of
Murder (1938)
Dr. Ehrlich's Magic
Bullet (1940)
Double Indemnity
(1944)
Woman in the
Window (1944)
Scarlet Street (1945)

* OSCARS
* ACADEMY
  AWARD
  NOMINATIONS

Mickey Rooney
1920-

Love Finds Andy
Hardy (1938)
Boys Town (1938)
Babes on
Broadway (1941)
The Human
Comedy (1943) ✳
Girl Crazy (1943)
National Velvet (1944)
Summer Holiday (1948)
The Strip (1951)
Requiem for a
Heavyweight (1962)

Frank Sinatra
1915-1998

Anchors Aweigh (1945)
On the Town (1949)
From Here to
Eternity (1953) ✳
Guys and Dolls (1955)
The Man With the
Golden Arm (1955) ✳
High Society (1956)
The Joker Is Wild (1957)
Pal Joey (1957)
The Manchurian
Candidate (1962)

James Stewart
1908-1997

Mr. Smith Goes to
Washington (1939) ✳
Destry Rides
Again (1939)
The Philadelphia
Story (1940) ✳
It's a Wonderful
Life (1946) ✳
Harvey (1950) ✳
Rear Window (1954)
The Man Who Knew Too
Much (1956)
Vertigo (1958)

Spencer Tracy
1900-1967

Boys Town (1938) ✳
Dr. Jekyll and Mr.
Hyde (1941)
Woman of the
Year (1942)
Adam's Rib (1949)
Father of the
Bride (1950) ✳
Pat and Mike (1952)
Bad Day at Black
Rock (1954) ✳
Judgment at
Nuremberg (1961) ✳

John Wayne
1907-1979

Stagecoach (1939)
Angel and the
Badman (1947)
Red River (1948)
Three Godfathers (1948)
She Wore a Yellow
Ribbon (1949)
The Quiet Man (1952)
The Searchers (1956)
The Man Who Shot
Liberty Valance (1962) ·
McClintock! (1963)

Jean Arthur
1905-1991

Mr. Deeds Goes to Town (1936)
The Ex-Mrs. Bradford (1936)
Easy Living (1937)
Mr. Smith Goes to Washington (1939)
The Devil and Miss Jones (1941)
Talk of the Town (1942)
The More the Merrier (1943) *
A Foreign Affair (1948)
Shane (1953)

Lauren Bacall
1924-

To Have and Have Not (1944)
The Big Sleep (1946)
Dark Passage (1947)
Key Largo (1948)
How to Marry a Millionaire (1953)
Woman's World (1954)
Written on the Wind (1956)
Designing Woman (1957)

Ingrid Bergman
1915-1982

Dr. Jekyll and Mr. Hyde (1941)
Casablanca (1942)
Gaslight (1944) *
Spellbound (1945)
Bells of St. Mary's (1945) *
Notorious (1946)
Anastasia (1956) *
Inn of the Sixth Happiness (1958)
Indiscreet (1958)

Claudette Colbert
1905-1996

The Smiling Lieutenant (1931)
Cleopatra (1934)
It Happened One Night (1934) *
Imitation of Life (1934)
Drums Along the Mohawk (1939)
Midnight (1939)
The Palm Beach Story (1942)
Since You Went Away (1944) *

Joan Crawford
1904-1977

Grand Hotel (1932)
The Women (1939)
A Woman's Face (1941)
Mildred Pierce (1945) *
Humoresque (1946)
Possessed (1947) *
Flamingo Road (1949)
Harriet Craig (1950)
Sudden Fear (1952) *
Whatever Happened to Baby Jane? (1962)

Dorothy Dandridge
1923-1965

Bright Road (1953)
Carmen Jones (1954) *
Island in the Sun (1957)
The Decks Ran Red (1958)
Porgy and Bess (1959)
Tamango (1959)

Bette Davis
1908-1989

Of Human Bondage (1934)
Jezebel (1938) *
Dark Victory (1939) *
The Letter (1940) *
The Little Foxes (1941) *
Now, Voyager (1942) *
Old Acquaintance (1943)
The Corn Is Green (1945)
All About Eve (1950) *
Whatever Happened to Baby Jane? (1962) *

Doris Day
1924-

Romance on the High Seas (1948)
Calamity Jane (1953)
Love Me or Leave Me (1955)
The Man Who Knew Too Much (1956)
Teacher's Pet (1958)
Pillow Talk (1959) *
Lover Come Back (1961)
That Touch of Mink (1962)
The Thrill of It All (1963)

Olivia de Havilland
1916-

The Adventures of Robin Hood (1938)
Gone with the Wind (1939) *
Hold Back the Dawn (1941) *
To Each His Own (1946) *
The Dark Mirror (1946)
The Snake Pit (1948) *
The Heiress (1949) *
My Cousin Rachel (1952)
Light in the Piazza (1962)

Marlene Dietrich
1901-1992

The Blue Angel (1930)
Shanghai Express (1932)
Blonde Venus (1932)
The Scarlet Empress (1934)
Destry Rides Again (1939)
A Foreign Affair (1948)
Stage Fright (1950)
Witness for the Prosecution (1957)
Judgment at Nuremberg (1961)

Irene Dunne
1898-1990

Roberta (1935)
Show Boat (1936)
Theodora Goes Wild (1936) *
The Awful Truth 1937) *
Love Affair (1939) *
My Favorite Wife (1940)
Penny Serenade (1941)
Anna and the King of Siam (1946)
Life With Father (1947)
I Remember Mama (1948) *

Alice Faye
1912-1998

On the Avenue (1937)
You Can't Have Everything (1937)
Alexander's Ragtime Band (1938)
Rose of Washington Square (1939)
Tin Pan Alley (1940)
That Night in Rio (1941)
Weekend in Havana (1941)
The Gang's All Here (1943)

Joan Fontaine
1917-

A Damsel in Distress (1937)
The Women (1939)
Rebecca (1940) *
Suspicion (1941) *
The Constant Nymph (1943) *
Jane Eyre (1944)
The Affairs of Susan (1945)
Ivy (1947)
Letter From an Unknown Woman (1948)
The Bigamist (1953)

Greta Garbo
1905-1990

Flesh and the Devil (1927)
Love (1927)
Anna Christie (1930) *
Mata Hari (1931)
Grand Hotel (1932)
Queen Christina (1933)
The Painted Veil (1934)
Anna Karenina (1935)
Camille (1937) *
Ninotchka (1939) *

Ava Gardner
1922-1990

The Killers (1946)
The Hucksters (1947)
One Touch of Venus (1948)
Show Boat (1951)
Mogambo (1953) *
Bhowani Junction (1956)
The Sun Also Rises (1957)
On the Beach (1959)
Seven Days in May (1964)
Night of the Iguana (1964)

* OSCARS
* ACADEMY AWARD NOMINATIONS

Judy Garland
1922-1969

The Wizard of Oz (1939)
Ziegfeld Girl (1941)
Meet Me in St. Louis (1944)
The Clock (1945)
The Harvey Girls (1946)
The Pirate (1948)
Easter Parade (1948)
In the Good Old Summertime (1949)
A Star Is Born (1954) ✷
Judgment at Nuremberg (1961) ✷

Greer Garson
1908-1996

Goodbye, Mr. Chips (1939) ✷
Pride and Prejudice (1940)
Blossoms in the Dust (1941) ✷
Mrs. Miniver (1942) ✷
Random Harvest (1942)
Madame Curie (1943) ✷
Mrs. Parkington (1944) ✷
The Valley of Decision (1945) ✷
Julius Caesar (1953)

Paulette Goddard
1911-1990

Modern Times (1936)
The Women (1939)
The Cat and the Canary (1939)
The Ghost Breakers (1940)
The Great Dictator (1940)
Hold Back the Dawn (1941)
So Proudly We Hail (1943) ✷
Kitty (1945)

Jean Harlow
1911-1937

Hell's Angels (1930)
Public Enemy (1931)
Platinum Blonde (1931)
Red-Headed Woman (1932)
Red Dust (1932)
Hold Your Man (1933)
Bombshell (1933)
Dinner at Eight (1933)
Libeled Lady (1936)
Saratoga (1937)

Susan Hayward
1918-1975

Deadline at Dawn (1946)
They Won't Believe Me (1947)
Smash-Up (1947) ✷
My Foolish Heart (1949) ✷
I Can Get It for You Wholesale (1951)
With a Song in My Heart (1952) ✷
I'll Cry Tomorrow (1955) ✷
I Want to Live (1958) ✷

Rita Hayworth
1918-1987

The Strawberry Blonde (1941)
Blood and Sand (1941)
You'll Never Get Rich (1941)
You Were Never Lovelier (1942)
Cover Girl (1944)
Tonight and Every Night (1945)
Gilda (1946)
The Lady From Shanghai (1948)
Pal Joey (1957)

Audrey Hepburn
1929-1993

Roman Holiday (1953) ✷
Sabrina (1954) ✷
Funny Face (1957)
Love in the Afternoon (1957)
The Nun's Story (1959) ✷
Breakfast at Tiffany's (1961) ✷
Charade (1963)
My Fair Lady (1964)

Katharine Hepburn
1907-2003

Stage Door (1937)
Bringing Up Baby (1938)
The Philadelphia Story (1940) ✷
Woman of the Year (1942) ✷
Adam's Rib (1949)
The African Queen (1951) ✷
Pat and Mike (1952)
Summertime (1955) ✷
Long Day's Journey Into Night (1963) ✷

Judy Holliday
1922-1965

Adam's Rib (1949)
Born Yesterday (1950) ✷
The Marrying Kind (1952)
It Should Happen to You (1954)
Phfft (1954)
The Solid Gold Cadillac (1956)
Bells Are Ringing (1960)

Grace Kelly
1928-1982

Fourteen Hours (1951)
High Noon (1952)
Mogambo (1953) ✷
Dial M for Murder (1954)
Rear Window (1954)
The Country Girl (1954) ✷
The Bridges at Toko-Ri (1954)
To Catch a Thief (1955)
The Swan (1956)
High Society (1956)

Veronica Lake
1919-1973

I Wanted Wings (1941)
Sullivan's Travels (1941)
This Gun for Hire (1942)
The Glass Key (1942)
I Married a Witch (1942)
So Proudly We Hail (1943)
Out of This World (1945)
Miss Susie Slagle's (1945)
The Blue Dahlia (1946)
Slattery's Hurricane (1949)

Vivien Leigh
1913-1967

A Yank at Oxford (1937)
Sidewalks of London (1938)
Gone With the Wind (1939) ✷
Waterloo Bridge (1940)
That Hamilton Woman (1941)
Caesar and Cleopatra (1945)
Anna Karenina (1948)
A Streetcar Named Desire (1951) ✷

Carole Lombard
1908-1942

Twentieth Century (1934)
Hands Across the Table (1935)
My Man Godfrey (1936) ✷
Swing High, Swing Low (1937)
Nothing Sacred (1937)
Made for Each Other (1939)
In Name Only (1939)
To Be or Not to Be (1942)

Myrna Loy
1905-1993

Love Me Tonight (1932)
The Thin Man (1934)
Libeled Lady (1936)
After the Thin Man (1936)
The Rains Came (1939)
The Best Years of Our Lives (1946)
The Bachelor and the Bobby-Soxer (1947)
Mr. Blandings Builds His Dream House (1948)
Cheaper by the Dozen (1950)

Dorothy McGuire
1918-2001

Claudia (1943)
A Tree Grows in Brooklyn (1945)
The Enchanted Cottage (1945)
The Spiral Staircase (1947)
Gentleman's Agreement (1947) ✷
Three Coins in the Fountain (1954)
Friendly Persuasion (1956)

Carmen Miranda
1909-1955

Down Argentine
Way (1940)
That Night in Rio (1941)
Weekend in
Havana (1941)
Springtime in the
Rockies (1942)
The Gang's All
Here (1943)
Greenwich Village (1944)
Doll Face (1945)
Copacabana (1947)
A Date With Judy (1948)
Nancy Goes to Rio (1950)

Marilyn Monroe
1926-1962

Don't Bother to
Knock (1952)
Niagara (1953)
Gentlemen Prefer
Blondes (1953)
How to Marry a
Millionaire (1953)
There's No Business Like
Show Business (1954)
The Seven Year Itch (1955)
Bus Stop (1956)
Some Like It Hot (1959)
The Misfits (1960)

Patricia Neal
1926-

John Loves Mary (1949)
The Fountainhead (1949)
The Hasty Heart (1950)
Three Secrets (1950)
The Breaking Point (1950)
The Day the Earth
Stood Still (1951)
A Face in the
Crowd (1957)
Breakfast at
Tiffany's (1961)
Hud (1963) ✱
In Harm's Way (1965)

Margaret O'Brien
1937-

Journey for
Margaret (1942)
The Lost Angel (1943)
The Canterville
Ghost (1944)
Meet Me in St.
Louis (1944)
Music for
Millions (1944)
Our Vines Have Tender
Grapes (1945)
The Unfinished
Dance (1947)

Maureen O'Hara
1920-

The Hunchback of Notre
Dame (1939)
How Green Was My
Valley (1941)
Sentimental
Journey (1946)
Miracle on 34th
Street (1947)
Sitting Pretty (1948)
The Quiet Man (1952)
The Long Gray
Line (1955)
The Parent Trap (1961)

Ginger Rogers
1911-1995

The Gay Divorcee (1934)
Top Hat (1935)
Swing Time (1936)
Stage Door (1937)
Bachelor Mother (1939)
The Primrose Path
(1940)
Kitty Foyle (1940) ✱
Tom, Dick and Harry
(1941)
The Major and the Minor
(1942)

Rosalind Russell
1908-1976

Craig's Wife (1936)
The Citadel (1938)
The Women (1939)
His Girl Friday (1940)
No Time for Comedy
(1940)
My Sister Eileen
(1942) ✱
Roughly Speaking
(1945)
Sister Kenny (1946) ✱
Auntie Mame (1958) ✱
Gypsy (1962)

Norma Shearer
1900-1983

The Trial of Mary Dugan
(1929)
The Divorcee (1930) ✱
Let Us Be Gay (1930)
A Free Soul (1931) ✱
Private Lives (1931)
Smilin' Through (1932)
The Barretts of Wimpole
Street (1934) ✱
Marie Antoinette
(1938) ✱
The Women (1939)
Escape (1940)

Barbara Stanwyck
1907-1990

Baby Face (1933)
Stella Dallas (1937) ✱
Golden Boy (1939)
Remember the
Night (1940)
The Lady Eve (1941)
Ball of Fire (1941) ✱
Lady of Burlesque (1943)
Double Indemnity
(1944) ✱
The Strange Love of
Martha Ivers (1946)
Sorry, Wrong Number
(1948) ✱

Gloria Swanson
1897-1983

Male and Female (1919)
The Affairs of
Anatol (1921)
Zaza (1923)
Madame
Sans-Gene (1925)
Sadie Thompson
(1928) ✱
Queen Kelly (1928)
The Trespasser
(1929) ✱
Sunset
Boulevard (1950) ✱

Elizabeth Taylor
1932-

Lassie Come
Home (1943)
Jane Eyre (1944)
National Velvet (1944)
Life With Father (1947)
Father of the Bride (1950)
A Place in the Sun (1951)
Giant (1956)
Cat on a Hot Tin
Roof (1958) ✱
Suddenly, Last
Summer (1959) ✱

Shirley Temple
1928-

Little Miss
Marker (1934)
Bright Eyes (1934)
The Little Colonel (1935)
Poor Little Rich Girl (1936)
Stowaway (1936)
Wee Willie Winkie (1937)
Heidi (1937)
Rebecca of Sunnybrook
Farm (1938)
The Little
Princess (1939)

Gene Tierney
1920-1991

The Shanghai
Gesture (1941)
Heaven Can Wait (1943)
Laura (1944)
Leave Her to
Heaven (1945) ✱
The Razor's Edge (1946)
The Ghost and Mrs.
Muir (1947)
The Iron Curtain (1948)
Whirlpool (1949)
Night and the City (1950)

Lana Turner
1920-1995

Ziegfeld Girl (1941)
Weekend at the
Waldorf (1945)
The Postman Always
Rings Twice (1946)
Green Dolphin
Street (1947)
Cass Timberlane (1947)
The Bad and the
Beautiful (1952)
Peyton Place (1957) ✱
Imitation of Life (1959)

Mae West
1892-1980

Night After Night (1932)
She Done Him
Wrong (1933)
I'm No Angel (1933)
Belle of the Nineties (1934)
Goin' to Town (1935)
Klondike Annie (1936)
Go West, Young
Man (1936)
Every Day's a
Holiday (1937)
My Little Chickadee (1940)

✱ OSCARS
✱ ACADEMY
  AWARD
  NOMINATIONS

Esther Williams
1923-

A Guy Named Joe (1943)
Bathing Beauty (1944)
Ziegfeld Follies (1945)
Easy to Wed (1946)
On an Island With
You (1948)
Neptune's
Daughter (1949)
Texas Carnival (1951)
Million Dollar
Mermaid (1952)
Dangerous When
Wet (1953)

Shelley Winters
1922-

A Double Life (1947)
A Place in the
Sun (1951) ✳
Phone Call From a
Stranger (1952)
Executive Suite (1954)
Night of the
Hunter (1955)
The Big Knife (1955)
The Diary of Anne
Frank (1959) ✳
A Patch of
Blue (1965) ✳

Natalie Wood
1938-1981

Miracle on 34th
Street (1947)
The Ghost and Mrs.
Muir (1947)
Rebel Without a
Cause (1955) ✳
The Searchers (1956)
Splendor in the
Grass (1961) ✳
West Side Story (1961)
Gypsy (1962)
Love With the Proper
Stranger (1964) ✳

Teresa Wright
1918-

The Little Foxes
(1941) ✳
Mrs. Miniver (1942) ✳
Pride of the
Yankees (1942) ✳
Shadow of a
Doubt (1943)
The Best Years of Our
Lives (1946)
Pursued (1947)
Enchantment (1948)
The Men (1950)
The Actress (1953)
Track of the Cat (1954)

Jane Wyman
1917-

Brother Rat (1938)
The Lost
Weekend (1945)
The Yearling (1946) ✳
Johnny Belinda
(1948) ✳
The Blue Veil (1951) ✳
So Big (1953)
Magnificent
Obsession (1954) ✳
All That Heaven
Allows (1955)
Miracle in the Rain (1956)

Busby Berkeley
1895-1976

Gold Diggers
of 1935 (1935)
They Made Me a
Criminal (1939)
Babes in Arms (1939)
Babes on
Broadway (1941)
For Me and My
Gal (1942)
The Gang's All Here
(1943)
Take Me Out to the Ball
Game (1949)

Frank Capra
1897-1991

Lady for a Day (1933) ✱
It Happened One
Night (1934) ✱
Mr. Deeds Goes
to Town (1936) ✱
Lost Horizon (1937)
You Can't Take It
With You (1938) ✱
Mr. Smith Goes to
Washington (1939) ✱
It's a Wonderful
Life (1946) ✱

Charlie Chaplin
1889-1977

The Kid (1921)
A Woman of
Paris (1923)
The Gold Rush (1925)
The Circus (1928)
City Lights (1931)
Modern Times (1936)
The Great
Dictator (1940)
Monsieur
Verdoux (1947)
Limelight (1952)

George Cukor
1899-1983

Dinner at Eight (1933)
David Copperfield (1935)
Camille (1937)
The Women (1939)
The Philadelphia
Story (1940) ✱
Gaslight (1944)
Adam's Rib (1949)
Born Yesterday
(1950) ✱
Pat and Mike (1952)
My Fair Lady (1964) ✱

Michael Curtiz
1886-1962

Captain Blood
(1935) ✱
The Adventures of
Robin Hood (1938)
Four Daughters
(1938) ✱
Angels With Dirty
Faces (1938) ✱
Yankee Doodle
Dandy (1942) ✱
Casablanca (1942) ✱
Mildred Pierce (1945)
Life With Father (1947)

Stanley Donen
1924-

On the Town (1949)
Royal Wedding (1951)
Singin' in the Rain (1952)
Seven Brides for Seven
Brothers (1954)
It's Always Fair
Weather (1955)
Funny Face (1957)
The Pajama Game (1957)
Indiscreet (1958)
Damn Yankees (1958)
Charade (1963)

John Ford
1894-1973

Stagecoach (1939) ✱
The Grapes of
Wrath (1940) ✱
How Green Was My
Valley (1941) ✱
My Darling
Clementine (1946)
The Quiet
Man (1952) ✱
Mister Roberts (1955)
The Searchers (1956)
The Man Who Shot
Liberty Valance (1962)

Howard Hawks
1896-1977

Scarface (1932)
Bringing Up Baby (1938)
His Girl Friday (1940)
Ball of Fire (1941)
To Have and Have
Not (1944)
The Big Sleep (1946)
Red River (1948)
I Was a Male War
Bride (1949)
The Thing (1951)
Gentlemen Prefer
Blondes (1953)

Alfred Hitchcock
1899-1980

The 39 Steps (1935)
The Lady
Vanishes (1938)
Shadow of a
Doubt (1943)
Notorious (1946)
Strangers on a
Train (1951)
Rear Window (1954) ✱
Vertigo (1958)
North by
Northwest (1959)
Psycho (1960) ✱
The Birds (1963)

Elia Kazan
1909-2003

A Tree Grows in
Brooklyn (1945)
Gentleman's
Agreement (1947) ✱
A Streetcar Named
Desire (1951) ✱
On the
Waterfront (1954) ✱
East of Eden (1955) ✱
A Face in the
Crowd (1957)
Splendor in the
Grass (1961)

Stanley Kubrick
1928-1999

Killer's Kiss (1955)
The Killing (1956)
Paths of Glory (1957)
Spartacus (1960)
Dr. Strangelove, or
How I Learned to Stop
Worrying and Love the
Bomb (1964) ✱

Joseph L. Mankiewicz
1909-1993

The Late George
Apley (1947)
The Ghost and Mrs.
Muir (1947)
A Letter to Three
Wives (1949) ✱
House of
Strangers (1949)
No Way Out (1950)
All About Eve (1950) ✱
Five Fingers (1952) ✱
Suddenly, Last
Summer (1959)

Vincente Minnelli
1903-1986

Cabin in the Sky (1943)
Meet Me in St.
Louis (1944)
The Clock (1945)
The Pirate (1948)
Father of the
Bride (1950)
An American in
Paris (1951) ✱
The Bad and the
Beautiful (1952)
The Band Wagon (1953)

Otto Preminger
1905-1986

Laura (1944) ✱
Where the Sidewalk
Ends (1950)
Carmen Jones (1954)
The Man With the Golden
Arm (1955)
The Court-Martial of Billy
Mitchell (1956)
Bonjour Tristesse (1958)
Anatomy of a
Murder (1959) ✱
Advise and
Consent (1962)

George Stevens
1904-1975

Alice Adams (1935)
Swing Time (1936)
Gunga Din (1939)
Woman of the
Year (1942)
The More the
Merrier (1943) ✱
I Remember
Mama (1948)
A Place in the
Sun (1951) ✱
Shane (1953) ✱

Preston Sturges
1898-1959

The Great
McGinty (1940)
Christmas in July (1940)
The Lady Eve (1941)
Sullivan's Travels (1941)
The Palm Beach
Story (1942)
The Miracle of
Morgan's Creek (1944)
Hail the Conquering
Hero (1944)
Unfaithfully Yours (1948)

Orson Welles
1915-1985

Citizen Kane (1941) ✱
It's All True (1942)
The Magnificent
Ambersons (1942)
The Stranger (1946)
The Lady From
Shanghai (1948)
Macbeth (1948)
Othello (1952)
Mr. Arkadin (1955)
Touch of Evil (1958)
The Trial (1962)

Billy Wilder
1906-2002

Double Indemnity
(1944) ✱
The Lost
Weekend (1945) ✱
Sunset Boulevard
(1950) ✱
Stalag 17 (1953)
Sabrina (1954) ✱
Witness for the
Prosecution (1957) ✱
Some Like It Hot (1959) ✱
The Apartment
(1960) ✱

Robert Wise
1914-

The Body Snatcher (1945)
The Set-Up (1949)
The Day the Earth
Stood Still (1951)
Executive Suite (1954)
Somebody Up There
Likes Me (1956)
I Want to Live (1958) ✱
West Side
Story (1961) ✱
The Haunting (1963)
The Sound of
Music (1965) ✱

William Wyler
1902-1981

These Three (1936)
Dodsworth (1936) ✱
Wuthering Heights
(1939) ✱
The Letter (1940) ✱
The Little Foxes
(1941) ✱
Mrs. Miniver (1942) ✱
The Best Years of Our
Lives (1946) ✱
The Heiress (1949) ✱
Roman Holiday
(1953) ✱
Ben-Hur (1959) ✱

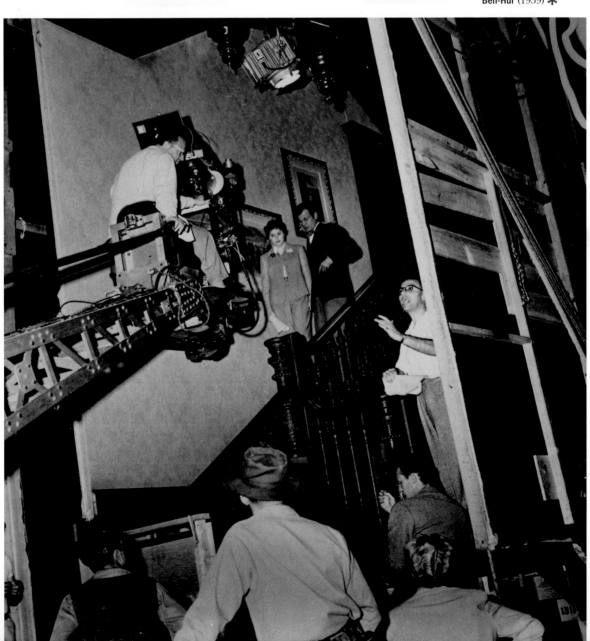

COVER

Cecil Kellaway, l., John Garfield, and Lana Turner in **The Postman Always Rings Twice**

p. 1: Joel McCrea in **Sullivan's Travels**

p. 2-3: George Sanders and Anne Baxter in **All About Eve**

p. 5: Clark Gable and Vivien Leigh in **Gone With the Wind**

p. 6-7: Barbara Stanwyck and Fred MacMurray in **Double Indemnity**

p. 8-9: Esther Williams

p. 10-11: (l. to r.) Tony Curtis (in wig on saxophone), Jack Lemmon (in wig on bass), Marilyn Monroe, c., in **Some Like It Hot**

MUST SEE

p. 12-13: (l. to r.) Paul Henreid, Ingrid Bergman, Claude Rains, and Humphrey Bogart in **Casablanca**

p. 14-15: Orson Welles in **Citizen Kane**

ALL ABOUT EVE

left: (l. to r.) Anne Baxter and Bette Davis, and George Sanders; **middle, left**: (l. to r.) Baxter, Davis, Marilyn Monroe, and Sanders; **middle, right**: Monroe; **right, top**: Baxter, l., and Davis; **right, bottom**: (l. to r.) Gary Merrill, Davis, Celeste Holm, and Hugh Marlowe

CASABLANCA

left: Humphrey Bogart and Ingrid Bergman; **middle, top**: Dooley Wilson (at piano); **middle, bottom**: (l. to r.) Claude Rains (in dark uniform), Paul Henreid, Bogart, and Bergman

CITIZEN KANE

left, bottom: (l. to r.) Joseph Cotten, Orson Welles, and Everett Sloane; **left, center**: Welles; **middle, top**: Dorothy Comingore and Welles; **right, bottom**: (l. to r.) Harry Shannon, George Coulouris, Buddy Swan, and Agnes Moorehead

DOUBLE INDEMNITY

left: (l. to r.) Barbara Stanwyck, Fred MacMurray, and Edward G. Robinson; **right, bottom**: Stanwyck and MacMurray

GONE WITH THE WIND

left: Vivien Leigh and Clark Gable; **middle, top**: Gable and Leigh; **middle, bottom**: Hattie McDaniel and Gable; **right, top**: (l. to r.) Leslie Howard, Leigh, and Olivia de Havilland; **right, bottom**: Howard and Leigh

ON THE WATERFRONT

left: Rod Steiger, l., and Marlon Brando; **right, bottom**: (l. to r.) Karl Malden, Brando, and Eva Marie Saint

THE PHILADELPHIA STORY

left: (l. to r.) James Stewart, Cary Grant, and Katharine Hepburn, and Ruth Hussey; **middle, top**: Hepburn and Grant; **middle, bottom**: Hepburn and Stewart

SOME LIKE IT HOT

left: Tony Curtis (in tub) and Marilyn Monroe; **middle, top**: Curtis, l., and Jack Lemmon; **middle, bottom left**: Lemmon and Joe E. Brown; **middle, bottom right**: Monroe and Curtis; **right**: Curtis, l., and Lemmon

SUNSET BOULEVARD

left: William Holden and Gloria Swanson; **right, top and bottom**: Swanson

THE WIZARD OF OZ

left: Judy Garland and Toto; **middle, bottom left**: Frank Morgan; **middle, bottom right**: Margaret Hamilton; **right bottom**: Billie Burke, l., and Garland

DRAMA

p. 36-7: (l. to r.) Russell Simpson, Jane Darwell, and Henry Fonda in **The Grapes of Wrath**

p. 38-9: Montgomery Clift and Elizabeth Taylor in **A Place in the Sun**

THE BEST YEARS OF OUR LIVES

left: (clockwise from top) Dana Andrews, Fredric March, and Harold Russell; **middle, bottom**: Russell; **right, bottom**: Myrna Loy, l., and Teresa Wright

EAST OF EDEN

left: James Dean, l., and Albert Dekker; **middle, top**: (l. to r.) Dean, Richard Davalos, and Julie Harris; **middle, bottom**: Dean and Harris; **right, top**: (l. to r.) Davalos, Dean, and Harris; **right, bottom**: Dean, l., and Raymond Massey

A FACE IN THE CROWD

left: Patricia Neal and Andy Griffith; **middle, top**: Griffith; **middle, bottom**: Griffith and Neal; **right, bottom**: Griffith (with guitar) and Neal

FROM HERE TO ETERNITY

left, top: Burt Lancaster and Deborah Kerr; **left, bottom**: Montgomery Clift; **right, bottom**: (l. to r.) Frank Sinatra, Clift, and Lancaster

GENTLEMAN'S AGREEMENT

left: (l. to r.) John Garfield, Gregory Peck, Dorothy McGuire, and Celeste Holm

GRAND HOTEL

left: Greta Garbo and John Barrymore

THE GRAPES OF WRATH

left: Jane Darwell and Henry Fonda; **right**: (l. to r.) Eddie Quillan, Dorris Bowdon, Fonda, Darwell, Russell Simpson, Frank Darien, O. Z. Whitehead, and John Carradine

THE LOST WEEKEND

left: Ray Milland and Jane Wyman; **middle**: Milland: **right, bottom**: Milland, l., and Howard Da Silva

MR. SMITH GOES TO WASHINGTON

left: James Stewart; **right, top**: Stewart and Jean Arthur; **right, bottom**: Claude Rains (seated) and Stewart

A PLACE IN THE SUN

left: Elizabeth Taylor and Montgomery Clift; **right, bottom**: Clift (in boat) and Raymond Burr (standing r.)

SUSPENSE

p. 60-1: (l. to r.) Leopoldine Konstantin, Ingrid Bergman, and Claude Rains in **Notorious**

p. 62: Dana Andrews and Gene Tierney in **Laura**

NOTORIOUS

top: Ingrid Bergman; **bottom**: Claude Rains

GASLIGHT

left: Charles Boyer and Ingrid Bergman

LAURA

left: Dana Andrews; **middle, bottom**: Vincent Price; **right, top**: Clifton Webb; **right, middle**: Andrews and Price; **right, bottom**: Gene Tierney and Andrews

REAR WINDOW

left: Grace Kelly and James Stewart: **middle, left**: Raymond Burr; **middle, right**: Alfred Hitchcock; **right, bottom**: Thelma Ritter and James Stewart

WITNESS FOR THE PROSECUTION

left: Tyrone Power and Marlene Dietrich; **right, top**: Elsa Lanchester (in nurse's cap) and Charles Laughton; **right, bottom**: Dietrich and Laughton

FILM NOIR

p. 72-3: Joseph Calleia (kneeling), George Macready (lying on floor), Steven Geray (behind bar), Glenn Ford, and Rita Hayworth (standing rear) in **Gilda**

p. 74: Burt Lancaster and Ava Gardner in **The Killers**.

GILDA

left: Glenn Ford, l., and George Macready; **middle**: Rita Hayworth; **right**: Hayworth and Ford

THE KILLERS

left: Ava Gardner and Burt Lancaster; **middle**: (l. to r.) Garry Owen (kneeling), Lancaster, and Charles D. Brown; **right, top**: Lancaster and Albert Dekker (hands raised); **right, bottom**: Gardner

OUT OF THE PAST

left: Robert Mitchum and Jane Greer; **right**: (l. to r.) Paul Valentine, Kirk Douglas, and Mitchum

THE POSTMAN ALWAYS RINGS TWICE

left: John Garfield and Lana Turner; **right, top**: Turner and Cecil Kellaway; **right, bottom**: Garfield, Turner, and Alan Reed

THE THIRD MAN

left: Orson Welles; **right**: Alida Valli, l., and Joseph Cotten, r.

GOOD GUYS & BAD GUYS

p. 84-5: Tony Curtis, l., and Sidney Poitier in **The Defiant Ones**

p. 86: Lew Ayres in **All Quiet on the Western Front**

PATHS OF GLORY

left and middle: Kirk Douglas

THE ADVENTURES OF ROBIN HOOD

left: Errol Flynn; **middle, bottom**: (l. to r.) Olivia de Havilland, Ian Hunter, and Flynn (kneeling); **right, top**: (l. to r.) Claude Rains, Basil Rathbone, and Melville Cooper; **right, bottom**: Rathbone, l., and Flynn

ALL QUIET ON THE WESTERN FRONT

left: Lew Ayres, l., and Louis Wolheim; **right, top**: Ayres and Ben Alexander; **right, center**: Ayres; **right, bottom**: Ayres, c., and William Bakewell, r.

THE DEFIANT ONES

left: Sidney Poitier, l., and Tony Curtis

WHITE HEAT

left and middle: James Cagney; **right, bottom**: Cagney and Margaret Wycherley

COMEDY

p. 96-7: Mae West and W. C. Fields in **My Little Chickadee**

p. 98-9: Carole Lombard and William Powell in **My Man Godfrey**

BORN YESTERDAY

left and right, top: William Holden and Judy Holliday; **right, bottom**: Broderick Crawford and Judy Holliday

BRINGING UP BABY

left: Cary Grant and Katharine Hepburn; **middle, top and bottom**: Grant and Hepburn; **middle, bottom**: Hepburn and Baby

DINNER AT EIGHT

left: Jean Harlow

DUCK SOUP

left bottom: Chico Marx; **left center**: (in front) Zeppo Marx, l., and Groucho Marx; **middle, bottom**: Margaret Dumont and Groucho; **right, bottom**: Groucho and dancing girls

HARVEY

left: James Stewart and Josephine Hull; **middle**: Hull: **right, top and bottom**: Stewart: **right, center**: Stewart and Dick Wessel

HIS GIRL FRIDAY

left: Rosalind Russell and Cary Grant; **middle, top**: (l. to r.) Porter Hall, Ernest Truex, Roscoe Karns, Russell, Regis Toomey, and Cliff Edwards; **middle, bottom**: Russell, Grant, Billy Gilbert, and Clarence Kolb; **right, bottom left**: John Qualen and Russell; **right, bottom right**: Russell

IT HAPPENED ONE NIGHT

left: Claudette Colbert and Clark Gable; **right**: Gable and Colbert

MY LITTLE CHICKADEE

left, top: (l. to r.) Mae West, W. C. Fields, and George Moran; **left, bottom**: Joseph Calleia and West; **middle, bottom**: Margaret Hamilton and Fields; **right**: West

MY MAN GODFREY

left: Carole Lombard and William Powell; **middle, bottom left**: (l. to r.) Gail Patrick, Alice Brady, Lombard, and Powell; **middle, bottom right**: (l. to r.) Powell, Eugene Pallette, and Jean Dixon; **right, bottom**: Powell and Brady

SULLIVAN'S TRAVELS

left: Joel McCrea and Veronica Lake; **middle**: Lake; **right, top**: McCrea (standing); **right, bottom**: McCrea and Lake

ROMANCE

p. 120-1: Audrey Hepburn and William Holden in **Sabrina**

p. 122: Bette Davis and Paul Henreid in **Now, Voyager**

LOVE AFFAIR
left: Irene Dunne and Charles Boyer; right: Dunne, l., and Maria Ouspenskaya

NOW, VOYAGER
left: Paul Henreid and Bette Davis; middle, top: Janis Wilson and Davis; middle, bottom: Davis and Claude Rains; right, top: (l. to r.) Henreid, Davis, and John Loder; right, bottom: Davis and Gladys Cooper

PRIDE AND PREJUDICE
left: (l. to r.) Bruce Lester, Greer Garson, Frieda Inescort, and Laurence Olivier; middle: Garson and Olivier; right, top: (top row) Marsha Hunt, l., and Heather Angel, (bottom row, l. to r.), Ann Rutherford, Garson, and Maureen O'Sullivan; right, bottom: Mary Boland and Edmund Gwenn

SABRINA
left: William Holden and Audrey Hepburn; middle, bottom: Hepburn and Humphrey Bogart

WUTHERING HEIGHTS
left: Laurence Olivier and Merle Oberon; right, bottom: (l. to r.) David Niven, Donald Crisp, Olivier, and Flora Robson, and Oberon

TEARJERKERS

p. 132-3: Roddy McDowall, l., and Walter Pidgeon in How Green Was My Valley

p. 134: Henry Travers, l., and James Stewart in It's a Wonderful Life

STELLA DALLAS
top: Barbara Stanwyck and Anne Shirley; bottom: John Boles and Stanwyck

GOODBYE, MR. CHIPS
left: Robert Donat (seated); middle, bottom left: Terry Kilburn; middle, bottom right: Greer Garson and Donat

HOW GREEN WAS MY VALLEY
left: (l. to r.) Donald Crisp, Roddy McDowall, and Sara Allgood; middle: (l. to r.) Walter Pidgeon, Crisp, and McDowall; right: Maureen O'Hara

IT'S A WONDERFUL LIFE
left: James Stewart and Donna Reed; middle, top: Henry Travers, l., and Stewart; middle, bottom: (l. to r.): Thomas Mitchell, Donna Reed, James Stewart, and Beulah Bondi; right: (l. to r.): Stewart, Mitchell (in glasses), and Lionel Barrymore (far r.)

A TREE GROWS IN BROOKLYN
left: Peggy Ann Garner and James Dunn; middle, top: Dorothy McGuire; middle, bottom: (l. to r.) McGuire, Ted Donaldson, Garner, and Dunn; right, top: Joan Blondell; right, bottom: Dunn and Garner

DAMSELS & DAMES

p. 144-5: (l. to r.) Jack Carson, Joan Crawford, and Ann Blyth in Mildred Pierce

p. 146: Dennie Moore, l., and Rosalind Russell in The Women

STAGE DOOR
left: (l. to r.); Gail Patrick, (brunette, seated), Constance Collier, Lucille Ball, Ginger Rogers, and Katharine Hepburn; middle: (l. to r.) Hepburn; right: Rogers

I'LL CRY TOMORROW
left: Susan Hayward; middle, top: Eddie Albert and Hayward; middle, bottom: Richard Conte and Hayward; right: Hayward

LOVE ME OR LEAVE ME
left: Doris Day and James Cagney; middle: Day; right, bottom: Day and Cagney

MILDRED PIERCE
left: Joan Crawford and Ann Blyth, and, in circle, Eve Arden; middle: Crawford; right: (l. to r.): Blyth, Zachary Scott, and Crawford

THE WOMEN
left: (l. to r.) Norma Shearer, Joan Fontaine, Rosalind Russell, Paulette Goddard, and Mary Boland; right, bottom: Virginia Weidler, l., and Crawford

ONE OF A KIND

p. 156-7: Carmen Miranda (sitting in wagon) and chorus girls in The Gang's All Here

p. 159: Charlie Chaplin (holding thermos) in Modern Times

CHARLIE CHAPLIN
left: Chaplin as the Little Tramp; right: Chaplin in Modern Times

JERRY LEWIS
left: Lewis; right, top: Lewis, l., and Robert Hirano in The Geisha Boy; right, bottom: Lewis and Harry the rabbit

CARMEN MIRANDA
left: Miranda, and chorus girls from The Gang's All Here; middle: (l. to r.) Charlotte Greenwood, Edward Everett Horton, and Miranda; right: Miranda and Horton

SHIRLEY TEMPLE
left and middle: Temple; right, top: Marcia Mae Jones (seated) and Temple in Heidi; right, bottom: Jean Hersholt and Temple

ESTHER WILLIAMS
left: Williams, and (l. to r.) Victor Mature, Williams, and Jesse White in Million Dollar Mermaid; right, top: Williams (suspended in air) and swimmers

MUSICALS

p. 170-1: Chorus boys and girls in 42nd Street

p. 172: Vera-Ellen and Gene Kelly in On the Town

42ND STREET
left, top: Ruby Keeler and Edward J. Nugent; left, bottom: (l. to r.) Ginger Rogers (in suspenders), Keeler, and Una Merkel; right, top: (l. to r.) Bebe Daniels, George Brent, Ruby Keeler, Warner Baxter, and Robert McWade

CARMEN JONES
left and middle: Dorothy Dandridge and Harry Belafonte; right, top: Dandridge, top; right, bottom: Pearl Bailey

MEET ME IN ST. LOUIS
left, top: Margaret O'Brien and Judy Garland; left, bottom: (l. to r.) Garland, Lucille Bremer, and Tom Drake; right, top: O'Brien and Garland; right, bottom: Bremer and Garland

ON THE TOWN
left, top and bottom: (l. to r.): Frank Sinatra, Betty Garrett, Jules Munshin, Ann Miller, Gene Kelly, and Vera-Ellen; right top: (l. to r.): Sinatra, Munshin, and Kelly (in front of ship); right, center: (l. to r.): Kelly, Sinatra, and Munshin; right, bottom: (l. to r.): Sinatra, Munshin, and Kelly

SINGIN' IN THE RAIN
left: (l. to r.) Donald O'Connor, Debbie Reynolds, King Donovan, Gene Kelly, and Jean Hagen; right, top: Kelly and Cyd Charisse; right, center and bottom: Kelly

WESTERNS

p. 182-3: Alan Ladd and Brandon de Wilde in Shane

p. 184: John Wayne in The Searchers

THE SEARCHERS
left, top: Vera Miles; left, bottom: Natalie Wood; right, top: John Wayne, l., and Jeffrey Hunter

HIGH NOON
left, bottom: Gary Cooper; left, top: Lloyd Bridges; middle, top: Grace Kelly; middle, bottom: Katy Jurado; right: Cooper

THE OX-BOW INCIDENT
left: Frank Conroy (in military uniform) and (l. to r.) prisoners Dana Andrews, Francis Ford (white hair), and Anthony Quinn; middle, bottom: Henry Fonda, l., and Harry Morgan; right: Jane Darwell

SHANE
left: Alan Ladd, l., and Brandon de Wilde; middle: de Wilde and his dog; right, top: (l. to r.) Ladd, Van Heflin, Jean Arthur, and de Wilde

STAGECOACH
left: (l. to r.) George Bancroft, John Wayne, and Louise Platt, and Claire Trevor; middle, left: Wayne; middle, right: Trevor and Wayne; right, top: (l. to r.) Trevor, Wayne, Andy Devine, John Carradine, Platt, Thomas Mitchell, Berton Churchill, Donald Meek, and Bancroft

SCI-FI & HORROR

p. 194-5: (l. to r.) Walter Pidgeon (screaming), Leslie Nielsen, and Anne Francis in Forbidden Planet

p. 196: Boris Karloff in Frankenstein

FORBIDDEN PLANET
top: (l. to r.) Jack Kelly, Earl Holliman, Warren Stevens, and Leslie Nielsen; left, bottom: Nielsen and Anne Francis; middle, bottom; Walter Pidgeon; right, bottom: Francis

THE DAY THE EARTH STOOD STILL
left, bottom: Patricia Neal and Michael Rennie; middle: Lock Martin, Neal, and Rennie; right: Rennie and Neal

FRANKENSTEIN
left: Boris Karloff; middle, top: Colin Clive; middle, bottom: Karloff and Marilyn Harris; right: Clive and Karloff

THE INVISIBLE MAN
left: E. E. Clive (in uniform) and Claude Rains (in bandages); middle, top: Rains and Gloria Stuart; middle, bottom: Rains, Una O'Connor, and Merle Tottenham (on stairs); right: Rains

KING KONG
left: Kong atop the Empire State Building; right, top: Fay Wray and Bruce Cabot; right, bottom: (l. to r.) Cabot, Wray, Robert Armstrong, and Kong

SCREEN TEAMS

p. 206-7: Spencer Tracy and Katharine Hepburn

p. 208-9: Mickey Rooney and Judy Garland

FRED ASTAIRE & GINGER ROGERS
left and right: Rogers and Astaire in Swing Time

HUMPHREY BOGART & LAUREN BACALL
left and middle, bottom: Bacall and Bogart in To Have and Have Not; right, top: Stephen Bogart with his parents and family dogs, (c) 1978 Sid Avery/MPTV; right, bottom: Bogart and Bacall

BOB HOPE & BING CROSBY
left: Crosby and Hope; middle, top: Hope and Crosby in Road to Morocco; right, bottom: Hope and Crosby in Road to Bali; right, top: (l. to r.) Dorothy Lamour, Crosby, Hope, and Dona Drake in Road to Morocco

WILLIAM POWELL & MYRNA LOY
left, top: Powell and Loy; left, bottom: Powell and Loy with Skippy (aka Asta); right, top: Loy and Powell at Grauman's Chinese Theater; right, bottom: Loy and Powell in The Thin Man

MICKEY ROONEY & JUDY GARLAND
left: Rooney and Garland; right, top and bottom: Garland and Rooney in Babes on Broadway

SPENCER TRACY & KATHARINE HEPBURN
left: Tracy and Hepburn; right, top and bottom: Tracy and Hepburn in Woman of the Year

YEARBOOK

p. 222-3: (l. to r.) Jimmy Stewart, Jean Arthur, and Frank Capra shooting Mr. Smith Goes to Washington
p. 227: bottom: Harpo Marx and Shirley Temple
p. 231: bottom: Marlene Dietrich in Witness for the Prosecution
p. 233: bottom: Ingrid Bergman and Joseph Cotten on the set of Gaslight

p. 234-5: Alfred Hitchcock shooting Rear Window
p. 239: Tony Curtis and Marilyn Monroe (in boat); Billy Wilder (on raft) shooting Some Like It Hot
p. 240: Charlie Chaplin and Paulette Goddard in Modern Times

Bacall, Lauren. *By Myself.* New York: Alfred A. Knopf, 1979.

Bergman, Ingrid and Alan Burgess. *Ingrid Bergman: My Story.* New York: Delacorte Press, 1980.

Bubbeo, Daniel. *The Women of Warner Brothers.* Jefferson, N.C.: McFarland, 2002.

Buford, Kate. *Burt Lancaster: An American Life.* New York: Alfred A. Knopf, 2000.

Cagney, James. *Cagney by Cagney.* New York: Doubleday, 1976.

Capra, Frank. *The Name Above the Title.* New York: MacMillan, 1971.

Crowe, Cameron. *Conversations With Wilder.* New York: Alfred A. Knopf, 1999.

Curtis, Tony with Barry Paris. *Tony Curtis: An Autobiography.* New York: Arrow, 1994.

Dickens, Homer. *The Films of Katharine Hepburn.* Secaucus, N.J.: Citadel Press, 1971.

Douglas, Kirk. *The Ragman's Son.* New York: Simon & Schuster, 1988.

Edwards, Anne. *Shirley Temple: America's Princess.* New York: William Morrow & Co., 1988.

Fields, Ronald. *W.C. Fields by Himself.* Englefield, N.J.: Prentice-Hall, 1973.

Eells, George and Stanley Musgrove. *Mae West.* New York: William Morrow & Co., 1982.

Gardner, Ava. *Ava: My Story.* New York: Bantam, 1990.

Garrett, Betty with Ron Rapoport. *Betty Garrett and Other Songs.* Lanham, Md.: Madison Books, 1998.

The Girl in the Hairy Paw. Edited by Ronald Gottesman and Harry Geduld. New York: Avon, 1976.

Guilaroff, Sydney with Cathy Griffin. *Crowning Achievement.* New York: General Publishing, 1996.

Harris, Warren G. *Audrey Hepburn.* New York: Simon & Schuster, 1994.

Higham, Charles. *Lucy: The Real Life of Lucille Ball.* New York: St. Martin's Press, 1986.

Higham, Charles and Roy Moseley. *Cary Grant: The Lonely Heart.* San Diego: Harcourt Brace Jovanovich, 1989.

Hirschhorn, Clive. *Gene Kelly.* Chicago: Henry Regnery Co., 1974.

Hollywood Album: Lives and Deaths of Hollywood Stars From the Pages of The New York Times. New York: Arno, 1979.

Hotchner, A.E. *Doris Day: Her Own Story.* New York: William Morrow & Co., 1975.

Huston, John. *An Open Book.* New York: Alfred A. Knopf, 1980.

Kaminsky, Stuart. *John Huston: Maker of Magic.* Boston: Houghton Mifflin, 1978.

Kanfer, Stefan. *Groucho: The Life and Times of Julius Henry Marx.* New York: Alfred A. Knopf, 2000.

Katz, Ephraim, revised by Fred Klein and Ronald Dean Nolen. *The Film Encyclopedia,* fourth edition. New York: HarperResource, 2001.

Lasky, Betty. *RKO: The Biggest Little Major of Them All,* second edition. Santa Monica, Calif.: Roundtable Publishing, 1989.

Lenburg, Jeff. *Peekaboo: The Story of Veronica Lake.* New York: St. Martin's Press, 1983.

Linet, Beverly. *Ladd: The Life, the Legend, the Legacy of Alan Ladd.* New York: Arbor House, 1979.

Linet, Beverly. *Susan Hayward: Portrait of a Survivor.* New York: Atheneum, 1980.

Louvish, Simon. *Man on the Flying Trapeze: The Life and Times of W.C. Fields.* New York: W.W. Norton & Co., 1997.

Maltin, Leonard. *Pyramid Illustrated History of the Movies: Carole Lombard.* New York: Pyramid Books, 1976.

McCabe, John. *Cagney.* New York: Alfred A. Knopf, 1997.

McGilligan, Patrick. *Alfred Hitchcock: A Life in Darkness and Light.* New York: HarperCollins, 2003.

Morella, Joe and Edward Epstein. *Judy: The Films and Career of Judy Garland.* Secaucus, N.J.: Citadel, 1969.

Moshier, W. Franklin. *The Alice Faye Movie Book.* New York: A&W Visual Library, 1974.

The Movie Buff's Book. Edited by Ted Sennett. New York: Pyramid Books, 1975.

Paris, Barry. *Garbo.* New York: Alfred A. Knopf, 1995.

Rogers, Ginger. *Ginger: My Story.* New York: HarperCollins, 1991.

Russell, Rosalind and Chris Chase. *Life Is a Banquet.* New York: Random House, 1977.

Shipman, David. *The Great Movie Stars: The Golden Years.* New York: Bonanza Books, 1970.

Spoto, Donald. *Laurence Olivier: A Biography.* New York: Harper Collins, 1992.

Stagg, Sam. *All About All About Eve.* New York: St. Martin's Press, 2000.

Stenn, David. *Bombshell: The Life and Death of Jean Harlow.* New York: Doubleday, 1993.

Stern, Lee Edward. *Pyramid Illustrated History of the Movies: The Movie Musical.* New York: Pyramid Books, 1974.

Swenson, Karen. *Greta Garbo: A Life Apart.* New York: Scribner, 1997.

Swindell, Larry. *Charles Boyer: The Reluctant Lover.* Garden City, N.Y.: Doubleday, 1983.

Temple, Shirley. *Child Star.* New York: McGraw-Hill, 1988.

Thomas, Bob. *Marlon: Portrait of the Rebel as an Artist.* New York: Random House, 1973.

Thomas, Tony and Jim Terry with Busby Berkeley. *The Busby Berkeley Book.* New York: Little Brown & Co., 1973.

Troyan, Michael. *A Rose for Mrs. Miniver: The Life of Greer Garson.* Lexington, Ky.: The University Press of Kentucky, 1999.

Turner, Lana. *Lana: The Lady, the Legend, the Truth.* New York: E.F. Dutton, 1982.

Vance, Jeffrey. *Chaplin: Genius of the Cinema.* New York: Abrams, 2003.

Wiley, Mason and Damien Bona. *Inside Oscar.* New York: Ballantine, 1986.

Williams, Esther with Digby Diehl. *The Million Dollar Mermaid.* New York: Simon & Schuster, 1999.

Young, Jeff. *Kazan: The Master Director Discusses His Films.* New York: Newmarket, 1999.

Zinman, David. *Fifty Classic Motion Pictures.* New York: Bonanza Books, 1970.

FROM THE START of this project I was blessed with the help of editor and fellow film addict Daniel Bubbeo, whose encyclopedic knowledge and love of classic films astounds me. His journalistic background and professionalism brought integrity, inspiring trust, and his agreeable disposition brought calm. His contributions were indispensable.

Grateful acknowledgment to all the actors and directors who participated in the book: to my friend, the exquisite Esther Williams, her husband, Edward Bell, and her personal assistant, Debbie Joseph; to Bonnie and Mike for always being there for me; and to dearest Anne Fletcher for her unconditional support and effervescent presence in my life.

Many others deserve my gratitude: At Bulfinch Press, my editor, Karyn Gerhard, for her enthusiasm for this project, her passion for old and obscure movies, and her unique vision, and production manager Pamela Schechter for her keen eye and technical expertise; photo editor Manoah Bowman for his hard work and vast knowledge of the golden age of cinema and its stunning black-and-white photography;

Silvio D'Aguanno for his artistic photographic enhancement and prepress work; Catherine Jeffery and Kelly McWilliam at IDPR for all their help; and Mikki Pallas and Lia Brandligt for their all-around amazing assistance.

Much appreciation to my family: Gary Rogers for his sage advice, suggestions, and loving patience. Margo and Matt Smithwick for asking for my list and being my guinea pigs—you are the type of insightful readers an author dreams of. Ben Smith for all his tech support, and Sam Smith for bestowing his love of black-and-white photography.

Much gratitude to my darling husband, Brendan, for sharing life's adventures, offering unending moral support to my project, and being the angel on my shoulder who gave me wings. And to my boy, Griffin, for being such a sweet baby.

Thank you to my best friend and mother, Miriam Smith, for taking this book from an idea to a reality with her incredible artistic vision, extraordinary talent, and many sleepless nights. Her belief in me made this book possible. She introduced me to the starry world of the movies and taught me to reach for the moon.

PHOTOGRAPHIC EDITOR Manoah Bowman would like to thank the following people: Robert Cushman at the Academy of Motion Picture Arts and Sciences Margaret Herrick Library for his invaluable assistance, without which this book would not have been possible; Karyn Gerhard for her unending enthusiasm; James Richman, who served as assistant photographic editor and also painstakingly retouched every photograph in this book; Matthew Tunia for generously loaning many photos from his expansive collection; Jennifer Kita, Maurice Davis, Tony Maietta, Anna Hrnjak, Ann Jastrab, and David Wills; and, most importantly, Afton Fraser and Miriam Smith for asking me to work on and be a part of their "dream" book.